BUSY COOK'S BOOK

FamilyCircle

Other Books by Family Circle:

The Best of Family Circle Cookbook
1986 Family Circle Cookbook
1987 Family Circle Cookbook
1988 Family Circle Cookbook

Family Circle Christmas Treasury
1987 Family Circle Christmas Treasury
1988 Family Circle Christmas Treasury

Family Circle Favorite Needlecrafts

Family Circle Hints, Tips & Smart Advice

To order **FamilyCircle** books, write to Family Circle Books,
110 Fifth Avenue, 4th Floor, New York, NY 10001

To subscribe to **FamilyCircle** magazine, write to Family Circle Subscriptions,
110 Fifth Avenue, New York, NY 10011.

Editorial Staff:

Editor, Family Circle Books: Carol A. Guasti
Editorial/Production Coordinator: Kim E. Gayton
Project Editor: David Ricketts
Editorial Assistant: Victoria Wachino
Book Design: Millsaps, Bosler & Stricker
Cover Illustration: Mark Desman
Typesetting: Gary Borden, Alison Chandler

Photographers: David Bishop, Michele Clement, Ronald G. Harris, Irwin Horowitz, James Kozyra, Laszlo, Karen Leeds, Bill McGinn, Rudy Muller, Paccione, Ron Scherwin, Jerry Simpson, Michael Skott, Gordon E. Smith

Marketing Staff:

Manager, Marketing & Development: Margaret Chan-Yip
Promotion Fulfillment Manager: Pauline MacLean Treitler
Administrative Assistant: Donna Sebring

Published by The Family Circle, Inc.
110 Fifth Avenue, New York, NY 10011
Copyright ©1988 by The Family Circle, Inc.

Manufactured in the United States of America

10 9 8 7 6 5 4 3 2 1

ISBN 0-933585-09-8

BUSY COOK'S BOOK

FamilyCircle

Table of Contents

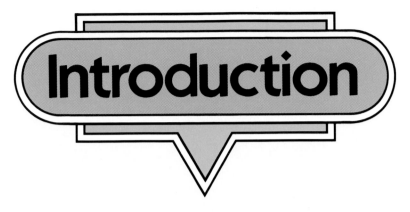

Introduction

Who *isn't* a busy cook these days? Men and women, married or single—even kids!—fit this category. According to Family Circle surveys, most people feel there just aren't enough hours in the day to get everything done. So wouldn't it be terrific if you could whip up a delicious dinner in just *minutes?* (And get out of the kitchen fast!)

That's what the Busy Cook's Book is all about. We gathered our most popular time-saving recipes, then divided them into sensible chapters that help you budget your time: Dishes to make in 15 minutes or less; 30 minutes or less; and dishes that take longer to cook, but don't need your constant attention. The clock starts when all the ingredients are on the counter, the cans are open and the vegetables are chopped.

Each main dish comes with a menu suggestion, so you won't have to guess at what makes a well-rounded meal. There are also dozens of make-ahead recipes that let you do most of the preparation beforehand; an easy entertaining chapter; jiffy desserts plus an entire chapter of step-by-step menus with shopping lists, work plans and recipes. *And every recipe has a complete nutrient analysis.* There are also "Quicktips" flagged in blue throughout the book. They'll help you maximize efficiency and improve your kitchen wisdom to make every second count.

This book will help you mix busy schedules with home-cooked meals. Turn to these pages when you're racing the clock, or when you need some extra free minutes at dinnertime. And keep it handy—you'll find yourself reaching for it whenever you want to make the most of your time in (and out of!) the kitchen.

Chapter 1 should really be called "rush hour meals". Once you've assembled all the ingredients, you can get dinner on the table in just *15 minutes!* These are the recipes to turn to when there's just no time to cook.

We've kept in mind real-life cooking priorities here. You'll find recipes that make good use of your microwave or toaster oven (so no preheating is necessary) as well as your stove top. Our repertoire of quarter-hour wonders includes satisfying pasta dishes, delicious stir-fries, hot sandwiches and main-dish salads. And when we say speedy, we mean it: In the time it takes to boil spaghetti, you can whip up Pasta with Chunky Tomatoes and Cheddar Cheese *(page 8);* our Stir-Fried Ham and Cashews *(page 14)* makes delicious short work of leftover ham.

For each main-dish recipe, you'll find menu suggestions that include a side dish and dessert. Some side dishes and desserts are easy toss-togethers from foods in your pantry or refrigerator; for others, we mark the dish with an asterisk (*) and tell you where to find the recipe in this book. When you get a moment, turn to chapters 5 and 7 and see for yourself the great go-withs and sweets a busy cook can whip up.

Fast and fabulous Shrimp Fried Rice (Chapter 1, page 12) is a tasty main dish — or perfect for a picnic or buffet. The quick-fix sauce in Green Beans with Spicy Pork Sauce (Chapter 2, page 63) is also delicious over hot rice or noodles. And stir-fried Emerald Scallops (Chapter 3, page 115) are equally wonderful served hot or cold.

Pasta

Fettuccine with Ham and Peas

Makes 6 servings.

Nutrient Value Per Serving: 848 calories, 36 g protein, 49 g fat, 65 g carbohydrate, 1,434 mg sodium, 238 mg cholesterol.

1	medium-size onion, finely chopped
3	tablespoons butter
2	cups thinly sliced mushrooms (about 8 ounces)
1½	cups heavy cream
2	cups 3 x ¼-inch strips cooked ham (about ⅔ pound)
1	package (10 ounces) frozen peas, thawed and drained
1	box (12 ounces) fettuccine
1	cup grated Parmesan cheese
½	teaspoon black pepper

1. Bring a large pot of water to boiling for the fettuccine.
2. Meanwhile, sauté the onion in the butter in a large skillet until the onion is softened but not browned, for about 5 minutes. Add the mushrooms and brown slightly, for about 4 minutes. Stir in the cream and simmer for 2 minutes.
3. Add the ham and the peas. Cook the mixture until heated through, stirring, for about 3 minutes.
4. Meanwhile, add the fettuccine to the boiling water and cook until *al dente*, firm but tender. Drain the fettuccine in a colander. Place the pasta in a large serving bowl.
5. Stir the Parmesan cheese into the sauce in the skillet. Add the sauce to the fettuccine along with the black pepper. Toss the pasta mixture gently to thoroughly mix. Serve immediately.

Menu Idea

Fettuccine with Ham and Peas*

Romaine and Chicory Salad

Strawberries with Cointreau and Whipped Cream

QUICK TIP

A Little Finely Chopped Onion, With Little Fuss
When a recipe calls for a small amount of grated or finely chopped onion, cut a slice off the top of an onion. Then cross-hatch the end of the main part of the onion with a paring knife in very thin straight-down cuts, first one way, then the other, cutting about ⅛ inch deep. Slice off this portion of the onion to use in the recipe and wrap the rest of the onion to use another time.

Fettuccine with Ham and Peas uses leftover ham or deli ham to cut preparation time. And the creamy rich mushroom sauce makes it special enough for any occasion.

5

Vermicelli with Seafood and Chicken

Menu Idea
Vermicelli with Seafood and Chicken*

Cucumber Salad

Breadsticks

Honeydew Melon Slices

1	pound vermicelli
2	cloves garlic, lightly smashed
2	tablespoons butter
1	tablespoon all-purpose flour
2	cups half-and-half
½	cup milk
1	cup shredded Monterey Jack cheese (4 ounces)
2	tablespoons grated Parmesan cheese
⅛	teaspoon white pepper
	Generous pinch ground hot red pepper
1	package (10 ounces) frozen peas, thawed
1	package (8 ounces) imitation crab meat substitute** from the freezer section, thawed according to package directions
2	cans (5 ounces each) chunk white chicken in water, drained

1. Cook the vermicelli in a large pot of boiling water, following the package directions, until *al dente*, firm but tender.
2. Meanwhile, sauté the garlic in the butter in a medium-size saucepan until golden, for about 2 minutes. Remove the saucepan from the heat and discard the garlic.
3. Stir the flour into the butter until smooth. Return the saucepan to the heat. Add the half-and-half and the milk. Bring to boiling, stirring, over medium heat until the mixture is thick and bubbly.
4. Add the Monterey Jack cheese, Parmesan cheese, white pepper and ground hot red pepper. Cook over low heat, stirring gently, until cheeses melt.
5. Stir in the peas, crab meat substitute and chicken. Cook over low heat until heated through, for about 3 minutes.
6. Drain the vermicelli in a colander and transfer to a large serving bowl. Add the sauce and toss until well mixed. Serve the vermicelli immediately.

**Note: *Crab meat substitute is a combination of pollack (a white fish), shellfish and other ingredients. It can be found in the seafood or frozen food section of your supermarket.*

Microwave Instructions
(for a 650-watt variable power microwave oven)

Directions: Place the garlic and the butter in a 2-quart microwave-safe casserole. Microwave, uncovered, at full power for 2 minutes. Remove the garlic. Stir in the flour until smooth; add the half-and-half and the milk. Cover the casserole. Microwave at full power for 5½ to 6½ minutes or until boiling. Whisk the mixture well. Add the Monterey Jack cheese, Parmesan cheese, white pepper and ground hot red pepper and stir until the cheeses melt. Stir in the peas, crab meat substitute and chicken. Cover the casserole. Microwave at full power for 4 minutes to heat the mixture through. Toss the sauce with the drained, cooked vermicelli.

QUICK TIP

Warm Plates
Slip the serving dishes into the oven to warm as you begin dinner preparation. Hot food on hot plates is a nice touch.

Spaghettini Salad

Garlic Bread

Menu Idea
Spaghettini Salad*
Garlic Bread*
Sautéed Peach
    Slices with
    Toasted Slivered
    Almonds

You can have your pasta and salad as one course in this unusual pasta salad. The crunchiness of the lettuce contrasts deliciously with the pasta.

Makes 4 servings.

Nutrient Value Per Serving: 556 calories, 16 g protein, 15 g fat, 89 g carbohydrate, 294 mg sodium, 0 mg cholesterol.

1	pound spaghettini
¼	cup good-quality olive oil
¼	cup red or white wine vinegar
½	teaspoon salt
¼	teaspoon pepper
8	cups mixed crisp salad greens, such as Bibb, watercress and arugula, washed and dried

1. Cook the spaghettini in a large pot of boiling salted water until *al dente*, firm but tender. Drain the spaghettini in a colander.
2. While the spaghettini is cooking, combine the oil, red or white vinegar, salt and pepper in a large bowl. Add the salad greens and toss well to combine all the ingredients. Add the drained spaghettini and toss again to mix in the spaghettini. Serve the salad immediately.

Warm from the oven, this bread is a wonderful accompaniment to any pasta dish.

Heat in 350° oven for 15 minutes.
Makes 8 servings.

Nutrient Value Per Serving: 216 calories, 5 g protein, 7 g fat, 32 g carbohydrate, 388 mg sodium, 17 mg cholesterol.

1	loaf French, Italian or sourdough bread
¼	cup (½ stick) butter or margarine
1	clove garlic, mashed

1. Preheat the oven to moderate (350°).
2. Cut the bread into ½-inch-thick slices and keep the slices in order.
3. Melt the butter or margarine and garlic in a small saucepan. Brush the butter generously over each slice of bread. Reshape the loaf on a large sheet of heavy-duty aluminum foil; wrap the loaf.
4. Heat the bread in the preheated moderate oven (350°) until hot and crisp around the edges, about 12 minutes. Loosen the foil packet for serving, but keep the bread in the foil to keep warm.

Variations: For a deliciously different garlic bread, try sprinkling Parmesan or mozzarella cheese on top for the last 5 minutes of baking (do not cover). Or add basil, parsley or oregano to the butter/garlic mixture before spreading on the bread.

QUICK TIP

Pasta Is Perfect
It's the ideal ingredient for the busy cook—takes just minutes to cook and pairs well with an infinite variety of sauces. The first step for any pasta recipe: Fill a large pot with hot tap water, cover with a lid and place the pot on a burner over high heat. While the water is coming to a boil for the pasta, proceed with the recipe.

Pasta with Chunky Tomatoes and Cheddar Cheese

Menu Idea

Pasta with Chunky Tomatoes and Cheddar Cheese*

Crusty Italian Bread

Shredded Romaine Lettuce Salad

Amaretti Cookies and Espresso

Freshly cooked hot pasta is tossed with chunks of uncooked tomato and shreds of sharp Cheddar cheese.

Makes 6 servings.

Nutrient Value Per Serving: 498 calories, 18 g protein, 19 g fat, 64 g carbohydrate, 411 mg sodium, 40 mg cholesterol.

2	pounds tomatoes (about 12 plum or 6 medium-size regular)
1	pound thin spaghetti
2	tablespoons vegetable or olive oil
1	large clove garlic, finely chopped
2	tablespoons butter or margarine
½	cup chopped parsley
¼	cup thinly sliced green onion
½	teaspoon salt
½	teaspoon pepper
1½	cups coarsely shredded sharp Cheddar cheese (6 ounces)

1. Cut the tomatoes in half crosswise. Gently squeeze out the seeds and remove the cores; discard the seeds and cores. Cut the tomatoes into ½-inch chunks and keep at room temperature. (This can be done several hours ahead.)
2. Cook the spaghetti following the package directions until *al dente*, firm but tender. Drain the spaghetti in a colander.
3. Meanwhile, heat the vegetable or olive oil in a small skillet over low heat. Add the garlic and sauté until softened but not colored, for about 2 minutes. Add the butter or margarine and melt. Remove the skillet from the heat.
4. Transfer the drained hot spaghetti to a large bowl. Add the butter or margarine mixture, tomatoes, parsley, green onion, salt and pepper. Toss to mix well. Add the Cheddar cheese and lightly toss to mix. (The trick is to evenly distribute the cheese before it melts too much; the cheese should hold its shape.) Serve immediately.

QUICK TIP

Great taste — no waste!
Transform that last half-inch of bottled French, blue cheese or Russian salad dressing! Just add 2 teaspoons of vinegar or lemon juice (or one of each if you prefer); recap and shake vigorously. Gradually add ½ cup of mayonnaise or sour cream, shaking as you add. A new dressing — quick and easy.

Rotelle with Shrimp and Lemon

Makes 4 servings.

Nutrient Value Per Serving:
752 calories, 33 g protein,
38 g fat, 69 carbohydrate, 428
mg sodium, 256 mg cholesterol.

12 ounces rotelle, or other spiral or corkscrew-shaped pasta
1 cup heavy cream
4 tablespoons (½ stick) butter or margarine
⅛ teaspoon ground hot red pepper
¼ cup grated Parmesan or Romano cheese
1 clove garlic, halved
1 pound medium-size fresh shrimp, shelled and deveined OR: 1 pound frozen, thawed and drained
1 cup finely chopped fresh herbs, such as parsley, basil, chives
   Grated rind of 1 large lemon (1 tablespoon)
   Juice of 1 large lemon (about 3 tablespoons)
1 tablespoon capers, coarsely chopped if large
   Lemon wedges *(optional)*
   Basil leaves *(optional)*

1. Cook the rotelle in boiling salted water in a large saucepan, following the package directions. Drain.
2. Meanwhile, combine the cream, 2 tablespoons of the butter, the red pepper and cheese in a small saucepan. Place the saucepan over low heat to heat through.
3. Sauté the garlic in the remaining 2 tablespoons of butter in a medium-size skillet; remove the garlic when it begins to brown. Add the shrimp and stir-fry until firm, pink and curled, for about 3 to 5 minutes. Quickly stir in the herbs, lemon rind and juice, and the capers. Remove the skillet from the heat.
4. Transfer the pasta to a warm serving bowl. Pour the hot cream sauce over the pasta; toss together until well blended. Spoon the shrimp mixture over the pasta; toss together. Garnish with the lemon wedges and basil leaves, if you wish.

Menu Idea
Rotelle with Shrimp and Lemon*
Crusty Italian Bread
Sliced Cucumbers with Vinegar
Almond Cookies

QUICK TIP

Rapid Reminder
Set out everything you'll need to use in a cooking project before beginning to cook and put them back in the cupboard or refrigerator or into the dishwasher as you use them. Your clean-up will be easier and there will be no doubt whether or not you remembered all the ingredients.

Skillet &
Stir-Fries

Two Beans, Tomatoes and Tuna

Makes 4 servings.

*Nutrient Value Per Serving:
288 calories, 14 g protein, 20 g
fat, 16 g carbohydrate, 832 mg
sodium, 10 mg cholesterol.*

1   large onion, thinly sliced
1   clove garlic, finely chopped
3   tablespoons good-quality
    olive oil
6   ripe plum tomatoes, peeled,
    quartered and seeded
    (about 1 pound)
¼   teaspoon salt
¼   teaspoon pepper
½   pound green beans,
    trimmed and steamed until
    crisp-tender
½   pound wax beans, trimmed
    and steamed until crisp-
    tender
16 black oil-cured olives
1   can (6½ ounces) tuna
    packed in oil, drained and
    flaked
¼   cup thinly sliced fresh basil
    leaves

1. Sauté the onion and the garlic
   in the oil in a large skillet over
   medium-high heat until
   softened, for about 3 minutes.
2. Add the tomatoes and season
   with the salt and the pepper.
   Cook the mixture, stirring
   occasionally, until the juices
   have evaporated, for about 2
   minutes.
3. Stir in the green and wax beans,
   olives and tuna. Cover and
   cook the mixture over low heat
   just until heated through. Add
   the basil. Serve warm.

Microwave Instructions
*(for a 650-watt variable power
microwave oven)*

Ingredient Changes: Reduce the
olive oil to 2 tablespoons.
Directions: Sprinkle the onion and
the garlic over the bottom of a
microwave-safe baking dish, about
11½ x 7½ inches. Pour on the oil.
Microwave, uncovered, at full
power for 3 minutes, stirring once.
Stir the tomatoes into the baking
dish. Arrange the green and wax
beans over the tomatoes in an even
layer. Cover the dish with
microwave-safe plastic wrap.
Microwave at full power for 6
minutes, stirring once. Stir in the
olives, tuna, salt and pepper.
Microwave, uncovered, at full
power for 30 seconds. Sprinkle the
mixture with the basil.

Menu Idea
Tomato Soup
**Two Beans,
    Tomatoes
    and Tuna***
Rye Bread
Fresh Fruit

*Low in calories and cholesterol, Two
Beans, Tomatoes and Tuna is a quick
fix on the stovetop or in the microwave.*

Shrimp Fried Rice

Menu Idea
Shrimp Fried Rice*

Sesame Seed Breadsticks

Mandarin Orange Sections Sprinkled with Granola

Serve this as a light main dish or make ahead for buffet or picnic fare. For less sodium, reduce the amount of soy sauce, eliminate it or use a light soy sauce.

Makes 4 servings.

Nutrient Value Per Serving: 490 calories, 16 g protein, 74 g fat, 52 g carbohydrate, 886 mg sodium, 206 mg cholesterol.

2	eggs, slightly beaten
1	tablespoon chopped green onion, green part only
6	tablespoons peanut or vegetable oil
2	tablespoons chopped green onion, white part only
½	cup slivered shiitake mushrooms OR: white mushrooms
1	cup peeled, deveined and cooked shrimp
4	cups cooked rice
3	tablespoons soy sauce
1	cup frozen green peas, thawed

1. Mix together the eggs and the chopped green part of the green onion.
2. Heat 1 tablespoon of the peanut or vegetable oil in a 9-inch skillet. Pour in the egg mixture. Cook, loosening the mixture from the bottom of the skillet but not stirring the mixture, until the egg is no longer wet on the top. Remove the skillet from the heat. Flip the egg mixture onto a plate. Cool slightly, then cut the egg mixture into strips.
3. Heat half the remaining oil in a wok or large skillet. Add the chopped white part of the green onion and the shiitake or white mushrooms and sauté for 3 minutes. Add the shrimp and sauté for 1 minute. Remove the shrimp mixture from the wok to a plate.
4. Heat the remaining oil in the wok. Add the rice and stir-fry until it is heated through and slightly golden. Add the soy sauce and stir-fry until the soy sauce is evenly absorbed.
5. Return the shrimp mixture to the wok along with the peas. Stir-fry until well mixed. Transfer the rice mixture to a serving bowl. Top with the egg strips. Serve the rice warm or at room temperature.

QUICK TIP

Stir-Frying: Cooking In A Flash
Stir-frying is an easy, quick-cooking technique. If you can, prepare ingredients (such as chopping vegetables) the day before. At dinnertime, assemble them near the stove top, and dinner will be ready in minutes.

12

Tomato Fried Rice

This Oriental-inspired dish is a great way to use up leftover rice.

Makes 4 servings.

Nutrient Value Per Serving: 354 calories, 10 g protein, 20 g fat, 35 g carbohydrate, 852 mg sodium, 274 mg cholesterol.

3   **medium-size tomatoes (about 1¼ pounds)**
4   **tablespoons vegetable oil**
4   **eggs, slightly beaten**
½   **cup thinly sliced green onion (about 6 medium-size green onions)**
1   **clove garlic, finely chopped**
1   **thin slice fresh gingerroot, finely chopped**
3   **cups cold cooked long-grain white rice****
3   **tablespoons soy sauce**
¼   **teaspoon pepper**

1. Cut the tomatoes in half crosswise. Squeeze out the seeds and remove the cores; discard the seeds and cores. Cut the tomatoes into 1-inch chunks.
2. Heat 1 tablespoon of the oil in a large skillet or wok over medium-high heat. Add the eggs and lightly scramble just until the eggs are set. Transfer the eggs to a dish.
3. Wipe the skillet clean. Add the remaining 3 tablespoons of oil. Add the green onion, garlic and gingerroot and sauté for 1 minute. Add the rice; stir-fry until the rice is heated through and well coated with the oil, for about 3 minutes. Add the tomatoes, soy sauce and pepper. Cook until hot, for about 1 minute. Gently stir in the scrambled eggs. Serve immediately.

**Note: If starting with uncooked rice, slowly add 1 cup of long-grain white rice to a large saucepan of boiling water. Cook until tender, for 12 to 15 minutes. Drain the rice and transfer to a bowl. Cool to room temperature. Refrigerate the rice, covered, overnight.

Menu Idea
Tomato Fried Rice*

Sesame Seed Breadsticks

Pineapple Cubes and Yogurt

Pressed For Garlic
No time to peel garlic? Place the unpeeled clove in a garlic press and squeeze directly into the food you're cooking.

13

Stir-Fried Ham and Cashews

Menu Idea
Stir-Fried Ham and Cashews*
Hot Cooked Rice
Bibb Lettuce Salad
Quick Lemon Mousse*
(page 230)

To lower the sodium in this recipe, use less soy sauce or eliminate it.

Makes 4 servings.

Nutrient Value Per Serving: 603 calories, 33 g protein, 42 g fat, 25 g carbohydrate, 2,328 mg sodium, 67 mg cholesterol.

¼   **cup light soy sauce**
⅓   **cup dry sherry**
1   **tablespoon rice wine vinegar**
2   **teaspoons Oriental sesame oil****
1   **teaspoon sugar**
2   **leeks, cut diagonally into 1-inch slices and rinsed well**
2   **medium-size cucumbers, peeled, quartered, seeded and cut diagonally into 1-inch slices**
1   **tablespoon peeled and finely chopped fresh gingerroot**
2   **cloves garlic, finely chopped**
4   **teaspoons cornstarch**
⅓   **cup water**
¼   **cup peanut oil**
1   **cup dry-roasted unsalted cashew nuts**
3   **cups diced cooked ham (1 pound)**
  Hot cooked rice *(optional)*

1. Combine the soy sauce, sherry, vinegar, Oriental sesame oil and sugar in a small bowl. Reserve.
2. Prepare the leeks, cucumbers, gingerroot and garlic. Stir together the cornstarch and the water in a small cup. Arrange all the ingredients near the stove top for easy access.
3. Heat the peanut oil in a large skillet. Add the cashews and fry until golden brown, for about 1 minute. Remove the cashews from the skillet with a slotted spoon to paper toweling to drain, leaving the oil in the skillet.
4. Add the leeks, cucumber, gingerroot and garlic to the skillet and stir-fry for 2 minutes. Add the reserved soy sauce mixture and stir-fry for 1 minute. Quickly restir the cornstarch mixture and add to the skillet. Cook until the sauce thickens, for about 1 minute.
5. Add the ham and the cashews and stir-fry for 2 to 3 minutes or until the mixture is heated through. Serve over hot cooked rice, if you wish.

**Note: Oriental sesame oil has more flavor and is darker in color than regular sesame oil. It can be found in the Oriental food section of many supermarkets or in Oriental specialty food stores.

QUICK TIP

Keeping Fresh Gingerroot Fresh
Refrigerate peeled fresh gingerroot in a jar, covered with dry sherry, or wrap in aluminum foil and store in the freezer indefinitely.

Stir-Fried Beef and Vegetables

Makes 4 servings.

*Nutrient Value Per Serving:
393 calories, 18 g protein, 30 g
fat, 13 g carbohydrate, 873 mg
sodium, 60 mg cholesterol.*

2   **tablespoons peanut or
    vegetable oil**
1   **clove garlic, pressed**
12 **ounces boneless sirloin
    steak, thinly sliced across
    the grain**
1   **large onion, cut into thin
    wedges**
2   **celery stalks, sliced**
1   **sweet red pepper, halved,
    seeded and cut into
    ¼-inch-wide strips**
4   **ounces mushrooms, washed
    and thinly sliced**
3   **tablespoons mild soy sauce**
3   **tablespoons water**
2   **tablespoons cornstarch**
1   **can (13¾ ounces) beef
    broth**
4   **ounces snow peas, trimmed
    Cooked vermicelli
    (optional)**

1. Heat 1 tablespoon of the oil in a large skillet or wok over high heat. Add the garlic and beef. Stir-fry until browned. Remove from the skillet with a slotted spoon.
2. Heat the remaining oil in the skillet. Stir-fry the onion, celery and the red pepper until the onion is tender, for about 4 minutes. Add the mushrooms; stir-fry for 2 minutes.
3. Combine the soy sauce, water and cornstarch in a small bowl. Stir into the skillet with the reserved beef and beef broth. Cook until the sauce thickens and becomes clear, for about 2 minutes.
4. Lower the heat. Add the snow peas; cook for 1 minute. Serve with the cooked vermicelli, if you wish.

Menu Idea
**Stir-Fried Beef and
  Vegetables***
Vermicelli
**Sesame Seed
  Breadsticks**
Banana Cake

Veggie Magic
If a recipe calls for a variety of vegetables, go to your freezer and use convenient bags of pre-cut mixed veggies. This will eliminate chopping and cut down on your preparation time.

Soups, Sandwiches &
Main-Dish Salads

Oriental Hot Pot

Makes 6 servings.

*Nutrient Value Per Serving:
271 calories, 29 g protein, 4 g
fat, 29 g carbohydrate, 1,273 mg
sodium, 44 mg cholesterol.*

2   **cans (13¾ ounces each)
      chicken broth**
1   **cup dry white wine**
¼   **cup soy sauce**
2   **tablespoons sugar**
2   **packages (3½ ounces each)
      Oriental soup noodles
      (without flavor packet)**
8   **ounces Oriental-style
      vegetables from salad bar,
      such as mushrooms,
      carrots, baby corn, sweet
      pepper, bean sprouts, pea
      pods**
8   **ounces firm bean curd, cut
      into ½-inch cubes**
1   **pound boneless, skinned
      chicken breasts, cut into
      2 x 1-inch pieces**
1   **bunch watercress, trimmed**
4   **green onions, cut into
       1-inch lengths**
      Chinese Mustard *(recipe
       follows)*
      Bottled plum sauce

1. Combine the broth, wine, soy sauce and sugar in a 5-quart skillet or a stove-top casserole. Break the noodles in half and add to the skillet along with the vegetables, curd and chicken. Bring the mixture to boiling. Reduce the heat to medium-low and cook for 3 minutes.
2. Remove the skillet from the heat. Stir in the watercress and the green onion. Serve immediately, with the Chinese Mustard and the plum sauce on the side.

Chinese Mustard: Mix together 1 tablespoon of dry mustard and 1 tablespoon of water in a small cup and let stand for 10 minutes.

Menu Idea
Oriental Hot Pot*
**Sesame Seed
   Breadsticks**
**Orange Sherbet
   with Fortune
   Cookies**

QUICK TIP

Fast Finder
Make finding your favorite recipes quick and easy. Stick colorful self-adhesive dots (found in stationery or dime stores) next to your favorite recipes in your cookbook. When you flip through the pages, the dots will catch your eye.

Chicken, vegetables and noodles in a tasty broth — this Oriental Hot Pot almost cooks itself! Buying cut-up vegetables at your local salad bar is a great time-saver.

Cioppino
(Fish Soup)

Menu Idea
Cioppino*
Crusty Italian Bread
Fruit Salad

QUICK TIPS

Two Ways To Peel Tomatoes
1. Add the tomatoes, a few at a time, to a large pot of boiling water. When the water returns to boiling, boil for 10 seconds for very ripe tomatoes, and for 20 seconds for firmer tomatoes. Remove the tomatoes with a slotted spoon. (If the skin splits, remove the tomato immediately.) Rinse the tomatoes under cold water to stop the cooking. Working from the bottom to the stem end, peel off the skin with a paring knife.
2. If you are peeling just a few tomatoes, stick a long, two-tined fork into the stem end of the tomato. Hold the tomato directly in a gas burner flame. Slowly rotate the tomato so all the sides begin to show a speckled brown color. Set the tomatoes aside to cool and then peel as above.

The soaking time for the clams is not included in the actual preparation time for this recipe.

Makes 8 servings.

Nutrient Value Per Serving:
209 calories, 26 g protein, 6 g fat, 11 g carbohydrate, 564 mg sodium, 99 mg cholesterol.

12	**well-scrubbed small clams, in their shells**
2	**carrots, thinly sliced**
1	**sweet green pepper, cored, seeded and chopped**
1	**large onion, chopped**
1	**clove garlic, finely chopped**
3	**tablespoons olive oil**
1	**can (16 ounces) whole tomatoes, broken up and with liquid**
1	**cup dry white wine**
1	**cup clam juice OR: fish stock OR: water**
1	**pound boneless haddock or cod steaks or fillets, cut into 1-inch pieces**
8	**ounces fresh or thawed frozen shrimp, shelled and deveined**
8	**ounces fresh scallops OR: thawed frozen crabmeat**
½	**teaspoon leaf basil, crumbled**
½	**teaspoon salt**
¼	**teaspoon pepper**

1. Let the clams soak in a bowl with enough cold water to cover for 1 hour to rid them of sand. Do not soak the clams overnight.
2. Sauté the carrot, green pepper, onion and garlic in the oil in a pressure cooker for 3 minutes, stirring often. Add the tomatoes with their liquid, wine, the clam juice, fish stock or water, haddock or cod, shrimp, scallops or crabmeat, basil, salt and pepper. Place the clams on top of the mixture. Cover the cooker with the lid, closing securely. Place the pressure regulator firmly on the vent pipe.
3. Heat the cooker until the pressure regulator attains a gentle rocking motion. Adjust the heat to maintain a slow, steady rocking motion of the regulator to prevent too much steam from escaping. Cook for 4 minutes.
4. Cool the cooker immediately under cold running water. When the air vent cover drops and no steam escapes when the pressure regulator is tilted, remove the pressure regulator.
5. Remove the lid and serve the soup immediately.

Cioppino, a savory soup of clams, shrimp, scallops and fish in a tomato broth, cooks quickly in a pressure cooker.

18

Tuna-White Bean Salad

Scallop Stew

Makes 4 servings.

Nutrient Value Per Serving: 261 calories, 24 g protein, 12 g fat, 17 g carbohydrate, 391 mg sodium, 37 mg cholesterol.

2   jars (6 ounces each) marinated artichoke hearts
1   pound fresh mushrooms, sliced
1   pound scallops
1   cup chopped parsley
¼   cup fresh lemon juice
    Salt and pepper, to taste

1. Drain the artichoke marinade into a large skillet. Reserve the artichoke hearts separately.
2. Cook the mushrooms in the marinade until tender, for about 3 minutes. Add the scallops, ½ cup of the parsley and the lemon juice. Cook, turning often, until the scallops are firm, for about 2 minutes. Stir in the reserved artichoke hearts and cook until heated through.
3. Garnish the stew with the remaining ½ cup of parsley. Serve the stew warm over hot cooked rice as a main dish, or at room temperature in lettuce cups as an appetizer. Season with the salt and pepper.

Makes 4 servings.

Nutrient Value Per Serving: 446 calories, 25 g protein, 22 g fat, 38 g carbohydrate, 986 mg sodium, 8 mg cholesterol.

1   can (19 ounces) cannellini beans, drained and rinsed
1   jar (2 ounces) sliced pimiento, drained
1   small red onion, quartered and thinly sliced
1   can (7 ounces) tuna, drained and coarsely flaked
¼   to ⅓ cup red wine vinegar
2   tablespoons lemon juice (1 lemon)
½   teaspoon finely chopped garlic
⅓   cup olive oil
½   teaspoon salt
¼   teaspoon pepper
2   tablespoons finely chopped parsley
    Lettuce leaves

1. Combine the beans, pimiento, onion and tuna in a medium-size bowl.
2. Combine ¼ cup of the vinegar, the lemon juice, garlic, oil, salt and pepper in a small bowl. Stir in the parsley. Pour the dressing over the bean mixture and toss gently to mix. Taste the salad and add the remaining vinegar, if you wish.
3. Serve the salad on lettuce leaves. Garnish with lemon wedges, if you wish.

Menu Idea
Scallop Stew*
Hot Cooked Rice
Strawberries with Cassis

Menu Idea
Tuna-White Bean Salad*
Crusty Italian Bread
Sliced Tomatoes
Lemon Sherbet

QUICK TIPS

More Juice For Your Money
To get more juice from oranges, lemons and limes, keep them at room temperature and roll them on a hard surface with your hand before squeezing.

Mushroom "Cellar"
Store mushrooms in a brown paper bag in the refrigerator for longer and fresher storage.

19

Homemade Chicken Soup with Pasta

Menu Idea
Homemade Chicken Soup with Pasta*
Crusty Italian Bread
Strawberries and Cream

Simmered with celery, carrots, peas and rotelle, Homemade Chicken Stock (page 184) becomes naturally delicious Homemade Chicken Soup with Pasta.

Makes 4 servings.

Nutrient Value Per Serving: 392 calories, 32 g protein, 10 g fat, 43 g carbohydrate, 571 mg sodium, 76 mg cholesterol.

2	stalks celery, diagonally sliced
3	small carrots, peeled and diagonally sliced
3	green onions, both white and green parts, diagonally sliced
½	teaspoon leaf tarragon, crumbled
½	to 1 teaspoon salt
6	cups Homemade Chicken Stock *(see recipe, page 184)* OR: canned chicken broth
4	ounces rotelle pasta, cooked according to package directions
2	cups cubed cooked chicken
1	cup frozen peas, thawed
¼	to ½ teaspoon white pepper

1. Combine the celery, carrot, green onion, tarragon, salt and stock or canned broth in a medium-size saucepan. Simmer the soup for 10 minutes or until the vegetables are crisp-tender.
2. Add the pasta, chicken, peas and white pepper. Simmer the soup until heated through. Serve immediately.

QUICK TIP

Salty Soup
If you've added too much salt to your soup while cooking, or canned chicken broth makes the soup taste too salty, add a peeled raw potato to the soup and simmer for a bit—the potato will absorb the salty flavor. Chop the potato and add to the soup, if you wish.

20

Bean and Spinach Soup

Skillet Chili

Makes 6 servings.

*Nutrient Value Per Serving:
158 calories, 11 g protein, 1 g
fat, 26 g carbohydrate, 870 mg
sodium, 0 mg cholesterol.*

2   cans (19 ounces each)
      cannellini beans, drained
1   can (13¾ ounces) chicken
      broth
½   cup water
¼   teaspoon pepper
2   cups finely shredded
      spinach
2   tablespoons fresh lemon
      juice
      Lemon slices, quartered, for
      garnish *(optional)*
      Sweet red pepper strips, for
      garnish *(optional)*

1. Combine the cannellini beans
   with the broth, working in
   batches if necessary, in the
   container of an electric blender
   or a food processor. Cover and
   whirl until the mixture is
   smooth. Pour the bean mixture
   into a medium-size saucepan.
   Add the water and the pepper.
   Bring the soup to boiling over
   medium heat. Cook the soup
   for 2 to 3 minutes, stirring
   occasionally.
2. Remove the saucepan from the
   heat. Stir in the spinach and the
   lemon juice. Garnish with
   lemon slices and red pepper
   strips, if you wish.

Makes 4 servings.

*Nutrient Value Per Serving:
246 calories, 24 g protein, 11 g
fat, 14 g carbohydrate, 581 mg
sodium, 72 mg cholesterol.*

1   pound packaged ground
      turkey, thawed if frozen
1   large sweet green pepper,
      halved, cored, seeded and
      chopped
1   medium-size onion,
      chopped
½   cup drained canned red
      kidney beans, rinsed
½   to 1 package (1¼ ounces)
      taco seasoning mix
      (depending on desired
      spiciness)
1   cup water
      Shredded lettuce *(optional)*
      Chopped tomatoes
      (optional)

1. Brown the turkey in a large,
   nonstick skillet, breaking up the
   turkey with a wooden spoon,
   until no pink remains, for about
   5 minutes. Carefully drain off
   the excess fat.
2. Add the green pepper, onion,
   kidney beans and seasoning
   mix to the meat in the skillet;
   stir in the water.
3. Bring the mixture to boiling.
   Lower the heat and simmer,
   uncovered, stirring frequently,
   for 3 to 5 minutes or until the
   onion is softened. Cover and
   simmer the chili for 5 minutes
   or until the green pepper is
   crisp-tender.
4. Serve the chili topped with
   shredded lettuce and chopped
   tomatoes, if you wish.

Menu Idea

**Bean and Spinach
  Soup***
**Cottage Cheese and
  Fruit Salad**
Crusty Italian Bread
**Espresso and
  Macaroons**

Menu Idea

Skillet Chili*
Taco Chips
**Sliced Banana with
  Kiwi Fruit**

Blue Cheese and Roasted Pepper Sandwich

Menu Idea

**Blue Cheese and
    Roasted Pepper
    Sandwich***

Coleslaw

**Ice Cream
    Sandwich**

A strongly-flavored sandwich for blue cheese lovers.

Makes 4 servings.

*Nutrient Value Per Serving:
471 calories, 15 g protein, 32 g
fat, 34 g carbohydrate, 1,184 mg
sodium, 32 mg cholesterol.*

1 **jar (8 ounces) marinated
    mushrooms**
6 **ounces blue cheese,
    crumbled (about 1 cup)**
1 **oval loaf (8 x 4 inches)
    pumpernickel bread,
    unsliced, or 6 slices
    pumpernickel bread**
1 **jar (7 ounces) roasted red
    peppers, drained**
4 **large leaves romaine lettuce**

1. Drain the mushrooms, reserving the marinade separately. Finely chop the mushrooms.
2. Mix together the mushrooms, blue cheese and 1 tablespoon of the marinade in a small bowl.
3. Cut the bread with a serrated knife into 3 equal horizontal slices. Brush a third of the reserved marinade over the bottom slice of the bread. Layer the remaining ingredients in the following order: half the blue cheese-mushroom mixture, half the roasted red peppers, 2 leaves of the lettuce, the middle slice of the bread, another third of the reserved marinade, the remaining blue cheese-mushroom mixture, the remaining roasted red peppers and the remaining 2 lettuce leaves. Brush the remaining marinade on the cut side of the top slice of the bread; place the slice on top of the sandwich. (If using sliced pumpernickel bread, make two sandwiches with the same layering.)
4. Slice the loaf into 4 equal portions and serve.

QUICK TIP

**Super-Quick
Coleslaw**
Use your food processor to chop up cabbage and carrots post-haste. (After you add the mayonnaise, sprinkle some poppy seeds on top for extra flavor!)

Grilled Open-Face Turkey Club

Broil for 2 to 3 minutes.
Makes 4 servings.

Nutrient Value Per Serving:
458 calories, 27 g protein, 27 g
fat, 29 g carbohydrate, 871 mg
sodium, 103 mg cholesterol.

¼ **cup (½ stick) unsalted**
   butter, softened
1 **tablespoon mayonnaise**
2 **teaspoons Dijon-style**
   mustard
8 **slices rye bread, lightly**
   toasted
½ **pound thinly sliced deli**
   roast turkey
1 **large ripe tomato, cut into**
   8 slices
8 **slices cooked bacon OR: ¼**
   cup real bacon bits
½ **cup shredded Swiss cheese**
   (2 ounces)

1. Adjust the oven rack 6 inches from the broiling element, if using a conventional oven. Preheat the broiler; preheating a toaster oven is not necessary.
2. Combine the butter, mayonnaise and mustard in a small bowl and blend well. Spread the mustard mixture evenly on one side of each bread slice.
3. Place the turkey over the mustard-coated side of each bread slice, dividing equally. Top each with 1 slice of the tomato and 1 slice of the bacon or ⅛ of the real bacon bits.
4. Place 4 of the bread slices on top of the other 4 slices, making 4 open-face double-decker sandwiches.
5. Sprinkle the Swiss cheese over the top of each sandwich, dividing equally. Place the sandwiches on a broiler or toaster oven pan.
6. Broil the sandwiches in the oven or a toaster oven for 2 to 3 minutes or until the Swiss cheese is melted.

Menu Idea

Grilled Open-Face
   Turkey Club*
Radish and Alfalfa
   Sprout Salad
Vanilla Ice Cream
   with Amaretti

Sandwich And Salad Combos Not Just For Lunch
Everyone racing in a different direction at dinner time? Sandwich, salad and a piece of fruit are a quick-to-fix, do-it-yourself supper on the run.

23

Zesty Jarlsberg Melts

Menu Idea

Zesty Jarlsberg Melts*

Belgian Endive Salad

Apple and Fruit-Flavored Yogurt

Bake at 375° for 8 to 10 minutes; broil for 2 to 3 minutes. Makes 4 servings.

Nutrient Value Per Serving: 273 calories, 11 g protein, 18 g fat, 21 g carbohydrate, 334 mg sodium, 18 mg cholesterol.

1 large ripe avocado, peeled, pitted, sliced and cut into chunks
3 tablespoons lime juice
1 small tomato, finely chopped
1 small onion, finely chopped
1 clove garlic, finely chopped
½ teaspoon ground cumin
  Salt, to taste
  Liquid red pepper seasoning, to taste
4 slices 7-grain bread, lightly toasted
4 slices cooked bacon, crumbled
½ cup shredded Jarlsberg cheese

1. Preheat a conventional oven to moderate (375°), if using; preheating a toaster oven is not necessary.
2. Combine the avocado, lime juice, tomato, onion, garlic, cumin, salt and liquid red-pepper seasoning in a medium-size bowl. Mix until well blended but still slightly chunky. Spread the avocado mixture over the bread slices. Place the bread slices on a broiler or toaster oven pan.
3. Bake the sandwiches in the preheated moderate oven (375°) or a toaster oven for 8 to 10 minutes or until the tops are golden. Remove the pan and sandwiches from the oven. Increase the oven temperature to broil.
4. Sprinkle each sandwich with the bacon and the Jarlsberg cheese, dividing equally. Broil for 2 to 3 minutes or until the bacon is crisp and the Jarlsberg cheese is melted.

QUICK TIPS

Soup 'N Sandwich
● Many supermarket bakeries produce excellent unsliced loaves of bread in a variety of sizes, shapes and flavors — 12-ounce or 1-pound loaves are perfect for "monster" sandwiches.
● If you have time, weight bread loaves for easier slicing. Cover round loaves with a 10-inch pie plate and oval loaves with a jelly-roll pan. Balance heavy canned goods on top.
● Use a long serrated knife for easy bread slicing.
● If you're preparing both a sandwich and soup for a quick meal, start the soup first. Assemble the sandwich while the soup is simmering.

Herbed Ham and Swiss Cheese Puffs

Liverwurst and American Cheese Melts

Bake at 375° for 8 minutes.
Makes 4 servings.

Broil for 2 to 3 minutes.
Makes 4 servings.

Nutrient Value Per Serving:
470 calories, 25 g protein, 34 g
fat, 16 g carbohydrate, 1,519 mg
sodium, 76 mg cholesterol.

Nutrient Value Per Serving:
688 calories, 27 g protein, 49 g
fat, 38 g carbohydrate, 1,885 mg
sodium, 158 mg cholesterol.

Menu Idea
Herbed Ham and
  Swiss Cheese
  Puffs*
Sliced Tomato
Nectarine Sorbet*
  (page 261)

2 cups chopped cooked ham
½ cup finely chopped celery
1 small red onion, finely
     chopped (about ⅓ cup)
¼ teaspoon rosemary,
     crumbled
¼ teaspoon leaf thyme,
     crumbled
⅛ teaspoon pepper
½ cup mayonnaise
½ cup shredded Swiss cheese
¼ cup grated Parmesan cheese
4 slices light rye bread, lightly
     toasted

¼ cup mayonnaise
¼ cup dairy sour cream
4 green onions, both white
     and green parts, finely
     chopped
8 slices pumpernickel bread,
     lightly toasted
16 slices (¼ inch thick)
     liverwurst (1¼ pounds)
16 slices American cheese

Menu Idea
Liverwurst and
  American Cheese
  Melts*
Potato Chips
Fresh Fruit

1. Preheat a conventional oven to
   moderate (375°), if using;
   preheating a toaster oven is not
   necessary.
2. Combine the ham, celery,
   onion, rosemary, thyme and
   pepper in a medium-size bowl.
   Add the mayonnaise, Swiss
   cheese and 1 tablespoon of the
   Parmesan cheese, and stir to
   mix well.
3. Spread the ham mixture over
   the bread slices, dividing
   equally. Sprinkle the
   sandwiches with the remaining
   Parmesan cheese. Place the
   sandwiches on a baking sheet
   or a toaster oven pan.
4. Bake in the preheated
   moderate oven (375°) or a
   toaster oven for 8 minutes or
   until the tops are lightly golden
   and puffed.

1. Adjust the oven rack 6 inches
   from the broiling element, if
   using a conventional oven.
   Preheat the broiler; preheating
   a toaster oven is not necessary.
2. Combine the mayonnaise, sour
   cream and green onion in a
   small bowl. Spread the
   mayonnaise mixture evenly on
   one side of each bread slice.
3. Place 2 slices of the liverwurst
   on the mayonnaise side of the
   bread slices. Top with 2 slices
   of the American cheese. Place
   the sandwiches on a broiler or
   toaster oven pan.
4. Broil the sandwiches for about
   2 to 3 minutes or until the
   American cheese is melted and
   lightly browned.

QUICK TIP

Toaster Oven
A toaster oven makes
quick grilled and
open-face cheese
melt sandwiches even
quicker—no oven
preheating.

25

Picante Chicken Salad

Menu Idea
Picante Chicken Salad*
Watermelon Ice*
(page 263)

Cilantro, also known as coriander and Chinese parsley, and jalapeño peppers are favorite seasoning ingredients in Southwestern cuisine. This salad is a perfect way to use leftover chicken.

Makes 4 servings.

Nutrient Value Per Serving: 514 calories, 33 g protein, 28 g fat, 37 g carbohydrate, 433 mg sodium, 75 mg cholesterol.

Cilantro Dressing:
1   **ripe tomato, peeled, seeded and chopped**
¼   **cup chopped fresh cilantro**
2   **tablespoons vegetable oil**
2   **tablespoons lime juice**
1   **tablespoon chopped pickled jalapeño pepper****
¼   **teaspoon salt**
⅛   **teaspoon pepper**

2   **cups shredded cooked chicken (about 14 ounces uncooked boneless breasts)**
6   **cups shredded lettuce (romaine or iceberg)**
1   **ripe avocado (about 14 ounces), halved, pitted, peeled and sliced lengthwise**
2   **ounces shredded Cheddar cheese (about ½ cup)**
⅓   **cup small red onion rings (½ small onion)**
8   **warm corn tortillas**

1. Prepare the Cilantro Dressing: Combine the tomato, cilantro, oil, lime juice, jalapeño pepper, salt and pepper in a medium-size bowl.
2. Add the chicken to the dressing and toss to mix well.
3. Arrange the shredded lettuce on a serving platter. Spoon the chicken over the lettuce. Arrange the avocado slices around the chicken. Sprinkle the salad with the Cheddar cheese and the red onion. Serve the salad with the warm tortillas.

****Note:** *Pickled or marinated jalapeño peppers can be found in the Mexican food section of many supermarkets.*

Cilantro Dressing Serving Suggestions: Make extra dressing and use with shrimp, beef, pork or cheese salads.

QUICK TIPS

Grate Ahead
Grate or shred cheeses ahead and store in screw-top jars in the refrigerator.

Terrific Tomatoes
To hasten the ripening of tomatoes, place them in a brown paper bag and leave them at room temperature until they reach the desired ripeness. Remember: *Never* refrigerate tomatoes!

Southeast Ham Salad

Ham, smoked or otherwise, has always been a favorite in the South.

Makes 4 servings.

Nutrient Value Per Serving: 274 calories, 20 g protein, 16 g fat, 15 g carbohydrate, 1,342 mg sodium, 48 mg cholesterol.

Sweet Pickle Mayonnaise Dressing:
- ¼ cup mayonnaise
- 1 tablespoon sweet relish
- 1 teaspoon dry mustard
- 1 teaspoon cider vinegar

- 2 large ripe tomatoes (about 10 ounces each)
- ¾ pound smoked ham, cut into ¼-inch pieces (about 3 cups)
- 1 small yellow squash, cut into ¼-inch pieces (about 1 cup)
- ½ cup cooked green peas
- ¼ cup chopped celery
- ¼ cup finely chopped red onion
- 8 lettuce leaves
  Parsley springs, for garnish (optional)

1. Prepare the Sweet Pickle Mayonnaise Dressing: Stir together the mayonnaise, relish, mustard and vinegar in a medium-size bowl.
2. Core and chop 1 of the tomatoes into ¼-inch pieces; add the tomato to the dressing. Add the ham, squash, peas, celery and onion to the dressing and toss to coat all the ingredients well.
3. Arrange the lettuce leaves on a serving platter. Spoon the salad over the leaves. Core and slice the remaining tomato and garnish the salad with the tomato slices, and with parsley sprigs, if you wish.

Sweet Pickle Mayonnaise Dressing Serving Suggestions: Make extra dressing and use with potato salad, coleslaw or tuna salad.

Menu Idea
Southeast Ham Salad*
Pickled Beets
Rolls
Peaches

QUICK TIPS

A Little Sprout Goes A Long Way
For extra zip, substitute alfalfa sprouts or "spicy" radish sprouts for lettuce.

Simple Substitution
Zucchini, yellow crookneck and straightneck squash share many of the same cooking qualities and may be substituted for each other in most recipes.

California Cheese Salad

Menu Idea

California Cheese
 Salad*
Sliced Beefsteak
 Tomatoes
Plums

This brightly colored salad features Monterey Jack, a cheese that originated in California.

Makes 4 servings.

*Nutrient Value Per Serving:
473 calories, 19 g protein, 42 g fat, 8 g carbohydrate, 414 mg sodium, 50 mg cholesterol.*

Basil Dressing:
¼   cup olive oil
¼   cup chopped fresh basil
2   tablespoons red wine
     vinegar
1   clove garlic, crushed
⅛   teaspoon pepper

8   ounces Monterey Jack
     cheese, cut into 1 x ¼-inch
     sticks
2   cups broccoli flowerets
     (4 ounces), blanched
½   cup walnut pieces
⅓   cup chopped ripe olives in
     brine** (12 large black
     olives)
8   leaves romaine lettuce
1   bunch arugula OR:
     watercress, trimmed of
     large stems
2   roasted sweet red peppers,
     cut into strips*** OR: 1 jar
     (7 ounces), drained and
     cut into strips, for garnish

1. Prepare the Basil Dressing: Whisk together the oil, basil, vinegar, garlic and pepper in a large bowl until well mixed.
2. Add the Monterey Jack cheese, broccoli, walnuts and olives to the dressing and toss to coat all the ingredients well.
3. For each serving, arrange the romaine and the arugula or watercress on a serving plate. Spoon one quarter of the cheese salad over the lettuce. Garnish with the roasted red pepper strips.

*Notes: **For the best flavor, use black Italian or Greek olives packed in brine. ***To roast sweet peppers, rub the outside skin with vegetable oil. Roast the peppers in a pan in a preheated hot oven (450°), turning once, for about 30 minutes or until the skin is blackened all over. Cool the peppers in the pan. Gently peel the blackened skin off the peppers with your fingers. Remove the stems and seeds.*

*Basil Dressing Serving
Suggestions:* Make extra dressing and use with salad greens or tomatoes when fresh basil is plentiful.

QUICK TIP

Choice Of The Cheese
To add a slightly spicier taste to salads or sandwiches, try a Monterey Jack with Jalapeño Pepper. Or, substitute an extra-sharp Cheddar.

Smoked Turkey Medley

Makes 4 servings (about 3 cups).

Nutrient Value Per Serving: 243 calories, 18 g protein, 9 g fat, 21 g carbohydrate, 645 mg sodium, 24 mg cholesterol.

1   can (15 ounces) black beans
8   ounces smoked turkey, cut into small cubes
1   jar (3¼ ounces) cocktail onions, with liquid
⅓   cup chopped red onion
2   tablespoons chopped parsley
2   tablespoons olive oil
¼   teaspoon pepper

1. Drain the black beans; rinse and drain the beans again. Place the beans in a medium-size bowl. Stir in the turkey, cocktail onions with their liquid, red onion, parsley, olive oil and pepper. Toss gently to mix well. Cover the bowl and refrigerate the salad for 1 hour to blend the flavors, if you wish.
2. Serve the salad with rye or pumpernickel bread, if you wish.

Bacon, Lettuce and Tomato Salad

This classic sandwich combination is even better in a salad.

Makes 4 servings.

Nutrient Value Per Serving: 417 calories, 11 g protein, 31 g fat, 26 g carbohydrate, 563 mg sodium, 26 mg cholesterol.

½   pound bacon, cut into 1-inch pieces
⅓   cup mayonnaise
¼   cup plain yogurt
2   tablespoons vegetable oil
1   tablespoon lemon juice
¼   teaspoon pepper
8   cups bite-size pieces iceberg lettuce
16   cherry tomatoes, halved
6   slices white or whole-wheat bread, toasted and cut into cubes

1. Fry the bacon in a medium-size skillet over medium heat until crisp and golden, turning occasionally. Transfer the bacon pieces with a slotted spoon to paper toweling to drain.
2. Combine the mayonnaise, yogurt, oil, lemon juice and pepper in a small bowl and whisk until the mixture is smooth.
3. Place the lettuce in a large, shallow salad bowl. Add the mayonnaise-yogurt dressing and toss until well blended. Mound the cherry tomatoes in the center of the salad. Surround the lettuce with the toasted bread cubes and the bacon.

Menu Idea

Tomato Soup
Smoked Turkey Medley*
Pumpernickel Bread
Brownies

Menu Idea

Bacon, Lettuce and Tomato Salad*
Toast with Basil Butter
Yogurt with Sliced Banana, Honey and Cashews

29

Chicken, Orange and Beet Salad

Roast Beef Salad Sandwiches

Menu Idea
Chicken, Orange
  and Beet Salad*
Flat Bread
Frozen Yogurt with
  Strawberries

Menu Idea
Roast Beef Salad
  Sandwiches*
Three-Bean Salad
Ice Cream

Makes 4 servings.

*Nutrient Value Per Serving:
244 calories, 23 g protein, 6 g
fat, 26 g carbohydrate, 405 mg
sodium, 62 mg cholesterol.*

Cumin Dressing:
½   cup orange juice
1   tablespoon ground cumin
2   teaspoons grated orange
     rind
2   teaspoons sugar
¼   teaspoon salt
⅛   to ¼ teaspoon ground hot
     red pepper

2   large oranges
½   pound fresh spinach,
     stemmed, washed and
     drained
2   cups cooked chicken**
1   can (16 ounces) sliced
     beets, drained
½   cup red onion slices, for
     garnish

1. Prepare the Cumin Dressing:
     Mix together the orange juice,
     cumin, orange rind, sugar, salt
     and ground hot red pepper in a
     small bowl until the sugar is
     dissolved.
2. Cut off the peel and the white
     membrane from the oranges.
     Cut out the sections and
     remove the seeds. Set the
     orange sections aside.
3. Arrange the spinach, chicken,
     orange sections and beets on a
     serving platter. Garnish with
     the red onion slices.
4. Pour the dressing over the
     salad just before serving.

**Note: *We used a rotisserie
chicken from the deli. Leftover
cooked chicken or canned chicken
may also be used.*

Makes 4 servings.

*Nutrient Value Per Serving:
420 calories, 21 g protein, 35 g
fat, 4 g carbohydrate, 345 mg
sodium, 82 mg cholesterol.*

2   green onions, quartered
¾   pound cooked beef, cut in
     ¾-inch cubes
⅓   cup mayonnaise
2   tablespoons sweet pickle
     relish
1   tablespoon lemon juice
½   teaspoon dry mustard
¼   teaspoon salt
     Rolls or sliced bread

1. Finely chop the green onions in
     a food processor. Add the beef
     and process just until finely
     chopped, 3 one-second pulses.
2. Combine the mayonnaise,
     relish, lemon juice, dry mustard
     and salt in a medium-size bowl.
     Add the beef mixture and stir
     until blended. Serve on rolls or
     sliced bread.

Mozzarella Tomato Salad

Walnut Pesto Dressing

Fresh basil glorifies summer's ripest tomatoes.

Makes 4 servings.

Nutrient Value Per Serving (without dressing): 297 calories, 20 g protein, 19 g fat, 14 g carbohydrate, 338 mg sodium, 66 mg cholesterol.

2 **heads Boston lettuce, washed**
¾ **pound mozzarella cheese, thinly sliced**
4 **medium-size ripe tomatoes, cored and sliced**
1 **large red onion, halved and sliced crosswise**
 Walnut Pesto Dressing (recipe at right)
 Walnut halves, for garnish

1. Arrange the lettuce leaves on 4 salad plates, dividing evenly.
2. Arrange the mozzarella cheese, tomatoes and onion on the lettuce in the 4 plates. Drizzle the Walnut Pesto Dressing over the salads. Garnish with the walnut halves.

Makes about 1 cup.

Nutrient Value Per Tablespoon: 71 calories, 2 g protein, 7 g fat, 2 g carbohydrate, 117 mg sodium, 2 mg cholesterol.

2 **cups fresh basil leaves**
1 **cup fresh parsley sprigs**
⅓ **cup walnut halves**
2 **cloves garlic**
⅓ **cup olive oil**
½ **teaspoon salt**
½ **cup freshly grated Parmesan cheese**

1. Combine the basil, parsley, walnuts, garlic, oil and salt in the container of a food processor. Cover and process on high speed until the mixture is smooth.
2. Transfer the mixture to a small bowl and stir in the Parmesan cheese until well blended. The dressing can be refrigerated for 2 or 3 days.

Menu Idea
Red Pepper Soup* *(page 167)*
Mozzarella Tomato Salad* with Walnut Pesto Dressing*
Flat Bread
Fresh Fruit

QUICK TIP

Pesto Pronto
You can make Walnut Pesto Dressing when basil is in fresh supply, and freeze it for winter months. Mix together all ingredients except the garlic and Parmesan cheese; place in a freezer-safe container and pour a thin layer of olive oil over the top. To thaw, immerse covered container in warm water. Add Parmesan cheese and garlic when thawed. Allow to sit 20 minutes for flavors to marry.

Mozzarella Tomato Salad is dressed with a pesto made from walnuts.

Mexican Salad

This main-dish salad is wonderful any time of year.

Makes 6 servings.

Nutrient Value Per Serving (without dressing): 547 calories, 17 g protein, 38 g fat, 41 g carbohydrate, 839 mg sodium, 40 mg cholesterol.

1   **to 2 heads romaine lettuce, rinsed, dried and torn into squares**
2   **cups shredded sharp Cheddar cheese (½ pound)**
2   **to 3 large tomatoes, diced**
1   **large red onion, diced**
1   **can (6 ounces) pitted ripe olives, drained and sliced**
1   **can (4 ounces) chopped green chilies**
1   **bag (8 ounces) corn tortilla chips, crumbled**
2   **avocados, peeled, pitted and diced**
     Creamy Salsa Dressing (recipe follows)

1. Place the romaine in a large serving bowl.
2. Add the Cheddar cheese, tomatoes, onion, olives and chilies. Gently toss the mixture to blend all the ingredients.
3. Top with the tortilla chips and the avocado. Serve with the Creamy Salsa Dressing on the side.

Creamy Salsa Dressing: Combine 1½ cups of mayonnaise, 1 can (7 ounces) of green chili salsa, ⅓ cup of catsup and ½ teaspoon of chili powder in a small bowl. Cover and chill, if you wish. *Makes about 2 cups. Nutrient Value Per Tablespoon: 79 calories, 0 g protein, 8 g fat, 1 g carbohydrate, 128 mg sodium, 6 mg cholesterol.*

A south-of-the-border delight, Mexican Salad is topped with Creamy Salsa Dressing.

Ham and Jarlsberg Salad

Don't feel like cooking? This Ham and Jarlsberg Salad fills you up without tying you to your kitchen. Serve with the Lemon Caraway Vinaigrette.

Menu Idea

Ham and Jarlsberg Salad* with Lemon Caraway Vinaigrette*

Caraway Seed Breadsticks

Peach and Blueberry Compote with Yogurt Sauce* *(page 251)*

Makes 4 servings.

Nutrient Value Per Serving (without dressing):
319 calories, 28 g protein, 17 g fat, 5 g carbohydrate, 1,110 mg sodium, 51 mg cholesterol.

	Romaine lettuce leaves
½	pound cooked ham, cubed
½	pound Jarlsberg cheese, cubed
1	pint cherry tomatoes, hulled and halved
	Lemon Caraway Vinaigrette (recipe follows)

Line a serving platter with the romaine leaves. Arrange the ham, Jarlsberg cheese and tomatoes over the lettuce. Drizzle with the Lemon Caraway Vinaigrette and toss.

Lemon Caraway Vinaigrette:
Combine 1 egg yolk, 1 small clove of garlic, crushed, 1 teaspoon of caraway seeds, ¼ cup of lemon juice and 1 teaspoon of grainy mustard in a small bowl. Slowly whisk in ¼ cup of olive oil and ¼ cup of vegetable oil. The dressing can be refrigerated for up to 2 days. *Makes about ¾ cup. Nutrient Value Per Tablespoon: 87 calories, 0 g protein, 10 g fat, 0 g carbohydrate, 6 mg sodium, 23 mg cholesterol.*

Tomatoes Stuffed with Ham Salad

Menu Idea
Tomatoes Stuffed with Ham Salad*
Crusty Italian Bread
Pecans with Gorgonzola Cheese

A spicy horseradish-mustard dressing adds zest to Tomatoes Stuffed with Ham Salad.

Makes 4 servings.

Nutrient Value Per Serving: 279 calories, 18 g protein, 19 g fat, 11 g carbohydrate, 1,419 mg sodium, 58 mg cholesterol.

Horseradish Mayonnaise:
- ⅓ cup dairy sour cream
- 2 tablespoons mayonnaise
- 3 teaspoons bottled horseradish
- 1 teaspoon Dijon-style mustard
- ⅛ teaspoon pepper

- ¾ pound deli baked ham, cut into small dice (about 2 cups)
- 1 cup chopped celery
- ¼ cup chopped black Greek olives**
- ¼ cup finely chopped dill pickle
- ¼ cup chopped parsley
- 4 medium-size ripe tomatoes
- 8 leaves Boston lettuce
- 8 whole black Greek olives, for garnish

1. Prepare the Horseradish Mayonnaise: Combine the sour cream, mayonnaise, horseradish, mustard and pepper in a large bowl.
2. Add the ham, celery, olives, pickle and 3 tablespoons of the parsley. Toss the mixture gently until all the ingredients are evenly coated.
3. Cut each tomato vertically into 6 wedges to within ½ inch of the bottom. Carefully spoon out the center membranes and seeds and save for another use. Stuff the tomatoes with the ham mixture. Serve on a platter lined with the Boston lettuce leaves. Garnish with the whole olives and the remaining chopped parsley.

**Note: *For best flavor, use black Greek olives packed in brine, but regular black ripe olives may be substituted.*

More Peppery Pepper
Pepper freshly ground from a peppermill has a lustier flavor than already ground or crushed pepper.

34

Ham Oriental

Finely shredded lettuce takes the place of rice, so this dish is low-calorie. And the deli ham makes it quick and easy.

Makes 4 servings.

Nutrient Value Per Serving:
286 calories, 23 g protein, 17 g fat, 11 g carbohydrate, 1,813 mg sodium, 118 mg cholesterol.

Oriental Dressing:
1	egg yolk
2	tablespoons vinegar
2	teaspoons sugar
1	teaspoon grated fresh gingerroot
	Pinch crushed red pepper flakes
2	tablespoons vegetable oil
1	teaspoon Oriental sesame oil**
2	tablespoons soy sauce
1	tablespoon water

¾	pound deli baked ham, cut into thin strips (about 2 cups)
1	medium-size cucumber, pared, halved, seeded and sliced
4	red radishes, sliced
1	cup bean sprouts, rinsed and drained
1	cup watercress sprigs
1	carrot, peeled and shredded (½ cup)
4	cups finely shredded iceberg lettuce (½ head)
¼	cup sliced green onion (2 green onions), for garnish

1. Prepare the Oriental Dressing: Combine the egg yolk, vinegar, sugar, gingerroot and red pepper flakes in the container of an electric blender. Cover the container and whirl on medium speed for 5 seconds. Gradually pour in the vegetable and Oriental sesame oils in a fine stream through the hole in the lid while blending on low speed. Pour the dressing into a small bowl. Stir in the soy sauce and the water until well mixed.
2. Mix together the ham, cucumber, radish, sprouts, watercress and carrot in a large bowl. Add the dressing and toss to mix all the ingredients. Place the shredded lettuce on a serving platter. Arrange the salad over the lettuce. Garnish the salad with the sliced green onion.

***Note:** Oriental sesame oil has more flavor and is darker in color than regular sesame oil. It can be found in the Oriental food section of many supermarkets or in Oriental specialty food stores.*

Menu Idea
Ham Oriental*
Sesame Seed Breadsticks
Ginger Melon*
(page 246)

QUICK TIP

Vegetable Vinaigrette
Vegetables such as carrots, green beans, lima beans, peas, corn or zucchini can be coated with vinaigrette, stored in the refrigerator and be ready at a moment's notice to add to salads. Whisk the vinaigrette together, pour over the cooked or raw vegetables, and allow at least six hours before serving, so that the flavors can marry. Marinated vegetables may be kept for at least a week in the refrigerator.

30 MINUTE DISHES

Chapter 2 presents dinner in 30 minutes or less—
a little less frantic than the 15-minute quick-fixes.
In the extra time, you can make more elaborate
pasta sauces, do wonders with chicken and work
miracles with fish.

For instance, in 30 minutes you can put together easy,
cooking-without-looking dishes such as Pasta with
Mushrooms and Ham *(page 40),* where the pasta and
sauce cook together. Or, stir-fry boneless chicken
chunks in Marinated Orange Chicken *(page 59)* for
dinner. If you've been meaning to add more fish to your
diet, our step-by-step primer for poaching fish *(page
70)* will take the mystery out of fish and give you
perfect results each time. Sample our Crab-Stuffed
Flounder *(page 68)* and Marjoram Poached Halibut
(page 75) to give you an idea of what we mean.

On the lighter side, you can try one of our main dish
salads such as Roast Beef Salad with Caper Dressing
(page 82) or match a salad with a soup for a speedy
meal.

The point is this: You can do an awful lot in a half
hour—but it takes the right recipes to do it!

*Orange and Onion Salad, top (page 83), is a colorful
complement to our hearty Roast Beef Salad with Caper
Dressing (page 82). For a spicy opener to any meal, try no-
cook Red Pepper Soup (Chapter 5, page 167.)*

Pasta

Pasta with Three "Peppers"

Pepperoni, pepperoncini and roasted peppers make this pasta dish a spicy standout.

Makes 6 servings.

Nutrient Value Per Serving: 558 calories, 21 g protein, 31 g fat, 48 g carbohydrate, 1,255 mg sodium, 78 mg cholesterol.

12	ounces penne or tubular pasta
½	teaspoon leaf rosemary, crumbled
8	ounces thinly sliced pepperoni
½	cup small pepperoncini (Tuscan pickled peppers; about 17)
1	jar (7 ounces) roasted red peppers, drained and coarsely chopped
3½	cups boiling water
1	cup heavy cream
1	cup grated Romano or Parmesan cheese

1. Arrange the pasta in a 10-inch skillet. Sprinkle the pasta with the rosemary. Layer on the pepperoni, pepperoncini and roasted red peppers.
2. Pour the boiling water over the contents of the skillet. Cover the skillet and bring to a full boil. Cook the mixture briskly over medium-high heat for 10 minutes or until the pasta is *al dente*, firm but tender.
3. Stir in the cream and the Romano or Parmesan cheese. Reheat gently. Serve immediately.

Menu Idea

Pasta with Three "Peppers"*

Romaine and Chicory Salad

Poppy Seed Breadsticks

Cookies and Coffee

QUICK TIP

Grated Cheese Accent
Not only pasta dishes, but soups, stews, salads and many other dishes benefit from a sprinkling of grated cheese. *Freshly* grated Parmesan, Romano, asiago or sardo hard cheeses have much more flavor than the packaged grated product. A hand-held grater produces grated cheese that is feathery light.

Pasta with Three "Peppers" has rich cream and hot peppers — a tantalizing combination. You don't have to boil the pasta separately; it goes right in with the meat and peppers.

Pasta with Mushrooms and Ham

Menu Idea

Pasta with Mushrooms and Ham*

Pear and Walnut Salad

Semolina Bread

Almond Cookies and Coffee-Flavored Liqueur

Makes 6 servings.

Nutrient Value Per Serving: 454 calories, 18 g protein, 18 g fat, 55 g carbohydrate, 659 mg sodium, 54 mg cholesterol.

1	clove garlic, halved
2	tablespoons butter
1	tablespoon olive oil
1	pound mushrooms, coarsely chopped
¼	pound cooked ham, coarsely chopped
1	large onion, coarsely chopped (1 cup)
½	teaspoon salt
¼	teaspoon crushed red pepper flakes
½	cup dry white wine
12	ounces penne, ziti or mostaccioli pasta
4	cups boiling water
½	cup grated Parmesan cheese
¼	cup finely chopped parsley
1	cup frozen lima beans, thawed
½	cup heavy cream

1. Sauté the garlic in the butter and the oil in a 10-inch skillet with at least a 2-quart capacity, until the garlic is lightly browned, for about 1 minute. Remove the garlic and discard. Add the mushrooms, ham and onion to the skillet. Sauté just until the mixture begins to color, for about 5 minutes. Add the salt, red pepper flakes and wine. Continue to cook the mixture just until the wine has evaporated.
2. Add the pasta and the boiling water to the skillet, stirring to distribute the ingredients evenly. Cover the skillet and simmer, stirring occasionally, for the least amount of time suggested in the package directions for cooking the pasta or until the pasta is *al dente*, firm but tender. Check the pasta halfway through the cooking time and add a little more water to the skillet, if necessary.
3. Combine the Parmesan cheese and the parsley in a small serving bowl.
4. Stir the lima beans and the cream into the pasta mixture. Heat the mixture gently for 30 seconds. Serve immediately. Pass the cheese-parsley mixture.

QUICK TIP

Start With Hot
Hot tap water comes to a boil much faster than cold. And *always* cover the pot—this traps the heat and, again, promotes a quick boil.

Pasta Primavera with Clams

This is a delicately seasoned dish that is best with fresh clams.

Makes 6 servings.

Nutrient Value Per Serving: 412 calories, 15 g protein, 10 g fat, 64 g carbohydrate, 190 mg sodium, 22 mg cholesterol.

2   cups coarsely chopped fresh, ripe, unpeeled tomatoes (about 1 pound)
2   cloves garlic, coarsely chopped
2   tablespoons coarsely chopped fresh basil leaves OR: 1½ teaspoons leaf basil, crumbled
¼   cup good-quality olive oil
¼   teaspoon salt
¼   teaspoon pepper
1   pound spaghettini
16 fresh littleneck clams, shucked, liquid reserved, clams thinly sliced (½ cup broth, ⅓ cup clams)
2   tablespoons finely chopped flat-leaf Italian parsley

1. Combine the tomatoes, garlic, basil, oil, salt and pepper in the container of an electric blender or a food processor. Cover and whirl until the mixture is a fairly smooth consistency but still with some texture.
2. Cook the spaghettini in a large pot of boiling salted water until *al dente*, firm but tender. Drain the spaghettini in a colander.
3. Bring the clam broth to boiling in a large skillet or Dutch oven over medium-high heat. Add the spaghettini and cook, tossing constantly, until all the clam broth has been absorbed, for about 3 minutes. Add the tomato mixture and the sliced clams. Continue cooking until the mixture is heated through and the clams are just cooked, tender and succulent, for about 4 minutes longer. Sprinkle with the parsley and serve.

Menu Idea

Pasta Primavera with Clams*
Escarole Salad
Garlic Bread*
   (page 7)
Cannoli Cream with Strawberries

QUICK TIP

Chopped Garlic On Hand
Chop a large quantity of garlic in a blender or food processor. Scrape into a glass jar with a screw-top lid, add enough olive oil to cover the garlic, screw on the top and refrigerate for up to several weeks.

Fusilli with Shrimp and Zucchini

Menu Idea
Fusilli with Shrimp and Zucchini *
Crusty Rolls
Raspberry Sherbet and Pound Cake

Makes 4 servings.

*Nutrient Value Per Serving:
531 calories, 20 g protein, 26 g
fat, 57 g carbohydrate, 391 mg
sodium, 66 mg cholesterol.*

1	**small dried red chili pepper**
½	**pound small shrimp, shelled, deveined and shells reserved**
6	**to 8 tablespoons olive oil**
6	**small shallots, thinly sliced**
1	**tablespoon peeled and chopped fresh gingerroot**
2	**large cloves garlic, finely chopped**
4	**large ripe tomatoes (1½ pounds), peeled, halved, seeded and chopped**
1	**teaspoon leaf oregano, crumbled**
1	**teaspoon leaf thyme, crumbled**
½	**teaspoon salt**
¼	**teaspoon pepper**
2	**medium-size zucchini (12 ounces), trimmed, quartered lengthwise and thinly sliced ¼ inch thick**
½	**pound fusilli pasta**
¼	**cup coarsely chopped fresh basil**
2	**tablespoons finely chopped parsley**

1. Sauté the chili pepper and the shrimp shells in 2 tablespoons of the oil in a large, heavy, deep skillet over medium-high heat, stirring constantly, until the shells turn a bright pink. Remove the shells and the chili pepper with a slotted spoon and discard.

2. Sauté the shrimp in the same skillet, adding an additional tablespoon of oil, if necessary. Scrape up any browned bits from the bottom of the skillet. Cook the shrimp for 3 minutes or until the shrimp turns pink and curls. Transfer the shrimp to a cutting board. Coarsely chop the shrimp, transfer it to a small bowl and reserve.

3. Sauté the shallots, gingerroot and garlic in 2 tablespoons of the oil in the skillet over low heat for 3 minutes or until the shallots soften.

4. Add the tomatoes, oregano, thyme, salt and pepper to the skillet. Cover the skillet and lower the heat. Simmer the mixture for 5 minutes or until the gingerroot is very soft.

5. Meanwhile, sauté the zucchini in 2 tablespoons of the oil, adding another tablespoon of oil if necessary, in a medium-size skillet until the zucchini is lightly browned. Add the zucchini to the tomato sauce. Simmer the sauce for 5 minutes. Keep the sauce warm over very low heat.

6. Cook the fusilli in a large saucepan of boiling water until *al dente*, firm but tender. Drain the fusilli in a colander and rinse briefly under cold running water. Return the fusilli to the saucepan it was cooked in.

7. Add the reserved shrimp and the tomato-zucchini sauce to the fusilli. Stir in the basil and the parsley. Serve immediately.

Penne with Tuna Sauce

Microwave Instructions
(for a 650-watt variable power microwave oven)

Ingredient Changes: Reduce the olive oil to 3 tablespoons, and the oregano and thyme to ½ teaspoon each.

Directions: Cook the fusilli conventionally, following the package directions. Place the chili pepper, shrimp shells and 2 tablespoons of the oil in a microwave-safe baking dish, about 12 x 8 inches. Cover the dish with microwave-safe plastic wrap, vented at one corner. Microwave the chili pepper and the shells at full power for 1 minute, 30 seconds. Remove the shells and the chili pepper and discard. Add the shrimp in one layer to the same dish. Cover the dish with microwave-safe plastic wrap. Microwave the shrimp at full power for 2 minutes, stirring once. Remove the shrimp and chop coarsely. Place the shrimp in a small bowl, cover the bowl and reserve the shrimp. Add the shallots, gingerroot and garlic to the same microwave-safe dish. Cover the dish with microwave-safe plastic wrap. Microwave at full power for 3 minutes. Stir in the tomatoes. Cover with microwave-safe plastic wrap. Microwave at full power for 3 minutes. Stir in the zucchini and the remaining tablespoon of oil. Cover the dish with microwave-safe plastic wrap. Microwave at full power for 4 minutes, stirring once. Remove the dish from the oven. Stir in the hot cooked fusilli, the shrimp, oregano, thyme, salt, pepper, basil and parsley.

Makes 6 servings.

Nutrient Value Per Serving: 469 calories, 18 g protein, 17 g fat, 61 g carbohydrate, 456 mg sodium, 17 mg cholesterol.

1   **medium-size onion, finely chopped**
¼   **cup good-quality olive oil**
2   **cups coarsely chopped fresh tomatoes**
2   **tablespoons chopped fresh mint OR: 1 teaspoon dried mint**
¼   **teaspoon salt**
⅛   **teaspoon pepper**
1   **can (6½ ounces) Italian-style tuna fish, packed in olive oil**
¾   **to 1 cup chicken broth**
1   **pound penne (short, tubular pasta)**
1   **tablespoon finely chopped parsley, for garnish**

1. Cook the onion in the oil in a medium-size skillet over medium heat until the onion is very soft, for about 8 minutes.
2. Add the tomatoes, mint, salt and pepper. Cover the skillet, lower the heat and simmer for 10 minutes. Transfer the mixture to an electric blender or a food processor. Cover and whirl until the mixture is puréed. Add the tuna and its oil to the blender; purée until smooth. Add enough of the broth to make the sauce the consistency of heavy cream.
3. While the sauce is cooking, cook the penne in boiling salted water until *al dente*, firm but tender; drain. Toss the penne with the sauce in a large serving bowl. Garnish with the parsley. Serve immediately.

Menu Idea
Penne with Tuna Sauce*

Boston and Romaine Lettuce Salad

Lemon Sponge Cake with Strawberry Sauce* *(page 241)*

QUICK TIP

Appliance Assistance
Busy cooks can cut time with electric slicers, blenders, food processors, electric mixers, microwave ovens, toaster ovens and the like.

43

Penne with Fresh Tomatoes

Menu Idea

Penne with Fresh
  Tomatoes*

Radish, Cucumber
  and Romaine
  Salad

Crusty Italian Bread

Mocha Amaretti
  Loaf* *(page 253)*

Makes 4 servings.

*Nutrient Value Per Serving:
582 calories, 17 g protein, 15 g
fat, 96 g carbohydrate, 155 mg
sodium, 0 mg cholesterol.*

---

10   ripe plum tomatoes
       (2 pounds)
¼   cup good-quality olive oil
1   clove garlic, finely chopped
¼   cup coarsely chopped fresh
       basil
¼   teaspoon salt
⅛   teaspoon pepper
1   pound penne (short, tubular
       pasta)
     Whole fresh basil leaves,
       for garnish *(optional)*

1. Blanch the tomatoes in a large pot of boiling water for 10 seconds. Drain the tomatoes in a colander and run under cold water. Peel the tomatoes. Cut the tomatoes in half lengthwise and remove the seeds. Slice each tomato into wedges lengthwise. Set aside. (If ripe tomatoes are not available, use 4 cups of sliced canned tomatoes.)

2. Heat the oil in a large skillet or Dutch oven over medium heat. Add the garlic. Cook, stirring. When the garlic begins to color, after about 1 minute, add the tomatoes, basil, salt and pepper. Cover the skillet, lower the heat and simmer until the tomatoes are tender but not falling apart, for about 8 minutes.

3. While the sauce is cooking, cook the penne in a large pot of boiling salted water until *al dente*, firm but tender. Drain the penne in a colander.

4. Add the penne to the tomato sauce and cook over high heat for 1 minute, stirring constantly. Garnish each portion with several whole fresh basil leaves, if you wish. Serve immediately.

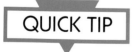

QUICK TIP

**Skillet Dish
Running Dry?**
When adding extra
liquid to a cooking
skillet dish, make
sure to heat the liquid
first so that the
mixture continues to
cook.

Pasta with Arugula Pesto

Arugula pesto is a tasty alternative to the more familiar basil pesto. Arugula is a slightly bitter leafy green.

Makes 4 servings.

Nutrient Value Per Serving: 568 calories, 17 g protein, 21 g fat, 80 g carbohydrate, 380 mg sodium, 2 mg cholesterol.

3   small potatoes (12 ounces), peeled, halved and thinly sliced
7   cups fresh arugula (leaves only), picked over, washed and dried**
2   to 3 cloves garlic, coarsely chopped
¼   cup (1½ ounces) pine nuts (pignoli)
5   tablespoons good-quality olive oil
2   tablespoons grated Parmesan cheese, plus extra for garnish
¾   teaspoon salt
¼   teaspoon pepper
¾   pound tubular pasta, such as penne

1. Cook the potatoes in a medium-size pot of boiling salted water until done. Drain the potatoes in a colander; reserve.
2. Combine the arugula, garlic, pine nuts, oil, Parmesan cheese, salt and pepper in the container of a food processor or an electric blender. Cover and whirl until the mixture is puréed to a creamy consistency. If the mixture is too dry, add a little more oil. Set aside 1 cup of the pesto for the pasta and reserve the remainder for another time or for Rigatoni Salad *(see recipe, page 46).* Save the pesto by placing in a jar or other container and adding ½ inch of olive oil to the surface. Cover the container and refrigerate.
3. Cook the pasta in a large pot of boiling salted water until *al dente,* firm but tender. Drain the pasta in a colander, reserving about ¼ cup of the pasta water. Thin the 1 cup pesto with the reserved pasta water until the pesto is the consistency of light cream. Add the pesto and the reserved potatoes to the pasta in a large serving bowl; toss well. Garnish the pasta with additional Parmesan cheese. Serve immediately.

**Note: *If you wish, you may substitute parsley (preferably flat-leaf Italian) for some of the arugula. Or, for a more traditional pesto, substitute 5 cups of fresh basil leaves, picked over, washed and dried, for the arugula.*

Menu Idea

Pasta with Arugula Pesto*

Red, Green and Yellow Sweet Pepper Vinaigrette

Chocolate Roll with Orange Ginger Meringue* *(page 234)*

Rigatoni Salad

Menu Idea
Rigatoni Salad*
Crusty Italian Bread
Chilled Peach
   and Blueberry
   Compote with
   Yogurt Sauce*
   (page 251)

Serve this salad at room temperature, and do not refrigerate. You may prepare the dish several hours in advance but, if you do, add the tomatoes and pesto at the last minute.

Makes 6 servings.

Nutrient Value Per Serving: 619 calories, 26 g protein, 35 g fat, 52 g carbohydrate, 851 mg sodium, 34 mg cholesterol.

¾ pound rigatoni
2 cups broccoli flowerets, in bite-size pieces
½ cup good-quality olive oil
2 cans (6½ ounces each) Italian-style tuna fish, packed in olive oil
1 cup thinly sliced green onion
3 tablespoons finely chopped flat-leaf Italian parsley
¾ teaspoon salt
¼ teaspoon pepper
2 teaspoons lemon juice
4 cups firm, ripe tomatoes (1½ pounds), at room temperature and cut into bite-size wedges
¼ cup pesto, the consistency of light cream *(see Pasta with Arugula Pesto, page 45)*

1. Cook the rigatoni in a large pot of boiling salted water. After 5 minutes, add the broccoli. Cook until the rigatoni is *al dente*, firm but tender. Drain the rigatoni and the broccoli in a colander and rinse under cold running water. Drain the rigatoni and the broccoli well.
2. Pour the rigatoni and the broccoli into a large bowl. Add the oil, tuna with its oil, green onion, parsley, salt, pepper and lemon juice. Toss until all the ingredients are well mixed. Add the tomatoes and the pesto, and toss the salad again. Serve.

Pasta with Zucchini and Black Olives

Makes 4 servings.

Nutrient Value Per Serving:
339 calories, 10 g protein, 11 g
fat, 52 g carbohydrate, 1,014 mg
sodium, 0 mg cholesterol.

1   pound zucchini, cut into
    ½-inch dice
2   tablespoons olive oil
1   clove garlic, finely chopped
¼   teaspoon crushed red
    pepper flakes
1   can (14 ounces) Italian-style
    whole tomatoes with their
    liquid, chopped
¼   cup Italian or Greek black
    olives, pitted and chopped
1   teaspoon salt
¼   teaspoon black pepper
8   ounces spaghetti, vermicelli
    or other pasta strands,
    broken into 3-inch pieces
3   cups boiling water
½   teaspoon leaf oregano,
    crumbled
¼   cup finely chopped parsley
    Grated Parmesan cheese

1. Sauté the zucchini in the oil in a 10-inch skillet with at least a 2-quart capacity, until the zucchini begins to soften, for about 3 minutes.
2. Add the garlic and the red pepper flakes to the skillet and cook for 1 minute. Add the tomatoes with their liquid, olives, salt and black pepper to the skillet. Cover the skillet and simmer for 5 minutes.
3. Add the pasta and the boiling water to the skillet, stirring to distribute the ingredients evenly. Cover the skillet and cook, stirring occasionally, for the least amount of time suggested in the package directions for cooking the pasta or until the pasta is *al dente*, firm but tender. Check the pasta halfway through the cooking time and add a little more water to the skillet, if necessary.
4. Add the oregano to the skillet and stir to combine. Remove the skillet from the heat. Sprinkle the pasta with the parsley. Serve immediately and pass the Parmesan cheese.

Menu Idea

Pasta with Zucchini and Black Olives*

Marinated Artichoke Hearts with Cherry Tomatoes

Crusty Italian Bread

Sliced Melon with Lemon Yogurt

Chicken

Chicken Parmesan with Noodles

Makes 4 servings.

*Nutrient Value Per Serving:
895 calories, 57 g protein, 33 g
fat, 89 g carbohydrate, 1,054 mg
sodium, 286 mg cholesterol.*

1   package (12 ounces) egg
       noodles
1   cup bottled spaghetti sauce
¼   cup all-purpose flour
       Pinch pepper
1   egg, slightly beaten
1   tablespoon water
½   cup packaged seasoned
       bread crumbs
¼   cup grated Parmesan cheese
½   teaspoon leaf oregano,
       crumbled
4   boneless, skinned chicken
       breast halves (1¼ pounds),
       lightly flattened
2   tablespoons olive oil
1   cup shredded mozzarella
       cheese (4 ounces)
1   tablespoon butter
¼   cup heavy cream
       Pinch white pepper

1. Cook the noodles following the
   package directions.
2. Meanwhile, heat the spaghetti
   sauce in a small saucepan over
   low heat.
3. Combine the flour and the
   pepper on a piece of wax paper.
   Combine the egg and the water
   in a shallow dish. Combine the
   bread crumbs, 2 tablespoons of
   the Parmesan cheese and the
   oregano on a second piece of
   wax paper.
4. Place the chicken in the flour
   mixture and turn to coat both
   sides evenly. Dip chicken in the
   egg mixture, then the crumbs,
   turning to coat both sides.
5. Heat the oil in a large skillet
   over high heat. Add the chicken
   and sauté on one side for 3
   minutes or until lightly
   browned. Turn the chicken
   over and sauté for 2 minutes
   longer.
6. Lower the heat to medium.
   Sprinkle the mozzarella cheese
   over the chicken. Cover the
   skillet and cook the chicken for
   2 minutes or until the
   mozzarella cheese is melted
   and the chicken is firm to the
   touch.
7. Meanwhile, drain the noodles in
   a colander. Add the butter and
   the cream to the pot used to
   cook the noodles. Heat the
   butter-cream mixture over
   medium heat until the butter is
   melted and the cream is
   bubbly. Add the noodles, the
   remaining Parmesan cheese
   and the white pepper; toss to
   combine all the ingredients.
8. Pour the noodles onto a serving
   platter. Sprinkle the noodles
   with additional Parmesan
   cheese, if you wish. Arrange the
   chicken over the noodles and
   spoon the spaghetti sauce over
   the chicken.

Menu Idea
**Chicken Parmesan
   with Noodles***
**Italian-Style Green
   Beans**
Garlic Bread*
   (page 7)
Amaretti Cookies

*Chicken Parmesan with Noodles is
topped with prepared spaghetti sauce
for even faster cooking.*

Chicken Cutlets Tampa

Menu Idea
Chicken Cutlets Tampa*

Broccoli with Toasted Almonds

Dinner Rolls

Chocolate Ice Cream with Ginger Snaps

```
QUICK TIP
```

To Cook Chicken Breasts Even Faster...
● Have all the ingredients and the utensils ready near the stove before you start cooking.
● To spruce up chicken breasts, use convenience foods, such as prechopped frozen onions and preshredded cheese.
● To flatten skinned chicken breasts quickly, place the boneless breasts between two sheets of wax paper and pound once or twice with a large, heavy saucepan.
● For fast, even heating, choose a wide-diameter saucepan or skillet.

Flattened chicken breasts are the quick-cook trick in this delectable chicken dish with its creamy orange sauce.

Makes 4 servings.

Nutrient Value Per Serving: 646 calories, 45 g protein, 22 g fat, 49 g carbohydrate, 589 mg sodium, 139 mg cholesterol.

1½	cups couscous**
1½	cups chicken broth
2	tablespoons butter
1	tablespoon oil
4	boneless, skinned chicken breast halves (1¼ pounds), flattened slightly
1	bunch green onions, trimmed, green and white parts sliced separately
¾	cup orange juice
½	cup heavy cream
¼	teaspoon salt
1	orange, thinly sliced

1. Cook the couscous using the broth and 1 tablespoon of the butter, following the package directions.
2. Melt the remaining tablespoon of butter and the oil together in a large skillet over medium-high heat. Add the chicken and sauté, turning once, until the chicken is golden and firm to the touch, for about 5 to 6 minutes. Remove the chicken to a plate. Cover the plate with aluminum foil to keep the chicken warm.
3. Add the white part of the green onion, the orange juice, cream and salt to the skillet. Boil the mixture over high heat, scraping up any browned bits from the bottom of the skillet, for 2 minutes to reduce the sauce and thicken. Add the orange slices and remove the skillet from the heat.
4. Stir the green part of the green onion into the cooked couscous. Spoon the couscous onto a serving platter. Arrange the chicken with the orange slices on the couscous. Spoon the orange sauce over the chicken.

**Note: *Couscous, sometimes referred to as "Moroccan pasta," is coarsely ground wheat granules and can be found in the rice and grain section of your supermarket.*

Creamy Ginger Chicken

By finishing this sauce with nonfat plain yogurt, instead of heavy or sour cream, you have an especially low-calorie entrée.

Makes 4 servings.

Nutrient Value Per Serving: 160 calories, 22 g protein, 4 g fat, 7 g carbohydrate, 204 mg sodium, 82 mg cholesterol.

1   **small onion, quartered**
2   **large cloves garlic, coarsely chopped**
1   **piece (1-inch cube) fresh gingerroot, peeled and coarsely chopped**
¼   **cup water plus 2 teaspoons**
1½   **pounds chicken thighs, skinned**
1   **large onion, sliced ½ inch thick and separated into rings**
½   **cup chicken broth**
1   **teaspoon cornstarch**
½   **cup nonfat plain yogurt**

1. Place the small onion, garlic, gingerroot and the ¼ cup of water in the container of a food processor or an electric blender. Cover and whirl until the mixture is smooth; reserve.
2. Fry the chicken, skinned side down, without any oil in a large, nonstick saucepan or Dutch oven. Cook over medium-high heat for about 3 to 5 minutes or until the chicken is crusty and very golden brown. Shake the pan back and forth to prevent sticking. Turn the chicken over and fry for 1 to 2 minutes longer or until the underside is brown. Push the chicken to one side of the pan.
3. Add the onion rings and cook, stirring constantly, until the edges of the onion rings are coated with the browned bits from the bottom of the pan, for about 2 minutes.
4. Stir in the broth. Lower the heat to very low. Cover the pan and simmer for 15 minutes or until the chicken is no longer pink. Transfer the chicken to a warm platter.
5. Remove the pan from the heat. Stir together the cornstarch and the 2 teaspoons of water in a small cup. Add to the saucepan along with the reserved gingerroot purée. Stir in the yogurt, 1 tablespoon at a time.
6. Return the pan to the heat and bring to boiling. Boil for 1 minute or just to thicken the mixture; do not overboil. Spoon the sauce over the chicken.

Menu Idea

Creamy Ginger Chicken*

White Rice

Red-Leaf Lettuce Salad

Lemon Sherbet and Almond Cookies

Chicken Grill with Hash Brown Potatoes

Menu Idea
Chicken Grill with Hash Brown Potatoes*
Coleslaw
Rice Pudding

This tasty mixed grill of chicken thighs, sausage and tomatoes is sparked with a piquant mustard and currant jelly sauce.

Makes 4 servings.

Nutrient Value Per Serving:
629 calories, 28 g protein, 36 g fat, 48 g carbohydrate, 650 mg sodium, 103 mg cholesterol.

2	tablespoons dry white wine OR: water
3	tablespoons currant jelly
1	tablespoon Dijon-style mustard
½	teaspoon leaf rosemary, crumbled
	Pinch pepper
1	bag (16 ounces) frozen hash brown potatoes
¼	cup vegetable oil
1	sweet green pepper, halved, cored, seeded and cut into ½-inch pieces
4	boneless chicken thighs (1 pound)
4	brown-and-serve sausage links (freeze remainder for another use)
2	tomatoes, halved crosswise Grated Parmesan cheese *(optional)*

1. Preheat the broiler. Lightly grease the broiler pan.
2. Combine the wine or water, jelly, mustard, rosemary and pepper in a small saucepan. Bring the mixture to boiling and boil, stirring, for 1 minute. Remove the saucepan from the heat.
3. Meanwhile, cook the hash brown potatoes following the package directions, using the oil. Add the green pepper for the final 5 minutes of cooking time.
4. Place the chicken, skin side down, in the lightly greased broiler pan. Brush the chicken with the sauce.
5. Broil the chicken 3 to 4 inches from the source of the heat for 6 minutes.
6. Turn the chicken over. Arrange the sausage and the tomatoes, cut side up, on the broiler pan. Brush the sausage, tomatoes and chicken with the sauce. Sprinkle the tomatoes with Parmesan cheese, if you wish.
7. Broil the chicken, sausage and tomatoes for about 7 minutes longer or until the chicken is no longer pink near the bone and the sausage is heated through. Turn the sausage after 3 minutes and brush the sausage and the chicken with the sauce, if needed. Serve the Chicken Grill with the hash browns.

QUICK TIP

Sauces From 'Round-The-World
Try some of the following "exotic" bottled sauces for basting broiled meats and poultry, or mixing with sour cream, yogurt or mayonnaise for sauces: Mexican picante sauce, chutney and Chinese hoisin sauce.

Chicken and Sesame Noodle Salad

Chinese-style sesame noodles can be the basis of a satisfying main dish when tossed with chicken. For lower sodium, use a light soy sauce.

Makes 8 servings.

Nutrient Value Per Serving: 465 calories, 78 g protein, 17 g fat, 51 g carbohydrate, 1,144 mg sodium, 47 mg cholesterol.

1½ **cups julienne-cut carrots**
1 **pound wheat-flour noodles (available wherever Oriental foods are sold) OR: 1 pound spaghetti**
½ **cup soy sauce**
½ **cup red wine vinegar**
⅓ **cup smooth peanut butter**
¼ **cup sesame paste (tahini)**
1 **to 2 tablespoons Oriental sesame oil**
3 **cups shredded cooked chicken**
½ **cup julienne-cut green onion**
Lettuce leaves

1. Bring a large pot of salted water to boiling. Place the carrots in a metal sieve or colander and immerse them in the boiling water. Boil the carrots for 1 minute or just until limp but not soft. Remove the sieve or colander from the water. Immediately place the carrots under cold running water.
2. Boil the noodles or spaghetti in water for 6 to 10 minutes for the noodles, for 10 to 12 minutes for the spaghetti, or until just tender. Drain the noodles in a colander and place under cold running water. Drain the noodles. Place in a large bowl. Add the soy sauce and the vinegar, and toss to coat well.
3. Combine the peanut butter, sesame paste and Oriental sesame oil in a small bowl.
4. Add the chicken, carrot, green onion and sesame dressing to the noodles in the bowl. Toss to blend the salad well.
5. Line 8 plates with the lettuce leaves. Top with the noodle mixture.

Menu Idea

Chicken and Sesame Noodle Salad*

Radish and Cucumber Salad

Pound Cake with Raspberry Purée

Tip-Top Toppings
For a quick and delicious topping, purée fresh fruit, such as raspberries, blueberries or strawberries, in a blender and keep it handy in the refrigerator. For an even faster low-calorie fruit topping, just open a jar of fruit baby food.

53

Stir-Fried Chicken with Chinese Noodles

Menu Idea

Stir-Fried Chicken
with Chinese
Noodles*

Spinach, Mandarin
Orange and Red
Onion Salad

Almond Cookies
and Coffee

Makes 4 servings.

*Nutrient Value Per Serving:
589 calories, 46 g protein, 12 g
fat, 71 g carbohydrate, 1,299 mg
sodium, 149 mg cholesterol.*

1   **package (10 ounces)
Chinese noodles OR: 12
ounces quick-cooking
capellini spaghetti**
2   **tablespoons oil**
4   **boneless, skinned chicken
breast halves (1¼ pounds),
cut crosswise into ½-inch-
wide strips**
1   **slice peeled fresh
gingerroot (⅛ inch thick)**
⅛   **teaspoon red pepper flakes**
1   **package (10 ounces) frozen
Oriental-style mixed
vegetables**
1   **cup chicken broth**
4   **green onions, trimmed and
both green and white parts
cut into 2-inch lengths**
3   **tablespoons soy sauce**
3   **tablespoons dry sherry OR:
dry vermouth**
2   **tablespoons cornstarch**
1   **can (8 ounces) water
chestnuts, drained**

1. Cook the noodles following
   package directions; drain well.
2. Meanwhile, heat the oil in a
   wok or large skillet over high
   heat. Add the chicken,
   gingerroot and red pepper
   flakes and stir-fry until the
   chicken turns white all over, for
   about 3 minutes. Remove the
   chicken with a slotted spoon to
   a bowl and reserve. Discard the
   gingerroot.
3. Add the frozen vegetables to
   the wok and stir-fry over high
   heat for 1 minute. Add the
   broth and cook for 3 minutes.
   Add the reserved chicken.
   Lower the heat to medium,
   cover the wok and cook,
   stirring once or twice, for 3
   minutes. Add the green onion;
   cook 1 minute longer or until
   vegetables are crisp-tender.
4. Combine the soy sauce, sherry
   or vermouth and cornstarch in
   a small bowl. Add the mixture
   to the wok along with the water
   chestnuts. Cook, stirring, until
   sauce is thickened and shiny,
   for about 1 minute. Pour the
   chicken and sauce over the
   drained noodles; toss to mix
   well. Serve immediately.

Spanish-Style Chicken and Rice

Chicken drumsticks and shrimp in a lightly spiced sauce are the stars of this dish. Use small chicken legs for quick cooking.

Makes 6 servings.

Nutrient Value Per Serving: 303 calories, 22 g protein, 11 g fat, 28 g carbohydrate, 366 mg sodium, 93 mg cholesterol.

Quick-cooking rice for 6
   servings
¼ teaspoon ground turmeric
¼ cup all-purpose flour
6 small chicken drumsticks
   (1¼ pounds)
2 tablespoons olive oil
2 cloves garlic, crushed
1 can (8 ounces) tomato
   sauce
¼ cup dry white wine
1 tablespoon lemon juice
1 sprig parsley
1 teaspoon leaf thyme,
   crumbled
⅛ teaspoon salt
⅛ teaspoon pepper
½ pound medium-size shrimp,
   peeled and deveined
   Lemon slices *(optional)*

1. Cook the rice following the package directions, adding the turmeric to the water.
2. Meanwhile, place the flour in a medium-size paper or plastic bag. Shake 3 drumsticks at a time in the bag to coat the drumsticks with the flour.
3. Heat the oil in a large skillet over high heat. Add the chicken and the garlic and brown the chicken quickly on all sides, for about 4 minutes.
4. Lower the heat to medium. Add the tomato sauce, wine, lemon juice, parsley, thyme, salt and pepper and stir to combine. Cover the skillet and cook for 8 minutes (the mixture should be gently boiling).
5. Add the shrimp to the skillet. Cook the mixture, uncovered, for 2 minutes longer or until the shrimp are pink and curled. Serve the chicken mixture over the rice. Garnish with lemon slices, if you wish.

Menu Idea

**Spanish-Style
  Chicken and
  Rice***
Broccoli
Caramel Flans

QUICK TIP

A Spice That Just Won't Quit
If you have added too much spice or herb to a dish, add more liquid and/or starchy foods, or a little sugar.

Warm Thai Chicken Salad

Menu Idea
Warm Thai Chicken Salad*
Fresh Fruit

Part of the uniqueness of Thai cuisine comes from the fondness for combining hot food with cold, as in this deliciously different salad.

Makes 4 servings.

Nutrient Value Per Serving: 564 calories, 55 g protein, 32 g fat, 16 g carbohydrate, 831 mg sodium, 115 mg cholesterol.

2   **tablespoons dry sherry**
2   **tablespoons soy sauce**
2   **tablespoons water**
4   **tablespoons corn oil**
1   **tablespoon light brown sugar**
1   **tablespoon creamy-style peanut butter**
¼   **to ¾ teaspoon crushed red pepper flakes**
1   **cup shredded carrot**
1   **cup shredded, peeled, seeded cucumber**
2   **tablespoons vinegar, preferably rice wine vinegar**
5   **boneless, skinned chicken breast halves (about 1¾ pounds), cut crosswise into strips**
2   **green onions, sliced**
2   **cloves garlic, finely chopped**
¾   **cup dry-roasted unsalted peanut halves**
8   **to 12 lettuce leaves**

1. Stir together the sherry, soy sauce, water, 1 tablespoon of the oil, the brown sugar, peanut butter and red pepper flakes in a small bowl. Blend the mixture well and set aside.
2. In a separate bowl, toss together the carrot, cucumber and vinegar. Cover the bowl and refrigerate until serving time.
3. Heat the remaining 3 tablespoons of oil in a wok or large skillet over medium-high heat. Add the chicken strips, green onion and garlic, half at a time, to the wok and stir-fry for about 3 minutes or until the chicken is cooked through. Remove the chicken from the wok. Add the peanuts and stir-fry for 1 minute. Add the reserved soy sauce mixture to the wok along with the chicken. Stir-fry for 1 minute or until the mixture is heated through. Remove the wok from the heat.
4. Arrange the lettuce leaves on 4 individual plates. Top with the carrot-cucumber mixture, dividing equally. Spoon the chicken mixture over each salad. Serve immediately.

QUICK TIP

Quick Fruit Salad
Spoon a little undiluted frozen orange juice concentrate (thawed), or other juice concentrate over cut-up fresh fruit.

Creole-Style Chicken Stew

Use a large, shallow saucepan to bring the liquids in this stew to a quick boil.

Makes 4 servings.

Nutrient Value Per Serving:
431 calories, 41 g protein, 16 g fat, 31 g carbohydrate, 1,075 mg sodium, 91 mg cholesterol.

1	**can (13¾ ounces) chicken broth**
1	**can (14½ ounces) stewed tomatoes**
1	**bag (16 ounces) frozen vegetables for stew**
1	**teaspoon leaf thyme, crumbled**
¼	**teaspoon liquid red-pepper seasoning**
	Pinch pepper
4	**sprigs parsley**
2	**tablespoons oil**
4	**boneless, skinned chicken breast halves (1¼ pounds), each cut into 6 pieces**
5	**brown-and-serve sausage links (½ package; wrap and freeze remainder for another use), each cut in half**
2	**cloves garlic, pressed**
1	**tablespoon all-purpose flour**
1	**package (10 ounces) frozen cut okra**
1	**tablespoon chopped parsley, for garnish (optional)**

1. Combine the broth, tomatoes, frozen vegetables, thyme, liquid red-pepper seasoning, pepper and parsley in a large saucepan. Bring the mixture to boiling over high heat. Lower the heat to medium. Cover the saucepan and cook for 5 minutes (the mixture should be gently boiling).
2. Meanwhile, heat the oil in a medium-size skillet over high heat. Add the chicken, sausage and garlic and stir-fry until the chicken turns white on all sides, for about 2 minutes. Remove the skillet from the heat. Sprinkle the flour over the chicken, stirring to coat the chicken.
3. When the vegetable mixture has cooked for 5 minutes, add the okra, breaking up the okra gently with a fork. Cover the saucepan and cook for 3 minutes.
4. Stir the chicken and sausage mixture into the stew. Cover the saucepan and simmer the stew for 5 minutes or until the vegetables are tender. Garnish the stew with chopped parsley, if you wish.

Menu Idea

Creole-Style Chicken Stew*
Corn Muffins
Mixed Green Salad
Chocolate Fudge Cake

QUICK TIP

Dress The Salad
Always keep on hand a variety of bottled salad dressings to make salad making easier: oil and vinegar types, creamy and herbal.

Honey Mustard Chicken with Rice and Broccoli

Menu Idea

Honey Mustard Chicken with Rice and Broccoli*

Berries with Fruit-Flavored Yogurt

This delicious chicken dish is prepared and served in foil packets. For foil-packet cooking information, see tips on opposite page.

Bake at 500° for 10 minutes. Makes 4 servings.

Nutrient Value Per Serving: 338 calories, 44 g protein, 3 g fat, 33 g carbohydrate, 128 mg sodium, 99 mg cholesterol.

2   teaspoons water
2   teaspoons dry mustard
1   tablespoon honey
    Nonstick vegetable cooking spray
4   boneless, skinned chicken breast halves (about 6 ounces each)
2   cups hot cooked rice
1   package (10 ounces) frozen chopped broccoli, thawed, drained and at room temperature

1. Combine the water and the mustard in a cup until smooth. Stir in the honey and reserve the mixture.
2. Preheat the oven to very hot (500°).
3. Tear off four 14 x 12-inch sheets of regular-weight aluminum foil. Spray the center of the lower half of each sheet with nonstick vegetable cooking spray.
4. Arrange 1 chicken breast half, skinned side up, on the sprayed surface of each sheet of foil. Make 3 diagonal slices, ¼ inch deep, about 1 inch apart, over the top of each chicken piece. Brush the honey mustard over the chicken, making sure to get the mixture inside the cut areas. Fold the upper half of the foil over the chicken, matching the edges. Fold the long edges over twice, fold the short ends over twice, to form a tightly sealed packet. Repeat the same procedure with the other packets. Arrange the packets on a large baking sheet.
5. Bake the chicken in the packets in the preheated very hot oven (500°) for 10 minutes.
6. Meanwhile, combine the rice and the broccoli in a serving bowl and keep warm.
7. Remove the foil packets to 4 dinner plates with the broccoli and the rice. Serve immediately. Let each diner cut open his or her own individual foil packet.

QUICK TIP

Non-Stick Honey
To measure honey or other sticky liquids, wipe the measuring spoon or measuring cup with vegetable oil first, or rinse with very hot water.

Marinated Orange Chicken

Cook It In Foil

It's calorie-wise cooking when you use packets of aluminum foil—no fattening oils or butter are necessary. Just spray a bit of nonstick vegetable cooking spray on the foil, add the meat, fish or poultry and bake. Because the foil packet holds in moisture, this method works especially well for lean cuts of meat—such as chicken, pork or turkey cutlets, and boneless pork loin—and for fish.

Tips

● Use regular aluminum foil; use only the amount needed for your portion.
● Two great ways to flavor foil-cooked food: For both methods, score the top of the meat, fish or poultry with a knife. Make three diagonal slices ⅛ to ¼ inch deep, about 1 inch apart.
—Brush the cut areas with a flavorful liquid, such as a mixture of lemon juice, salt, sage, paprika and ground hot red pepper; fresh herb vinaigrette; or bottled salad dressing. Then wrap and bake.
—Marinate the food for at least 20 minutes, discard the marinade, wrap the food and bake. Two easy marinades: lime juice and spicy taco sauce; low-fat buttermilk with garlic and fresh rosemary.

For a lower sodium meal, use light soy sauce.

Makes 6 servings.

Nutrient Value Per Serving: 188 calories, 28 g protein, 4 g fat, 9 g carbohydrate, 739 mg sodium, 66 mg cholesterol.

1	cup orange juice
3	tablespoons soy sauce
1	clove garlic, finely chopped
½	teaspoon grated orange rind
¼	teaspoon ground ginger
1½	pounds boneless, skinned chicken breasts, cut into ½-inch cubes
1	tablespoon vegetable oil
1	tablespoon cornstarch
1	package (6 ounces) frozen Chinese pea pods, thawed

1. Stir together the orange juice, soy sauce, garlic, orange rind and ginger in a bowl. Add the chicken cubes. Cover the bowl and let the chicken marinate for 15 minutes.
2. Heat the oil in a 10-inch nonstick skillet. Remove the chicken from the marinade with a slotted spoon and add to the skillet. Stir-fry for 2 minutes or until the chicken is pale white.
3. Measure ½ cup of the marinade into a glass measure and stir in the cornstarch until the mixture is smooth. Pour the cornstarch mixture into the skillet. Heat to boiling, stirring constantly. Boil, stirring for 1 minute.
4. Add the pea pods to the skillet. Lower the heat, cover the skillet and simmer until the pods are crisp-tender, for about 1 minute. Serve the chicken and pea pods over rice, if you wish.

Menu Idea

Marinated Orange Chicken*
Rice
Raspberry Sherbet

Beef and Pork

Sliced Beef with Snow Peas

Makes 2 servings.

Nutrient Value Per Serving: 686 calories, 25 g protein, 60 g fat, 12 g carbohydrate, 991 mg sodium, 54 mg cholesterol.

½ **pound flank steak OR: beef tenderloin**
⅓ **cup plus 2 tablespoons peanut or vegetable oil**
2 **tablespoons red wine OR: sherry**
1 **tablespoon water**
1 **tablespoon plus 1 teaspoon cornstarch**
¼ **cup water**
1 **tablespoon oyster sauce**
½ **teaspoon salt**
 Few drops Oriental sesame oil
 Pinch ground white pepper
4 **thin slices peeled fresh gingerroot**
2 **cloves garlic, mashed**
¼ **cup snow peas**
¼ **cup sliced fresh mushrooms**
1 **can (8 ounces) sliced bamboo shoots, drained**
1 **green onion, chopped**
1 **cup water**
 Hot cooked rice
 Chinese parsley and slivers of sweet red pepper, for garnish (optional)

1. Trim the fat from the meat and cut the meat into thin strips, using a long sharp knife. (The meat is much easier to slice thinly if partially frozen; place the meat in the freezer for 10 minutes to firm up before slicing.)
2. Combine the 2 tablespoons of peanut or vegetable oil, 1 tablespoon of the wine or sherry, the 1 tablespoon of water and the 1 teaspoon of cornstarch in a shallow glass dish. Add the meat and turn to coat well. Set aside.
3. Combine the remaining tablespoon of cornstarch, the ¼ cup of water, the oyster sauce, the remaining tablespoon of wine or sherry, the salt, Oriental sesame oil and white pepper in a small bowl. Mix well and set aside.
4. Heat a wok or large skillet. Add the remaining ⅓ cup of peanut or vegetable oil and heat. Add the gingerroot, garlic and reserved meat and stir-fry until the meat is almost cooked.
5. Add the snow peas, mushrooms, bamboo shoots and green onion. Stir-fry for 1 minute.
6. Add the 1 cup of water and bring to boiling. Add the reserved oyster sauce mixture; stir-fry quickly to blend the sauce and coat the meat and vegetables. Remove the mixture to a platter.
7. Serve with the hot cooked rice. Garnish with Chinese parsley and red pepper slivers, if you wish.

Menu Idea

Sliced Beef with Snow Peas*

Hot Cooked Rice

Shredded Carrot Salad

Orange Sections with Liqueur

A Cantonese dinner for two—Sliced Beef with Snow Peas and rice.

61

Sausages Creole

Hungarian Sausage Skillet

Menu Idea
Sausages Creole*
Hot Cooked Rice
Peasant Bread
Sherbet with Butter
  Cookies

Menu Idea
Hungarian Sausage
  Skillet*
Parslied Noodles
Rye Bread
Cherry Cheese Tart*
  (page 259)

Makes 4 servings.

*Nutrient Value Per Serving:
414 calories, 19 g protein, 29 g
fat, 17 g carbohydrate, 1,062 mg
sodium, NA mg cholesterol.***

1	pound reduced-fat knockwurst
2	tablespoons vegetable oil
1	large sweet green pepper, halved, cored, seeded and finely chopped
2	stalks celery, finely chopped
1	large onion, finely chopped
1	can (15 ounces) tomato sauce (no salt added)
⅛	teaspoon black pepper
⅛	teaspoon ground hot red pepper

1. Simmer the knockwurst in water to cover in a deep skillet for 5 minutes. Drain off the water; let the knockwurst cook slightly in the skillet. Cut each knockwurst crosswise into sixths.
2. Heat the oil in a large skillet. Add the green pepper, celery and onion and sauté until the vegetables are tender but not browned, for about 5 minutes.
3. Stir in the tomato sauce, black pepper and ground hot red pepper. Mix in the knockwurst. Cover the skillet and simmer for 5 minutes or until the mixture is hot. Serve over hot cooked rice, if you wish.

Note: *Cholesterol amounts were not available for this recipe.*

Makes 4 servings.

*Nutrient Value Per Serving:
472 calories, 19 g protein, 37 g
fat, 17 g carbohydrate, 1,184 mg
sodium, 79 mg cholesterol.*

2	medium-size sweet green peppers
2	medium-size onions (¾ pound)
1	tablespoon vegetable oil
1	tablespoon Hungarian paprika
1	can (16 ounces) whole tomatoes with their liquid
⅛	teaspoon pepper
1	pound kielbasa (25% less sodium), cut into 4 pieces
2	tablespoons chopped parsley

1. Halve and seed the green peppers. Cut each pepper into 8 wedges. Halve the onions and cut each onion half into 8 wedges.
2. Sauté the green peppers and the onion in the oil in a large skillet for 3 minutes, stirring often; do not brown them. Sprinkle the vegetables with the paprika and cook for 1 minute, stirring constantly. Add the tomatoes with their liquid and the pepper. Bring the mixture to boiling. Add the kielbasa. Lower the heat, cover the skillet and cook for 10 minutes.
3. Sprinkle with the parsley and serve with rye bread.

Green Beans with Spicy Pork Sauce

The quickly prepared sauce in Green Beans with Spicy Pork Sauce can also be served over hot cooked rice.

Makes 4 servings.

Nutrient Value Per Serving:
453 calories, 21 g protein, 35 g fat, 15 g carbohydrate, 848 mg sodium, 83 mg cholesterol.

1½	**cups chopped onion**
¼	**cup peeled and finely chopped fresh gingerroot**
1	**tablespoon finely chopped garlic**
2	**tablespoons peanut oil**
3	**tablespoons soy sauce**
1	**pound coarsely ground pork**
½	**teaspoon Oriental sesame oil****
½	**to 1 teaspoon chili oil OR: ¼ teaspoon red pepper flakes**
1	**pound green beans, trimmed**

1. Sauté the onion, gingerroot and garlic in the oil in a large skillet over medium heat until soft.
2. Add the soy sauce and the pork. Cook, stirring, until the pork loses its pink color.
3. Stir in the Oriental sesame oil and the chili oil or red pepper flakes. Lower the heat. Continue cooking, stirring occasionally, for 15 minutes. Taste and adjust the seasonings.
4. Meanwhile, steam the green beans until they are barely tender. Immediately place the green beans under cold running water.
5. Mix the pork sauce with the green beans. Serve at room temperature.

**Note: *Oriental sesame oil is darker in color and stronger in flavor than regular sesame oil. It can be found in the Oriental food section of many supermarkets or in Oriental specialty food stores.*

Menu Idea

Green Beans with Spicy Pork Sauce*

Chinese Noodles

Honeydew Melon and Cantaloupe with Toasted Almonds

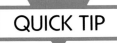

QUICK TIP

Picking Perfect Melons
Pick the sweetest melons by fragrance and make sure the blossom end is somewhat indented and soft to pressure. Cantaloupes are yellowish, with thick, coarse veins; honeydew should be creamy or yellowish-white.

Savory Stuffed Peppers

Menu Idea
Savory Stuffed
  Peppers*
Peasant Bread
Vanilla Pudding

These Savory Stuffed Peppers are filled with rice, tender veal, beef and kielbasa.

Cooking these stuffed peppers with sauerkraut in a pressure cooker makes them especially moist.

Makes 6 servings.

Nutrient Value Per Serving:
434 calories, 24 g protein, 24 g
fat, 30 g carbohydrate, 1,625 mg
sodium, 127 mg cholesterol.

6	medium-size sweet green peppers
8	ounces lean ground beef
8	ounces ground veal
8	ounces kielbasa, coarsely chopped
½	cup raw rice
2	small onions, chopped
¾	teaspoon salt
½	teaspoon pepper
1	clove garlic, finely chopped
1	egg
1	can (6 ounces) tomato paste
1	can (8 ounces) tomato sauce
1	cup water
1	can (16 ounces) sauerkraut

Onion Burgers

1. Cut the tops from the green peppers; seed and derib the green peppers.
2. Combine the beef, veal, half the kielbasa, the rice, onion, salt, pepper, garlic, egg and 3 tablespoons of the tomato paste in a medium-size bowl and mix well. Divide mixture evenly into the peppers.
3. Combine the remaining tomato paste, the tomato sauce and water in a small bowl; mix well.
4. Drain and rinse the sauerkraut with cold water. Squeeze out the excess moisture.
5. Place a cooking rack in the pressure cooker. Pour half the tomato sauce mixture into the cooker. Spread half the sauerkraut over the rack. Place the green peppers on top of the sauerkraut. Scatter the remaining kielbasa between the green peppers. Sprinkle the remaining sauerkraut over the green peppers and pour the remaining tomato sauce mixture over all. Check to make certain the vent pipe in the lid is clear. Place the lid on the cooker and close securely. Place the pressure regulator firmly on the vent pipe.
6. Heat the cooker until the pressure regulator attains a gentle rocking motion. Adjust the heat to maintain a slow, steady rocking motion of the regulator to prevent too much steam from escaping. Cook for 13 minutes.
7. Remove cooker from heat and let cool until pressure is completely reduced. (The air vent cover will drop and no steam will escape when the pressure regulator is tilted.) Remove the lid and serve the green peppers with the sauce and sauerkraut.

Makes 4 servings.

Nutrient Value Per Serving: 175 calories, 11 g protein, 10 g fat, 9 g carbohydrate, 307 mg sodium, 34 mg cholesterol.

2   **cups finely chopped onions (2 large onions)**
2   **teaspoons vegetable oil**
½   **pound lean ground beef**
½   **teaspoon salt**
¼   **teaspoon pepper**
2   **tablespoons all-purpose flour**
    Shredded Cheddar cheese (optional)
    Toasted hamburger buns

1. Sauté the onions in 1 teaspoon of the oil in a large heavy skillet, stirring frequently, until tender and lightly colored, for about 10 minutes. Cool to room temperature.
2. Combine the beef, sautéed onions, salt and pepper in a medium-size bowl. Shape into 4 equal patties, pushing onions firmly into the patties.
3. Place the flour on a piece of wax paper. Coat the patties with the flour.
4. Panfry the burgers in the remaining teaspoon of oil in a skillet, until crisp and golden brown on one side, for about 3 minutes. Turn; cook for another 1 or 2 minutes or until desired doneness. For cheeseburgers, sprinkle the shredded cheese over the burgers after turning; cover the skillet for the last 1 or 2 minutes. Serve on the toasted hamburger buns.

Menu Idea
Onion Burgers*
Cottage Fries
Coleslaw
Cheesecake

QUICK TIP

Make Ahead Burgers
For a real time saver, prepare burgers as per your favorite recipe. Wrap them well in aluminum foil or plastic wrap and refrigerate. About 30 minutes before you're ready to cook them, remove the patties from the refrigerator and allow them to come to room temperature. Proceed as the recipe directs.

65

Fish

Marinated Fish Brochettes with Toasted Noodles

Marinating is not included in the preparation time for this recipe.

Broil for 10 minutes.
Makes 6 servings.

Nutrient Value Per Serving:
232 calories, 23 g protein, 14 g
fat, 3 g carbohydrate, 104 mg
sodium, 44 mg cholesterol.

¼ cup olive oil
¼ cup freshly squeezed lime
    juice
2   tablespoons finely chopped
    fresh coriander OR: finely
    chopped parsley
1   tablespoon finely chopped
    shallots
¼   teaspoon fresh Thai
    peppers, finely chopped
    OR: pinch crushed red
    pepper flakes
1½ pounds swordfish, halibut,
    tuna or other firm-textured
    fish, cut into 1¼-inch
    chunks
4   ounces uncooked spaghetti
2   tablespoons olive oil
2   cups chicken broth
1   large sweet red pepper, cut
    into 1-inch squares
12 small button mushrooms
1   large sweet yellow pepper,
    cut into 1-inch squares
    Salt and freshly ground
    black pepper, to taste

1. Combine the ¼ cup of oil, the lime juice, coriander or parsley, shallots and Thai peppers or red pepper flakes in a shallow glass dish. Add the fish and marinate for 1 hour. Drain the fish, reserving the marinade.
2. Break the spaghetti into 2-inch lengths. Add the spaghetti to a large skillet with the 2 tablespoons of oil. Cook over medium heat, stirring often, until the spaghetti is golden brown. Add the broth, cover the skillet and cook until the spaghetti is *al dente,* firm but tender. Keep the spaghetti warm.
3. Arrange a red pepper square, mushroom, yellow pepper square and fish chunk on each of 6 metal or wooden skewers. Repeat with the trio of vegetables.
4. Brush the fish and vegetable kabobs with the remaining marinade. Season the kabobs with the salt and freshly ground black pepper.
5. Broil the kabobs for 5 minutes on each side or until the fish flakes easily when tested with a fork. Serve the fish over the spaghetti with green beans and additional red and yellow pepper squares. Garnish with broiled baby eggplant, if you wish.

Menu Idea

Marinated Fish Brochettes with Toasted Noodles*
Green Beans
Broiled Baby Eggplant
Papaya with Lime

Whether broiled or grilled, these Marinated Fish Brochettes are delicious with Toasted Noodles.

Crab-Stuffed Flounder

Menu Idea

Crab-Stuffed
  Flounder*
Herb-Seasoned
  Rice
Green Beans
Peach Crown*
  (page 255)

*Bake at 350° for 18 to 20
minutes.
Makes 4 servings.*

*Nutrient Value Per Serving:
256 calories, 28 g protein, 13 g
fat, 49 g carbohydrate, 599 mg
sodium, 114 mg cholesterol.*

1   small onion, chopped
       (¼ cup)
¼   cup chopped celery
¼   cup chopped sweet red
       pepper
4   tablespoons (½ stick) butter
       or margarine
¼   pound crabmeat, picked
       over and flaked
½   cup soft bread crumbs
3   teaspoons lemon juice
½   teaspoon salt
⅛   teaspoon pepper
       Few drops liquid red-
         pepper seasoning
4   small flounder fillets (about
       4 ounces each)
       Paprika
       Lemon wedges, for garnish
       Parsley sprigs, for garnish

1. Preheat the oven to moderate
   (350°). Butter a small, shallow
   baking dish.
2. Sauté the onion, celery and red
   pepper in 2 tablespoons of the
   butter or margarine in a
   saucepan until the vegetables
   are soft, for about 2 minutes.
   Mix in the crabmeat, bread
   crumbs, 1 teaspoon of the
   lemon juice, the salt, pepper
   and liquid red-pepper
   seasoning.
3. Place the fillets, skin side up, on
   the counter. Mound the crab
   mixture in the center of the
   fillets. Overlap the ends of the
   fillets over the top of the
   stuffing. Fasten the fish with
   wooden picks. Place the rolled
   fillets in the prepared dish.
4. Melt the remaining 2
   tablespoons of butter or
   margarine in a small saucepan;
   stir in the remaining lemon
   juice. Pour the butter-lemon
   juice mixture over the fish and
   sprinkle with the paprika.
5. Bake the fish in the preheated
   moderate oven (350°) for 18 to
   20 minutes or until the fish just
   begins to flake when pierced
   with a fork. Garnish the fish
   with the lemon wedges and the
   parsley sprigs, and serve with
   herb-seasoned rice, if you wish.

Microwave Instructions
*(for a 650-watt variable power
microwave oven)*

Directions: Combine the onion,
celery, red pepper and 2
tablespoons of the butter or
margarine in a shallow, microwave-
safe baking dish large enough to
hold the 4 fish rolls. Cover the dish
tightly. Microwave the vegetables at
full power for 4 minutes. Add the
crabmeat, bread crumbs, 1
teaspoon of the lemon juice, the
salt, pepper and liquid red-pepper
seasoning; mix well. Assemble the
rolls as directed above. Place the
rolls in the same baking dish. Cover
the rolls with the butter-lemon
juice mixture and sprinkle the tops
with the paprika. Cover the dish
tightly. Microwave the fish at full
power for 4 minutes.

Flounder with Kidney Bean Salsa

*Bake at 400° for 7 to 10 minutes.
Makes 6 servings.*

*Nutrient Value Per Serving:
197 calories, 25 g protein, 3 g
fat, 18 g carbohydrate, 111 mg
sodium, 99 mg cholesterol.*

Kidney Bean Salsa:
½   cup chopped tomato
¼   cup chopped onion
1   teaspoon finely chopped,
     seeded fresh jalapeño
     pepper
1   small clove garlic, finely
     chopped
1   tablespooon red wine
     vinegar
2   cups cooked dried red
     kidney beans, no salt
     added (not canned)
     Lettuce cups *(optional)*

Flounder:
½   cup lowfat plain yogurt
1   egg, slightly beaten
1   tablespoon all-purpose
     flour
     Pinch ground hot red
     pepper
6   flounder fillets (about 1½
     pounds)
     Additional ground hot red
     pepper OR: paprika
     (optional)

1. Prepare the Kidney Bean Salsa: Combine the tomato, onion, jalapeño pepper, garlic and vinegar in a small bowl. Add the kidney beans and mix. Reserve.
2. Preheat the oven to hot (400°).
3. Prepare the Flounder: Whisk together the yogurt and the egg in a small saucepan. Whisk in the flour and the ground hot red pepper until smooth. Cook the sauce, stirring constantly, over very low heat for 3 to 4 minutes or until thickened slightly (do not boil). Remove the saucepan from the heat.
4. Fold the flounder fillets in half crosswise. Arrange the fish in a single layer on an aluminum foil-lined broiler pan.
5. Bake the fish in the preheated hot oven (400°) for 7 to 10 minutes or until the center of the fish just begins to flake when touched with a fork. Carefully transfer the fillets with a spatula to individual plates. Spoon about 2 tablespoons of the yogurt sauce over each fillet. Sprinkle the tops of the fillets with ground hot red pepper or paprika, if you wish. Serve the salsa in lettuce cups, if you wish.

Menu Idea

**Flounder with
   Kidney Bean
   Salsa***
Leafy Lettuce
Hot Cooked Rice
Orange Sherbet

Busy Cook's Primer: How To Poach Fish

Poaching on the Stove Top—Fillets or Steaks

1. Butter a deep skillet or similar pan large enough to hold the fish in a single layer without touching. If using fillets, fold them in half crosswise to make an attractive package for serving. Measure the thickness of the fish *(see "Foolproof Cooking Rule" at right).*

2. Pour enough Classic Court Bouillon *(see recipe, page 71)* into the skillet so the fish will be just barely covered by the liquid. Bring the liquid to boiling.

3. Add the fish to the liquid. Return to a simmer and adjust the heat to maintain the simmer. Cover the top of the fish with a buttered piece of wax paper, buttered side down. Cover the skillet.

4. Simmer the fish for 10 minutes per measured inch of thickness. Do not let the liquid boil.

5. Lift the cooked fish with a slotted spatula from the skillet, draining the fish well over the skillet. Drain the fish briefly on paper toweling. Place the fish on a serving platter, cover loosely with aluminum foil and keep warm in a preheated very slow oven (175°) if making an acompanying sauce.

Foolproof Cooking Rule

The Department of Fisheries of Canada developed this standard rule for cooking fish: Cook the fish for exactly 10 minutes per measured inch of thickness or depth of the fish. If cooking a whole fish, lay it on its side and measure its height or depth. This rule applies to any method of cooking fish— poaching, sautéing, steaming, broiling, etc.

Test for Doneness

Fish should be opaque, just beginning to flake when touched with a fork, and a wooden skewer inserted in the thickest portion of the fish should slide in easily.

Classic Court Bouillon

Take the time to prepare Classic Court Bouillon ahead and keep it on hand in the freezer. Use it to add delicious flavor to poached fish or fish soups and stews.

Makes about 2 quarts.

Nutrient Value Per ½ Cup:
3 calories, 0 g protein, 0 g fat,
1 g carbohydrate, 3 mg sodium,
0 mg cholesterol.

1 large onion, sliced
1 large carrot, scraped and sliced
1 stalk celery, sliced
2 green onions, trimmed and sliced
6 sprigs parsley
1 teaspoon leaf thyme, crumbled
1 bay leaf
6 cups water
2 cups dry white wine*
6 white peppercorns

1. Combine the onion, carrot, celery, green onion, parsley, thyme, bay leaf and water in a 4-quart nonaluminum saucepan or pot. Bring the liquid to boiling. Lower the heat and simmer for 10 to 15 minutes.
2. Add the wine and simmer for 15 minutes. Add the peppercorns for the last 5 minutes of simmering. Skim off any foam from the liquid and discard.
3. Strain the bouillon through a strainer or colander lined with a double thickness of dampened cheesecloth or paper toweling. Discard the solids in the cheesecloth.

4. Refrigerate the bouillon for up to 3 days, or freeze in freezer bags or ice cube trays for up to 6 months. Use Classic Court Bouillon to poach fish or in making fish soups and stews.

*Note: This amount of wine added halfway through the simmering produces a slightly acidic stock good for poaching strongly flavored fish, such as salmon, swordfish, tuna and mackerel. For a milder Court Bouillon, add the wine at the very beginning of the simmering.

Other Poaching Liquids
Milk and Lemon: Combine 1 part milk with 6 parts lightly salted water in the pan to be used for poaching. Add 4 to 6 lemon slices, rinds and seeds removed, to the pan. Add the fish and poach. This poaching liquid is especially good for white fish.
White Wine and Water: To poach strongly flavored fish, combine equal parts of white wine and water in the pan to be used for poaching. Add a few thin onion slices.

Poaching on the Stove Top—Whole Fish

Select a 3- to 4-pound whole fish (we used a red snapper) to serve four. Have the fish gutted; remove the head and the tail, if you wish. (The head and tail will, however, add more flavor to the poaching liquid.)

1. Cut one or two pieces of cotton string to encircle the fish and tie the string loosely around the fish.
2. Place the fish in a fish poacher, roasting pan, flameproof baking dish or casserole large enough to hold the fish and a rack. Set the fish on the rack in the poacher.
3. Add enough poaching liquid to the poacher so the liquid covers the fish by about ¾ inch. Cover the poacher.

4. Place the poacher over 2 burners on the stove top. Bring the liquid almost to boiling over medium heat. Quickly lower the heat and simmer for 10 minutes per measured inch of thickness of the fish.
5. Remove the fish from the poacher. Working from the head to the tail with your fingers and a small knife, peel off the skin.
6. With a long thin knife, divide one side of the fish into 4 fillets, cutting just to the backbone along the center of the length and the width. Holding the knife at an angle, carefully scrape along the backbone to remove each of the fillets.
7. Carefully lift off the backbone and repeat the filleting with the other side.

Poaching Fish in the Oven

1. Butter a shallow, flameproof baking dish that will hold the fish in a single layer.
2. Pour enough poaching liquid into the pan to barely cover the fish. Bring the liquid to boiling on top of the stove.
3. Add the fish to the liquid. Cover the top of the fish with a buttered piece of wax paper, buttered side down.
4. Immediately place the dish in a preheated moderate oven (375°). Oven-poach the fish for 10 minutes per measured inch of thickness.
5. Remove the fish with a slotted spatula and let it drain off the poaching liquid.

Easy Fish Sauce

Makes 1 cup.

Nutrient Value Per Tablespoon:
9 calories, 0 g protein, 1 g fat,
0 g carbohydrate, 0 mg sodium,
2 mg cholesterol.

1   tablespoon unsalted butter
1   tablespoon all-purpose
     flour
1   cup Classic Court Bouillon,
     hot *(see recipe, page 71)*

Melt the butter in a small saucepan over medium heat. Whisk in the flour until smooth and cook, whisking, for 2 minutes. Slowly whisk in the Classic Court Bouillon. Bring the sauce to boiling, whisking. Lower the heat and simmer, whisking frequently, for 2 minutes. The sauce should lightly coat the back of a metal spoon. Spoon the sauce over or around poached fish.

Variations
Herb: Stir in ¼ cup of chopped fresh herbs, such as tarragon, chervil or thyme.
Tomato: Stir in ¼ cup of chopped, seeded, peeled tomato.
Cream: Stir in 1 to 2 tablespoons of heavy cream.

Yogurt-Dill Sauce

Makes about 1 cup.

Nutrient Value Per Tablespoon:
7 calories, 1 g protein, 0 g fat,
1 g carbohydrate, 8 mg sodium,
1 mg cholesterol.

¾   cup lowfat plain yogurt
2   to 4 tablespoons Classic
     Court Bouillon *(see recipe,*
     page 71)
¼   cup chopped fresh dill

Whisk the yogurt in a medium-size bowl until very smooth. Slowly whisk in the amount of Classic Court Bouillon you wish to use to achieve the desired thickness for the sauce. Scrape the yogurt mixture into a small saucepan. Warm the sauce over medium heat, whisking. Remove the saucepan from the heat. Stir in the dill. Spoon the sauce over or around poached fish.

QUICK TIP

Curdled Yogurt Sauce
If your yogurt-based sauce has curdled, it means you've overheated the sauce. Yogurt should be gently folded into the other sauce ingredients and then *gently* reheated. At the first sign of separation, transfer the sauce to a cool bowl over an ice bath, or add 1 ice cube directly to the sauce mixture. Reheat *slowly* over hot water. If the sauce is fully separated, add 1½ teaspoons of cornstarch per 2 cups of cooled, curdled sauce. Mix well and reheat slowly in a lightweight saucepan, stirring gently. If the sauce is beyond saving, use as a marinade for fish or poultry, or mix with leftover cooked vegetables.

Tomato Basil Butter Sauce

Lemon-Dijon Marinade

Makes 4 servings.

Nutrient Value Per Tablespoon: 189 calories, 1 g protein, 20 g fat, 3 g carbohydrate, 8 mg sodium, 54 mg cholesterol.

2   cups Classic Court Bouillon (*see recipe, page 71*)
6   to 8 tablespoons unsalted butter, cut into small pieces
1   small tomato, peeled, seeded and chopped
¼   cup chopped fresh basil

1. Boil the Classic Court Bouillon in a medium-size saucepan over high heat until the liquid is reduced to ¼ cup. Remove the saucepan from the heat.
2. Whisk the butter into the liquid, piece by piece, incorporating each piece, but not allowing it to melt completely, before adding the next. The sauce should be creamy and frothy. Stir in the tomato and the basil. Spoon the sauce around or over the poached fish.

This tangy marinade will enhance the taste of any firm-fleshed fish. It can also be used to cook chicken or fish in foil packets.

Makes 1 cup.

Nutrient Value Per Tablespoon: 66 calories, 1 g protein, 7 g fat, 1 g carbohydrate, 359 mg sodium, 0 mg cholesterol.

½   cup vegetable oil
⅓   cup soy sauce
¼   cup lemon juice
2   teaspoons Dijon-style mustard
1   teaspoon grated lemon rind
1   clove garlic, finely chopped

Combine the oil, soy sauce, lemon juice, mustard, grated lemon rind and garlic in a small bowl, blending well. Pour the marinade over fish steaks in a glass baking dish. Cover the dish and marinate in the refrigerator for 3 hours before grilling or broiling.

QUICK TIP

Red Pepper Mayonnaise For Cold Poached Fish
Let the poached fish cool in the poaching liquid. Remove the fish from the liquid and drain. Wrap the fish in plastic wrap and refrigerate it until serving time. Serve the cold poached fish with Red Pepper Mayonnaise: Mix 2 cups of homemade or store-bought mayonnaise with a 7-ounce jar of roasted red peppers, drained and puréed in an electric blender or a food processor. Add a little lemon juice and a pinch of ground hot red pepper, if you wish. Use the mayonnaise in cold fish salads, too.

Tuna with Red Rice

Makes 6 servings.

Nutrient Value Per Serving:
285 calories, 19 g protein, 21 g
fat, 6 g carbohydrate, 1,016 mg
sodium, 44 mg cholesterol.

2 tablespoons olive oil
¾ cup chopped frozen onion
½ cup chopped frozen sweet green pepper
1½ teaspoons bottled finely chopped garlic in oil
1½ cups long-grain white rice
1 bottle (8 ounces) clam juice
½ cup dry white wine
¾ cup water
1 cup canned crushed tomatoes, with their liquid
⅓ cup pimiento-stuffed green olives (about 2 ounces), cut in half
½ cup grated Romano or Parmesan cheese
2 cans (6½ ounces each) solid white tuna packed in oil, undrained and flaked
1 lemon, cut into 6 wedges

1. Heat the oil in a 10-inch skillet. Add the onion, green pepper, garlic, rice, clam juice, wine, water, tomatoes with their liquid and olives to the skillet. Bring the mixture to a rolling boil. Reduce the heat to low. Cover the skillet and simmer the mixture for 20 to 25 minutes or until the rice is tender.
2. Stir ¼ cup of the Romano or Parmesan cheese and the tuna into the rice with a fork. Sprinkle with the remaining Romano or Parmesan cheese. Serve with the lemon wedges.

Marjoram Poached Halibut

A tasty marjoram-flavored sauce transforms and enhances the fish flavor; even fish-haters will like this dish.

Makes 4 servings.

Nutrient Value Per Serving:
223 calories, 27 g protein, 5 g
fat, 19 g carbohydrate, 1,056 mg
sodium, 64 mg cholesterol.

2 leeks, chopped OR: 2 large onions, chopped (2 cups)
2 cloves garlic, minced
1 tablespoon butter or margarine
1 can (35 ounces) plum tomatoes
1 tablespoon chopped fresh marjoram OR: 1 teaspoon leaf marjoram, crumbled
1 teaspoon salt
¼ teaspoon pepper
4 halibut steaks (4 ounces each)

1. Sauté the leeks and garlic in the butter in a large skillet until soft. Drain the liquid from the tomatoes into the skillet; cook, stirring often, until the liquid is reduced by half.
2. Stir in the tomatoes, marjoram, salt and pepper breaking up the tomatoes with the back of a wooden spoon.
3. Place the fish on the tomato mixture, spooning part of the sauce over the fish; lower the heat. Cover the skillet; simmer for 10 minutes, or until the fish flakes easily.

Menu Idea
Tuna with Red Rice*
Arugula Salad
Breadsticks
Broiled Grapefruit

Menu Idea
Marjoram Poached Halibut*
Boiled New Potatoes
Fresh Asparagus
Quick Lemon Mousse*
(page 230)

75

Other Speedy
Entrées

Mini Frittatas Primavera with Red Pepper Sauce

Make the egg batter ahead, then spoon into the muffin cups and bake just before serving. Try your own combination of vegetables for the filling.

Bake at 400° for 4 to 5 minutes; broil for about 1 minute.
Makes 4 servings (16 frittatas).

Nutrient Value Per Serving: 220 calories, 12 g protein, 16 g fat, 8 g carbohydrate, 640 mg sodium, 416 mg cholesterol.

Red Pepper Sauce *(see recipe, page 78)*

1/3	cup finely chopped sweet red pepper (1/2 medium-size)
1/2	cup thinly sliced green beans (about 3 ounces)
1	teaspoon vegetable oil
1/2	teaspoon butter
2	cloves garlic, finely chopped
6	eggs
2	tablespoons plain yogurt
1	tablespoon Dijon-style mustard
1/8	teaspoon ground hot red pepper
1	to 2 tablespoons finely snipped fresh chives OR: finely chopped green onion, both white and green parts
	Nonstick vegetable cooking spray
8	teaspoons grated Romano or Parmesan cheese

Make the batter ahead for these Mini Frittatas Primavera and serve them with Red Pepper Sauce.

1. Prepare the Red Pepper Sauce. Keep the sauce warm in a small saucepan over very low heat.
2. Preheat the oven to hot (400°).
3. Sauté the red pepper and the green beans in the oil and the butter in a medium-size skillet over medium heat for 4 to 5 minutes or until softened. Add the garlic and sauté for 30 seconds or until fragrant. Remove from the heat.
4. Lightly beat the eggs in a medium-size bowl. Combine the yogurt, mustard and ground hot red pepper in a small bowl. Add a little of the eggs and whisk until the yogurt mixture is smooth. Whisk the yogurt mixture back into the eggs in the medium-size bowl. Add the chives or green onion and the sautéed green bean mixture.
5. Heat a muffin pan with twelve 2-inch cups in the preheated hot oven (400°) for 1 minute or until warm. Remove from the oven; spray with nonstick vegetable cooking spray.
6. Spoon 2 tablespoons of the egg mixture into each cup.
7. Bake in the preheated hot oven (400°) for 4 to 5 minutes or just until the frittatas are set but still wiggly on top. Remove the pan from the oven; increase the temperature to broil.
8. Sprinkle 1/2 teaspoon of the Romano or Parmesan cheese over each frittata. Place the pan 5 inches from the source of the broiler heat. Broil for 1 minute or until the frittatas are lightly golden and slightly puffed. Remove the frittatas from the pan and keep warm. Repeat to make 4 more frittatas.
9. To serve, spoon the Red Pepper Sauce around the frittatas.

Menu Idea

Mini Frittatas Primavera* with Red Pepper Sauce* *(page 78)*

Cannellini Bean Salad with Chopped Red and Green Onion

Flat Bread

Lime Cheesecake* *(page 247)*

QUICK TIP

Double-Batch Cooking

Make double batches of recipes when you have the time. You'll avoid an extra shopping trip and cleanup. Refrigerate or freeze the extra for another meal.

Red Pepper Sauce

Pastrami and Onion Sandwich

Menu Idea
Green Onion and Potato Soup

Pastrami and Onion Sandwich*

Dill Pickles

Apple Pie

Serve chilled as a dip with raw vegetables, or warm as a sauce.

Makes about 1 cup.

Nutrient Value Per Tablespoon: 13 calories, 0 g protein, 1 g fat, 1 g carbohydrate, 93 mg sodium, 0 mg cholesterol.

2 green onions, chopped (2 tablespoons)
1 tablespoon olive oil
2 medium-size sweet red peppers, halved, seeded and cut into ½-inch pieces
1 cup drained, canned whole tomatoes, chopped
½ teaspoon salt
2 teaspoons chopped fresh basil OR: ½ teaspoon leaf basil, crumbled
½ teaspoon lemon juice

1. Sauté the green onion in the oil in a medium-size skillet for 2 minutes or until softened. Add the red pepper and sauté over low heat for 3 minutes or until slightly wrinkled.
2. Add the tomatoes and the salt. Simmer, covered, for 10 to 15 minutes or until the red pepper is very soft. Add the basil and the lemon juice and cook for 1 minute more.
3. Scrape the pepper mixture into the container of an electric blender or a food processor. Cover and whirl until the mixture is a coarse purée. To serve, heat the sauce in a small saucepan over low heat until warm.

Adjust the horseradish in this recipe to suit your taste.

Makes 4 servings.

Nutrient Value Per Serving: 320 calories, 23 g protein, 13 g fat, 35 g carbohydrate, 1,455 mg sodium, 65 mg cholesterol.

8 slices caraway rye bread
4 ounces soft cream cheese
6 to 12 teaspoons bottled horseradish, drained
12 ounces thinly sliced pastrami from the deli
¼ teaspoon pepper
4 outer leaves iceberg lettuce
½ cup thinly sliced onion
4 thin slices tomato

1. Layer the following ingredients on one slice of the bread to make one sandwich: 1½ tablespoons of the cream cheese, 1 to 2 teaspoons of the horseradish, 3 ounces of the pastrami, a pinch of the pepper, 1 lettuce leaf, 1 slice of the bread, 1½ tablespoons of the cream cheese, 1 to 2 teaspoons of the horseradish, ¼ cup of the onion, 2 slices of the tomato, 1 slice of the bread, 1½ tablespoons of the cream cheese, 1 to 2 teaspoons of the horseradish, 3 ounces of the pastrami, a pinch of the pepper, 1 lettuce leaf and 1 slice of the bread.
2. Repeat with the remaining ingredients to make a second sandwich.
3. Cut each sandwich in half and serve one half to each diner.

Hearty Pasta E Fagioli

A hearty bean and pasta soup. The soup will thicken as it stands.

Makes 6 servings (2 cups each).

Nutrient Value Per Serving:
368 calories, 20 g protein, 4 g
fat, 60 g carbohydrate, 1,856 mg
sodium, 2 mg cholesterol.

2 cloves garlic, finely
    chopped
1 tablespoon olive oil
12 ounces (½ of 24-ounce
    package) frozen vegetables
    for stew**
3 cans (13¾ ounces each)
    chicken broth
1 can (14 ounces) Italian-style
    plum tomatoes
1½ teaspoons leaf sage,
    crumbled
1 teaspoon leaf oregano,
    crumbled
    Pinch pepper
½ teaspoon salt
4 ounces pasta (½ of 8-ounce
    package wheels, small
    shells or broken spaghetti)
1 can (19 ounces) cannellini
    beans, undrained
1 can (19 ounces) red kidney
    beans, undrained
1 can (11 ounces) lima beans,
    drained
¼ cup chopped parsley
2 tablespoons grated
    Parmesan cheese

1. Sauté the garlic in the oil in a Dutch oven or kettle over medium heat for 1 minute.
2. Add the vegetables, broth, tomatoes, sage, oregano, pepper and salt. Bring the mixture to boiling over high heat, breaking up the tomatoes with a wooden spoon. Lower the heat. Cover the Dutch oven and simmer for 10 minutes.
3. Add the pasta and the cannellini, kidney and lima beans. Bring the mixture to boiling. Lower the heat and simmer for 15 minutes or until the pasta is tender.
4. Stir the parsley into the pasta e fagioli. Sprinkle each serving with some of the Parmesan cheese.

**Note: *If the stew vegetables are large, let them thaw at room temperature for 30 minutes and cut them into bite-size pieces.*

Menu Idea
Hearty Pasta E Fagioli*
Garlic Bread*
(page 7)
Walnut Pie

79

Speedy Jambalaya

Curried Chicken and Rice Salad

Menu Idea
Speedy Jambalaya*
Cornbread
Pecan Ice Cream

Menu Idea
Curried Chicken
  and Rice Salad*
Wheat Crackers
Peaches and Cream

To make this dish less spicy, substitute regular ham for the spicy ham; and eliminate the ground hot red pepper.

Makes 6 servings.

Nutrient Value Per Serving: 435 calories, 18 g protein, 19 g fat, 47 g carbohydrate, 916 mg sodium, 90 mg cholesterol.

¼ cup (½ stick) butter
¾ cup frozen chopped onion
¾ cup frozen chopped sweet green pepper
1 package (10 ounces) frozen brown-and-serve sausage links, quartered
¼ pound spicy ham, thickly sliced and cubed
1 teaspoon sweet paprika
¼ teaspoon ground hot red pepper
2 bay leaves
1 bottle (8 ounces) clam juice
1 cup chicken broth
1 cup water
1 cup low-sodium canned crushed tomatoes
2 tablespoons Worcestershire sauce
1½ cups frozen shrimp (half 12-ounce package)
1½ cups long-grain white rice

1. Melt the butter in a 10-inch skillet. Add the onion, green pepper, sausage, ham, paprika, ground hot red pepper, bay leaves, clam juice, broth, water, tomatoes and Worcestershire sauce; bring to a boil.
2. Add the shrimp and the rice to the skillet, stirring to combine all the ingredients. Cover the skillet, reduce the heat to medium-low and simmer the jambalaya for 20 minutes. Remove and discard the bay leaves. Serve immediately.

Makes 8 servings.

Nutrient Value Per Serving: 429 calories, 28 g protein, 31 g carbohydrate, 22 g fat, 282 mg sodium, 80 mg cholesterol.

½ cup mayonnaise
½ cup prepared mayonnaise-type salad dressing
½ cup raisins
3 tablespoons mango or other chutney
2 tablespoons curry powder
1 tablespoon lemon juice
4½ cups cubed cooked chicken (2½ to 3 pounds whole chicken breasts)
2 cups cooked rice (¾ cup uncooked converted rice)
¼ cup thinly sliced green onions
1 banana, cut into ¼-inch-thick rounds *(optional)*
¼ cup peanuts
¼ cup flaked coconut

1. Combine the mayonnaise, salad dressing, 2 tablespoons of the raisins, the chutney, curry powder and lemon juice in the container of an electric blender. Cover; whirl until the dressing is a smooth purée.
2. Combine the chicken pieces, rice, green onion and remaining raisins in a large bowl. Blend in the curry dressing. Cover the salad and chill.
3. To serve, arrange the salad in a serving bowl or on a platter. Garnish with the banana, if you wish, the peanuts and the coconut.

QUICK TIP

Grease Slick
If there is too much grease or fat floating on top of a soup, stew or casserole and you are serving it right away, float lettuce leaves on top and replace them as they absorb the grease. Or blot the fat with a cheesecloth-wrapped ice cube. If the dish is to be served at a later time, refrigerate it and remove the fat layer after it congeals on top.

Black Bean Chili with Tortilla Chips

Warm chips at 300° for 3 to 5 minutes.
Makes 4 servings.

Nutrient Value Per Serving: 359 calories, 17 g protein, 12 g fat, 51 g carbohydrate, 640 mg sodium, 19 mg cholesterol.

2   cans (16 ounces each) black beans, with their liquid
1   can (8 ounces) tomato sauce
1   cup frozen chopped sweet green pepper
2   tablespoons bottled salsa jalapeño (or ¼ cup salsa picante)
1   tablespoon chili powder
½   teaspoon ground cumin
1   cup crushed tortilla chips (2 ounces)
½   cup dairy sour cream
½   cup shredded Monterey Jack cheese
2   cups shredded iceberg lettuce (about ½ head)
    Salsa, for garnish

1. Combine the black beans with their liquid, tomato sauce, green pepper, salsa, chili powder and cumin in a 2-quart saucepan. Bring to a boil. Lower the heat to medium and cook for 15 minutes or until the flavors are well blended.
2. Preheat the oven to slow (300°).
3. Place the tortilla chips on a cookie sheet and warm the chips in the preheated slow oven (300°) for 3 to 5 minutes or until the chips are crisped and fragrant.
4. To serve, divide the chips evenly among 4 bowls. Spoon the chili over the chips. Garnish the chili with the sour cream, Monterey Jack cheese, lettuce and additional salsa.

Sensational Cheese Sandwiches

Bake at 350° for 20 to 25 minutes.
Makes 12 servings.

Nutrient Value Per Serving: 463 calories, 24 g protein, 26 g fat, 33 g carbohydrate, 1,285 mg sodium, 89 mg cholesterol.

12   Kaiser rolls
¾   cup (1½ sticks) butter, softened
⅓   cup horseradish mustard
2   tablespoons finely chopped onion
2   teaspoons poppy-seeds
1½   pounds thinly sliced boiled ham
12   slices Swiss cheese (about 12 ounces)

1. Preheat the oven to moderate (350°).
2. Slice the rolls and set aside. Combine the butter, mustard, onion and poppy-seeds in a small bowl.
3. Spread the butter mixture on the cut sides of the rolls.** Divide the ham and the cheese evenly among the rolls. Wrap the rolls individually in aluminum foil, sealing tightly. Place the rolls on a baking sheet.
4. Bake the rolls in the preheated moderate oven (350°) for 20 to 25 minutes or until heated through. Serve the rolls immediately.

**Note: *Save any remaining butter mixture for another use.*

Menu Idea

Black Bean Chili with Tortilla Chips*
Cucumber Salad
Watermelon

Menu Idea

Sensational Cheese Sandwiches*
Coleslaw
Chocolate Cake

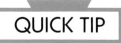
QUICK TIP

Easy Grater
Thoroughly chill soft cheeses, such as Swiss or Monterey Jack, before shredding or grating. A little vegetable oil brushed on the grater will help to make it nonstick.

Roast Beef Salad

Menu Idea
Roast Beef Salad*
with Caper
Dressing*
Orange and Onion
Salad* *(page 83)*
Crusty French
Bread
Cheesecake

Use cooked steak or deli roast beef for this salad.

Makes 6 servings.

Nutrient Value Per Serving:
325 calories, 31 g protein, 19 g
fat, 7 g carbohydrate, 207 mg
sodium, 94 mg cholesterol.

1½ **pounds rare cooked beef**
1   **sweet red pepper, halved,**
    cored, seeded and thinly
    sliced
1   **sweet yellow or green**
    pepper, halved, cored,
    seeded and thinly sliced
3   **green onions, trimmed and**
    cut into 1-inch pieces
8   **pimiento-stuffed olives,**
    sliced
    Caper Dressing *(recipe*
    follows)
1   **large cucumber, scored and**
    sliced
4   **firm ripe tomatoes, sliced**

1. Cut the beef into 2 x ½ x ½-inch
   pieces. Place the beef in a bowl.
   Add the pepper slices, green
   onion and olive slices. Pour ½
   cup of the Caper Dressing over
   the beef mixture and toss to
   combine.
2. Line a serving platter with the
   cucumber and tomato slices.
   Fill the center with the beef
   mixture. Pass the remaining
   Caper Dressing.

Caper Dressing

Makes ⅔ cup.

Nutrient Value Per Serving:
98 calories, 0 g protein, 11 g fat,
0 g carbohydrate, 52 mg
sodium, 0 mg cholesterol.

3   **tablespoons red wine**
    vinegar
2   **teaspoons Dijon-style**
    mustard
1   **clove garlic, crushed**
½   **cup fruity olive oil**
1   **tablespoon drained capers,**
    crushed
    Salt, to taste
    Freshly ground pepper, to
    taste

Combine the red wine vinegar, the
mustard and the crushed garlic in a
small bowl. Add the salt and the
freshly ground pepper to taste. Add
the fruity olive oil in a slow stream,
beating with a wire whisk. Stir in
the crushed drained capers.
Remove the garlic before pouring
the dressing.

Orange and Onion Salad

Salade Niçoise

For a richer salad, add 1 ripe avocado, cubed, just before serving.

Makes 4 servings.

Nutrient Value Per Serving: 170 calories, 2 g protein, 14 g fat, 12 g carbohydrate, 7 mg sodium, 0 mg cholesterol.

1   medium-size head leaf lettuce
2   navel oranges
1   medium-size red onion
1   tablespoon lemon juice
¼   teaspoon dry mustard powder
⅛   teaspoon sugar
     Salt and freshly ground pepper, to taste
¼   cup fruity olive oil
1   tablespoon finely chopped fresh parsley *(optional)*

1. Separate the lettuce into leaves and wash the leaves well. Dry the leaves and tear them into a large bowl.
2. Cut the peel and the white pith from the oranges. Working over a bowl to catch the juice, section the oranges; reserve the orange juice. Peel and slice the onion. Arrange the orange sections and the onion slices over the lettuce in the bowl. Cover the salad with damp paper toweling. Chill the salad.
3. Combine 2 tablespoons of the reserved orange juice, the lemon juice, mustard, sugar, salt and pepper in a small bowl. Slowly beat in the oil. Stir in chopped fresh parsley, if you wish.
4. Pour the dressing over the salad and toss gently to mix.

Makes 6 servings.

Nutrient Value Per Serving (without vinaigrette): 259 calories, 27 g protein, 10 g fat, 16 g carbohydrate, 1,579 mg sodium, 37 mg cholesterol.

2   cups cut green beans
2   large boiling potatoes
2   ripe tomatoes
2   sweet green peppers
     Lettuce leaves
2   cups chunked tuna fish
½   cup anchovies, diced
1   cup oil-cured black olives
     Basil Vinaigrette *(recipe follows)*

1. Steam the green beans for 3 minutes or until barely tender. Reserve the water. Remove the beans from the saucepan and rinse in cold water. Drain well.
2. Cook the potatoes in the same water until tender. Drain the potatoes. When cool enough to handle, peel and cube.
3. Core and dice the tomatoes. Seed and dice the peppers.
4. Arrange the lettuce leaves on 6 salad plates. Top with the remaining ingredients. Serve with the Basil Vinaigrette.

Basil Vinaigrette: Combine 1 cup olive oil, ⅓ red wine vinegar, 4 leaves basil, chopped, 2 cloves garlic, 1 egg white, ½ teaspoon salt and pepper to taste in a blender or food processor; whirl until smooth. *Makes 1⅓ cups. Nutrient Value Per Tablespoon: 93 calories, 0 g protein, 10 g fat, 0 g carbohydrate, 55 mg sodium, 0 mg cholesterol.*

Menu Idea

Salade Niçoise with Basil Vinaigrette*
Semolina Bread
Pears with Jarlsberg Cheese

QUICK TIP

Less Sodium In Your Salad
For the Salade Niçoise, you can reduce the amount of sodium by using fewer anchovies (or eliminating them), and substituting low-sodium tuna for regular tuna.

83

DISHES IN 30 TO 55 MINUTES

Chapter 3 helps you put dinner on the table in 35 to 55 minutes. That may not *seem* like busy cooking, but here's the plus: many of these recipes actually give you 15 to 20 minutes of *free time,* while a sauce simmers, a casserole bakes or a dish braises on the stove. Which means you can go on to other things—catch up on tasks, or just take a break and relax.

What can you make in this time? How about homemade pizza, such as Pizza Rustica *(page 91)* or Tricolor Pizza *(page 90).* Making it at home will save you money—as will buying whole chickens on sale, and cutting them into parts at home. Try this money-saving technique for New Zealand Chicken with Blue Cheese Sauce *(page 93).* Pork is one entrée that needs time to cook thoroughly, so it's ideal for this chapter. Braised Stuffed Pork Chops *(page 101)* or savory Potato, Pepper and Kielbasa Casserole *(page 102)* are two delicious examples.

Whatever recipe you choose, these dishes will set you free of the kitchen for part of the time. And that's good news for busy cooks!

Sausage and Eggplant Ragoût (page 103), combines sweet Italian sausage and garden-fresh eggplant and zucchini. Two Beans, Tomatoes and Tuna (Chapter 1, page 11) is a 15-minute miracle of quick cooking. Try something different with zucchini—Crisp Zucchini Pancakes (Chapter 5, page 157).

Pasta & Pizza

Sweet Pepper Pasta

A bright red pepper sauce coats the bow-tie pasta.

Makes 4 servings.

Nutrient Value Per Serving: 635 calories, 18 g protein, 17 g fat, 104 g carbohydrate, 528 mg sodium, 0 mg cholesterol.

¼ **cup good-quality olive oil**
2 **medium-size onions, halved and thinly sliced**
3 **pounds sweet red peppers, halved, cored, seeded and cut into ½-inch-thick strips**
2 **tablespoons chopped fresh mint OR: 1 teaspoon dried mint**
½ **teaspoon salt**
¼ **teaspoon pepper**
1 **to 1½ cups chicken broth**
1 **pound bow-tie pasta, penne or ziti**
2 **tablespoons chopped flat-leaf Italian parsley, for garnish**

1. Heat the oil in a large skillet or Dutch oven over high heat. Add the onion and the red peppers and cook, stirring often, until the edges of the onion begin to brown, for about 15 minutes. Lower the heat to medium. Add the mint, salt and pepper to the skillet. Cook until the red peppers are tender, for about 15 minutes. Add 1 cup of the broth to the skillet. Cover the skillet and cook for 5 minutes longer.
2. Remove 12 slices of the cooked red peppers and set aside. Place the remaining pepper mixture in the container of a food processor or, working in batches, of an electric blender. Cover and whirl until the mixture is the consistency of a thick tomato sauce. If the sauce is too thick, add some of the remaining ½ cup of broth.
3. While the sauce is cooking, cook the pasta in a large pot of boiling salted water until *al dente*, firm but tender. Drain the pasta in a colander. Add the pasta to the sauce in the skillet. Toss to mix well. Serve the pasta garnished with the reserved slices of red pepper and the chopped parsley.

Menu Idea
Sweet Pepper Pasta*
Breadsticks
Boston and Red Leaf Lettuce Salad
Nectarines

QUICK TIP

No Tears Onions
Peel onions under cold running water to avoid the tears. Be sure to blot the onions dry with paper toweling.

Clockwise from bottom left: Sweet Pepper Pasta is spiced with sweet red peppers, fresh mint and onions; arugula replaces the usual basil in the pesto in Pasta with Arugula Pesto (page 45); crisp broccoli and plump tomatoes combine with chunks of tuna to make a colorful Rigatoni Salad (page 46).

Blue Cheese Electric Skillet Lasagne

Menu Idea

Blue Cheese Electric Skillet Lasagne*
Crusty Italian Bread
Escarole Salad
Spumoni Ice Cream

No need to precook the lasagne noodles.

Makes 6 servings.

Nutrient Value Per Serving:
599 calories, 29 g protein, 25 g fat, 63 g carbohydrate, 1,033 mg sodium, 140 mg cholesterol.

3 **cups bottled spaghetti sauce with beef**
1½ **cups water**
½ **teaspoon leaf oregano, crumbled**
2 **cups shredded mozzarella cheese (8 ounces)**
1 **cup cottage cheese**
4 **ounces blue cheese, crumbled**
⅓ **cup chopped parsley**
2 **eggs, slightly beaten**
12 **lasagne noodles, uncooked Grated Parmesan cheese** *(optional)*

1. Combine the spaghetti sauce, water and oregano in a medium-size bowl and mix well.
2. Combine 1 cup of the mozzarella cheese, the cottage cheese, blue cheese, parsley and eggs in another bowl and stir well to mix.
3. Spread ¾ cup of the spaghetti sauce mixture over the bottom of a nonstick 11-inch-square electric skillet. Place 4 of the lasagne noodles over the sauce. Spread the noodles with half the cheese mixture and drizzle with 1¼ cups of the spaghetti sauce mixture. Place 4 more lasagne noodles on top of the sauce at right angles to the noodles below. Spread with the remaining cheese mixture and drizzle with another 1¼ cups of the spaghetti sauce mixture. Top with the remaining noodles, again placing them at right angles to the ones below. Cover with the remaining 1¼ cups of the spaghetti sauce mixture. Sprinkle with the remaining cup of mozzarella cheese. Press down the whole lasagne lightly with your hands to level the mixture and to cover everything with the sauce.
4. Cover the skillet with the lid. Place a small wad of aluminum foil under one corner of the lid to hold it slightly open, about ⅛ inch, or open the vent in the lid, if there is one.
5. Set the temperature control at 225°. Cook the lasagne for 45 minutes. Turn the heat off. Let the lasagne stand, covered, for 15 minutes.
6. Sprinkle the lasagne with Parmesan cheese, if you wish. Cut the lasagne into 6 portions to serve.

QUICK TIP

Microwave Your Herbs
Use your microwave to dry fresh herbs. Wash and pat the herbs dry on paper toweling. Measure 1½ cups of leaves (without the stems). Spread them on a double thickness of paper toweling and microwave at full (100%) power for four to five minutes, stirring several times.

Easy Pissaladiere

This delicious, Mediterranean-style onion and anchovy pizza makes a perfect main dish for family or company—and all the ingredients you'll need are in your cupboard!

Bake at 425° for 5 minutes, then at 375° for 15 minutes.
Makes two 12-inch pizzas (8 slices each).

Nutrient Value Per Serving: 189 calories, 5 g protein, 8 g fat, 26 g carbohydrate, 434 mg sodium, 5 mg cholesterol.

2   **pounds yellow onion, peeled and thinly sliced**
2   **cloves garlic, peeled**
2   **tablespoons olive oil**
2   **tubes (10 ounces each) refrigerated pizza dough**
1   **jar (15½ ounces) meatless spaghetti sauce**
2   **cans (2 ounces each) flat anchovy fillets, drained**
1   **can (6 ounces) pitted black olives, drained**

1. Sauté the onion and the garlic in the oil in a large skillet over low heat until the onion is slightly softened, for about 2 to 3 minutes. Cover the skillet and cook until very soft but not browned, for about 20 minutes.
2. Preheat the oven to hot (425°).
3. Open one of the tubes of dough and unroll the dough. Pat onto a 12-inch pizza pan or large cookie sheet following the package directions. Repeat with the second tube.
4. Spread half the spaghetti sauce over one dough, leaving a ½-inch border around the edge. Top with half the onion mixture, decorate with 1 can of the anchovies and half a can of the pitted black olives. Repeat with the second pizza.
5. Place the pizzas on 2 shelves of the preheated hot oven (425°). Bake for 5 minutes. Exchange the shelf positions of the pizzas. Lower the oven temperature to moderate (375°). Bake the pizzas for 15 minutes or until the pizza crusts are golden.

Menu Idea

Cups of Minestrone

Easy Pissaladiere*

Tossed Green Salad

Sliced Apples with Cheese

QUICK TIP

Easy Clean Up
To clean up oven spills, pour salt on the area, dampen it slightly and allow it to sit for up to half an hour. Spills should wipe up easily.

Tricolor Pizza

Menu Idea
Antipasto Platter*
*(half recipe,
page 172)*
Tricolor Pizza*
Melon Slush*
(page 269)

*Bake at 425° for 20 minutes.
Makes 6 servings (one 14-inch
pizza).*

*Nutrient Value Per Serving:
324 calories, 13 g protein, 15 g
fat, 35 g carbohydrate, 688 mg
sodium, 25 mg cholesterol.*

3   **tablespoons olive oil**
5   **cups thinly sliced leeks,
      white and green parts
      (4 medium-size or 3 large)**
¼   **teaspoon salt**
4   **ounces thinly sliced
      prosciutto OR: quality
      smoked ham, cut into
      ¼-inch strips**
1   **tube (10 ounces)
      refrigerated pizza dough**
1   **large sweet red pepper,
      cored, seeded and cut into
      strips**
4   **ounces coarsely shredded
      mozzarella cheese
      (1½ cups)
      Freshly ground black
      pepper**

1. Preheat the oven to hot (425°). Place the oven rack in the lowest position.
2. Heat the oil in a large skillet. Add the leeks and the salt and toss to coat with the oil. Cover the skillet and simmer for 8 minutes, stirring occasionally, until the leeks are tender. Stir the prosciutto or ham into the skillet. Set the skillet aside, uncovered.
3. Open the tube and unroll the dough. Place the dough in a 14-inch pizza pan. Pat the dough with your hands to stretch the dough to the edge of the pan.
4. Spread the leek mixture over the pizza dough. Top the dough with the red pepper strips.
5. Bake the pizza in the preheated hot oven (425°) on the lowest shelf for 15 minutes. Sprinkle the top of the pizza with the mozzarella cheese. Continue baking the pizza for 5 minutes longer or until the crust is lightly browned on the edges. Sprinkle the black pepper over the top. Cut the pizza into 6 wedges and serve hot.

*Quick-fix, fancy Tricolor Pizza is topped
with leeks, prosciutto and sweet red
peppers.*

Pizza Rustica Pie

The flavor of this two-crusted pie, with prosciutto and a variety of cheeses, is best when the pie is served lukewarm or at room temperature.

Bake at 375° for 45 to 50 minutes.
Makes 6 servings.

Nutrient Value Per Serving: 550 calories, 19 g protein, 35 g fat, 41 g carbohydrate, 977 mg sodium, 173 mg cholesterol.

Pastry dough for two-crust 9-inch pie
3 **eggs, slightly beaten**
1 **cup marinara sauce, homemade or store-bought**
1 **teaspoon leaf oregano, crumbled**
1½ **cups ricotta cheese**
¼ **cup coarsely shredded Provolone**
¼ **cup grated Romano or Parmesan cheese**
2 **ounces prosciutto, thinly sliced and shredded**
2 **ounces mortadella, thinly sliced and shredded**

1. Preheat the oven to moderate (375°).
2. Roll out half the pastry dough to fit into a 9-inch pie plate and fit the pastry into the plate. Roll out the remaining pastry dough to make a top crust and reserve.
3. Reserve 1 tablespoon of the eggs to glaze the pie. Combine the marinara sauce and the oregano in a large bowl. Stir in about half the remaining eggs. Place the ricotta cheese in another bowl and stir in the remaining eggs, the Provolone, the Romano or Parmesan cheese, prosciutto and mortadella. Pour the marinara mixture over the ricotta and marbelize with a few strokes of a rubber scraper.
4. Spoon the filling into the pastry-lined pie plate, spreading into an even layer. Cover the pie with the top crust. Brush the edges of the bottom crust with a little water to seal the edges together. Flute the pastry edges or press together with the tines of a fork. Brush the top with the reserved 1 tablespoon of egg.
5. Bake the pie in the preheated moderate oven (375°) for 45 to 50 minutes or until the top crust is puffed and browned.

Menu Idea
Pizza Rustica Pie*
Green Beans and Radish Vinaigrette
Strawberries with Raspberry Sauce

Chicken

New Zealand Chicken with Blue Cheese Sauce

Blue cheese adds pizzazz to baked chicken.

Bake at 375° for 40 minutes.
Makes 4 servings.

Nutrient Value Per Serving:
550 calories, 47 g protein, 35 g
fat, 10 g carbohydrate, 858 mg
sodium, 176 mg cholesterol.

1	broiler-fryer (about 3 pounds), cut up
½	teaspoon salt
¼	teaspoon pepper

Blue Cheese Sauce:

1	tablespoon butter
1	tablespoon all-purpose flour
½	cup chicken broth
½	cup dry white wine
3	ounces crumbled blue, Roquefort, Gorgonzola or Stilton cheese
1	teaspoon leaf thyme, crumbled
¼	cup heavy cream
2	tablespoons chopped parsley
2	kiwifruit, peeled and sliced

1. Preheat the oven to moderate (375°). Arrange the chicken in a shallow baking pan. Season the chicken with the salt and the pepper.
2. Bake the chicken in the preheated moderate oven (375°) for 40 minutes or until the juices run clear and the meat is no longer pink near the bone.
3. Ten minutes before the chicken is done, prepare the Blue Cheese Sauce: Melt the butter in a small saucepan. Stir in the flour until smooth. Stir in the broth and the wine. Cook the sauce, stirring, over medium-high heat until the mixture is bubbly and thickened, for about 3 minutes.
4. Stir the blue cheese and the thyme into the sauce until the blue cheese is melted. Reduce the heat to low. Stir in the cream and the parsley. Stir to heat the sauce through; do not boil. Keep the sauce warm over low heat until the chicken is done.
5. To serve, arrange the chicken on a platter with the kiwi slices. Pass the blue cheese sauce.

Menu Idea

New Zealand
** Chicken with Blue**
** Cheese Sauce***
Baby Carrots
Radicchio
Buttermilk Rolls
Fresh Fruit
** Compote**

Two favorite chicken dishes from around the world include: top, New Zealand Chicken with Blue Cheese Sauce, flavored with white wine and thyme and surrounded by kiwifruit and baby carrots; and Greek Chicken (page 98), stuffed with a delicately spiced spinach and feta cheese filling and served on a bed of savory rice.

Apricot Wild Rice and Chicken

Menu Idea

Apricot Wild Rice and Chicken*

Steamed Carrots

Sesame Seed Breadsticks

Vanilla Ice Cream with Butterscotch Sauce

The nutty flavor of wild rice is the perfect match for the sweetness of the apricots. A great buffet dish!

Bake at 350° for 25 minutes. Makes 6 servings.

Nutrient Value Per Serving: 427 calories, 33 g protein, 13 g fat, 39 g carbohydrate, 640 mg sodium, 105 mg cholesterol.

1   box (6¼ ounces) fast-cooking long grain and wild rice OR: 2 cups wild rice
½   teaspoon salt *(optional)*
6   tablespoons butter
9   canned whole skinless apricots, pitted
3   whole boneless, skinned chicken breasts (each about 9 ounces), halved
¼   cup apricot brandy OR: apricot nectar
¼   teaspoon pepper

1. Preheat the oven to moderate (350°). Grease a 13½ x 8½ x 2-inch glass casserole.
2. Prepare the rice following the package directions, adding the ½ teaspoon of salt if using plain wild rice.
3. Stir 2 tablespoons of the butter into the rice until melted. Coarsely chop 6 of the apricots and stir the apricots into the rice. Spoon the rice mixture into the prepared casserole.
4. Sauté the chicken breast halves in the remaining 4 tablespoons of butter in a skillet until golden, for about 2 minutes on each side.
5. Halve the remaining 3 apricots. Arrange the chicken pieces on top of the rice mixture in the casserole with the apricot halves arranged between the breasts. Pour the apricot brandy or nectar over the top.
6. Bake the chicken casserole, uncovered, in the preheated moderate oven (350°) for 25 minutes or until the chicken is no longer pink in the center. Season the chicken with the pepper. Serve immediately.

QUICK TIP

Hot Stuff!
For an extra-elegant topping for ice cream or pound cake, heat your bottled sauces. Just a few seconds in your microwave (without the jar cap) or place the bottle in a saucepan of hot water as you sit down to dinner—either way your fudge or butterscotch will taste especially wonderful.

Chicken Breasts with Prosciutto and Spinach

Frozen spinach soufflé makes a quick filling for chicken breasts.

Bake at 350° for 20 minutes. Makes 6 servings.

Nutrient Value Per Serving: 305 calories, 32 g protein, 17 g fat, 4 g carbohydrate, 606 mg sodium, 104 mg cholesterol.

3 **whole large boneless, skinned chicken breasts**
1 **package (12 ounces) frozen spinach soufflé, still frozen**
3 **thin slices prosciutto, halved**
2 **tablespoons olive or vegetable oil**
1 **cup dry white wine**
1 **cup chicken broth**
½ **cup heavy cream**
 Watercress, for garnish

1. Preheat the oven to moderate (350°).
2. Halve the chicken breasts, crosswise. With a meat mallet or the back of a heavy chef's knife, pound the meat to a ¼-inch thickness.
3. Cut enough of the frozen soufflé to make six ½-inch-wide strips. Save the remaining soufflé in the freezer for another use.
4. Place a half slice of the prosciutto on each chicken breast half. Top with a spinach soufflé strip. Fold over the long edges of the chicken breast to cover the soufflé and fasten with wooden picks.
5. Brown the chicken rolls in the oil in a large, ovenproof skillet for about 2 minutes, turning the rolls occasionally.
6. Add the wine and the broth to the skillet; bring the mixture to boiling. Cover the skillet.

7. Bake the chicken rolls in the preheated moderate oven (350°) for 20 minutes or until the chicken is no longer pink.
8. Remove the rolls from the skillet and let stand. Keep warm.
9. Skim the fat from the liquid in the skillet. Reduce the liquid by half over medium heat. Add the cream and simmer until slightly thickened.
10. Cut the chicken rolls crosswise into 1-inch-thick slices. Arrange the slices on a serving platter. Remove the wooden picks and garnish with the watercress. Pass the sauce separately.

Menu Idea
Chicken Breasts with Prosciutto and Spinach*
Mashed Potatoes with Garlic
Green Beans with Almonds
Grapes

Foods from your freezer add the easy touch to delicious Chicken Breasts with Prosciutto and Spinach and our colorful Broccoli and Artichoke Salad (page 181).

Chicken Normandy

Menu Idea
Chicken Normandy*
Green Beans with Walnuts
Leafy Green Salad
Chocolate Mousse

This dish is a trademark of the Normandy region of France.

Makes 4 servings.

Nutrient Value Per Serving: 661 calories, 42 g protein, 48 g fat, 15 g carbohydrate, 530 mg sodium, 188 mg cholesterol.

1   **broiler-fryer (about 3 pounds), cut up**
3   **tablespoons corn oil**
½   **teaspoon salt**
¼   **teaspoon pepper**
8   **small white onions, peeled OR: 1 small onion, thinly sliced**
½   **cup apple juice**
¼   **cup chicken broth**
1   **bay leaf**
2   **small apples, cored and thinly sliced**
2   **tablespoons butter**
¼   **cup apple brandy OR: cognac**
1   **tablespoon all-purpose flour**
½   **cup heavy cream Watercress or parsley sprigs, for garnish (optional)**

1. Brown the chicken in the oil in a large, heavy skillet, working in batches if necessary, for about 5 minutes per side. As the pieces brown, remove them to a plate. Season the chicken with the salt and the pepper.

2. In the same skillet, brown the onion for about 3 minutes. Carefully pour off the excess fat. Return the chicken to the skillet. Add the apple juice, broth and bay leaf; bring to a boil. Cover the skillet, lower the heat and simmer. Remove the chicken breasts from the skillet after 15 minutes and test for doneness; keep warm. Cook the remaining chicken pieces for another 15 minutes or until it is no longer pink near the bone.

3. Meanwhile, sauté the apple slices in the butter in a separate skillet for 3 to 4 minutes or until tender. Set the apple slices aside until the chicken is done.

4. Remove the chicken and onion to a shallow serving dish with sides. Cover the dish and keep warm. Skim the fat from the juices in the skillet; remove the bay leaf. Measure out ¾ cup of the pan juices and refrigerate the remaining juices for another use. In the skillet, stir together the ¾ cup of juices and the brandy or cognac. Boil vigorously for 3 minutes.

5. Reduce the heat to low. Stir the flour into the cream in a small cup. Stir the flour mixture into the brandy mixture in the skillet along with the apple slices. Cook gently for 1 minute more to heat the sauce through; do not boil. Ladle the sauce over the chicken. Garnish with watercress or parsley, if you wish.

QUICK TIP

Fast Flour
Keep a large shaker full of flour near the stove for those times when you need only a pinch or a spoonful. This saves the time and bother of opening a big canister and you can avoid spilling flour on your counter or stove.

Chicken with Almonds

Chicken with Mushroom Rosemary Sauce

Bake at 350° for 40 to 45 minutes. Makes 4 servings.

Nutrient Value Per Serving: 519 calories, 43 g protein, 36 g fat, 8 g carbohydrate, 277 mg sodium, 131 mg cholesterol.

2   whole boneless, skinned chicken breasts (each about 9 ounces), halved
4   ounces Jarlsberg or Swiss cheese, cut into 4 sticks, each about 3½ x ½ inch
¼   cup (½ stick) butter
2   tablespoons dry sherry
1   cup ground almonds (4 ounces)

1. Preheat the oven to moderate (350°).
2. Pound the chicken breasts between sheets of wax paper with the side of a wooden meat mallet until the chicken is thin and as even as possible.
3. Place one stick of the Jarlsberg or Swiss cheese in the middle of each breast on the bone side. Starting with a short end, roll up the chicken breasts, jelly-roll fashion, tucking in the sides. Secure the breasts with a wooden pick, or tie with kitchen twine.
4. Melt the butter in a small saucepan. Stir in the sherry. Remove the saucepan from the heat. Dip the chicken in the butter mixture, then roll in the almonds. Pour any remaining butter mixture into a 9-inch pie plate. Place the chicken rolls in a single layer in the pie plate.
5. Bake the chicken rolls, uncovered, in the preheated moderate oven (350°) for 40 to 45 minutes or until the chicken is no longer pink and the nuts are toasted. Serve immediately.

Makes 6 servings.

Nutrient Value Per Serving: 363 calories, 31 g protein, 23 g fat, 7 g carbohydrate, 350 mg sodium, 111 mg cholesterol.

3   pounds chicken thighs
½   teaspoon salt
½   teaspoon pepper
1   tablespoon vegetable oil
1   medium-size onion, chopped
3   cloves garlic, chopped
2   4-inch sprigs fresh rosemary OR: 1 teaspoon crumbled dried
12 ounces mushrooms, cut into ¼-inch-thick slices (about 4 cups)
½   cup dry white wine
3   tablespoons tomato paste

1. Salt and pepper the chicken. Brown half, skin-side down first, in the oil in a large, heavy-bottomed casserole over medium-high heat, for about 3 minutes per side; remove. Repeat with the other thighs.
2. Lower heat to medium. Pour off all but 1 tablespoon of fat. Add the onion and garlic. Cook, stirring, until onion is softened, for about 4 minutes. Stir in the rosemary and mushrooms and cook, until mushrooms are softened, for 3 to 4 minutes. Stir in the wine and tomato paste.
3. Return the chicken to the pan and stir to coat with the sauce. Simmer, covered, for 25 minutes. Uncover the pot. Bring to a boil and cook until the liquid is reduced by half, for about 10 minutes. The sauce should be the consistency of a thick glaze. Remove the rosemary sprigs before serving.

Menu Idea

Chicken with Almonds*
Hot Cooked Rice
Sautéed Snow Peas
Lemon Sherbet

Menu Idea

Chicken with Mushroom Rosemary Sauce*
White Rice
Sliced Tomato Salad
Fresh Fruit Compote

97

Greek Chicken

Menu Idea
Greek Chicken*
Herbed Rice
Broccoli
Caramel Flan

Fan out slices of the stuffed chicken breast on an earthenware platter to create an appetizing centerpiece for a buffet.

> *Bake at 350° for 40 minutes. Makes 8 servings.*

> *Nutrient Value Per Serving: 244 calories, 43 g protein, 6 g fat, 2 g carbohydrate, 304 mg sodium, 146 mg cholesterol.*

1   package (10 ounces) frozen chopped spinach, thawed and excess liquid squeezed out
4   ounces feta cheese, drained well and crumbled (1 cup)
1   egg, slightly beaten
1   teaspoon leaf basil, crumbled
½   teaspoon leaf rosemary, crumbled
½   teaspoon dillweed, crumbled
8   boneless, skinned chicken breast halves (3 pounds)

1. Preheat the oven to moderate (350°). Butter a 13 x 9 x 2-inch baking pan.
2. Stir together the spinach, feta cheese, egg, basil, rosemary and dillweed in a medium-size bowl. Set the mixture aside.
3. Place the chicken breast halves between sheets of wax paper. Pound the breasts with the smooth side of a meat mallet or the bottom of a frying pan to a ¼-inch thickness. Lay the chicken breast halves, skinned side down, on a board. Top each with a scant ¼ cup of the spinach filling. Roll up the breasts, starting with a narrow end and folding the long sides toward the center while rolling. Place the chicken rolls, seam side down, in the prepared

baking pan. Butter a sheet of aluminum foil large enough to cover the pan. Place the foil, buttered side down, over the chicken rolls and seal the edges.
4. Bake the chicken rolls in the preheated moderate oven (350°) for 40 minutes or until the chicken is firm to the touch and cooked through. Remove the rolls to a cutting board. Slice each roll crosswise into about 6 equal rounds. Arrange the rounds on a platter with your favorite packaged rice mix or orzo, if you wish.

Microwave Instructions
(for a 650-watt variable power microwave oven)

Ingredient Changes: Use small chicken breasts weighing a total of about 2¼ pounds.
Directions: Prepare the spinach stuffing and assemble the chicken rolls as above. Place the rolls, seam side down, in spoke fashion in a 10-inch microwave-safe pie plate. Cover the plate with a sheet of wax paper. Microwave the rolls at full power for 8 minutes or until the chicken is tender, rearranging the rolls after 4 minutes. Let the rolls stand for 5 minutes before serving.
Nutrient Value Per Serving: 197 calories, 33 g protein, 5 g fat, 2 g carbohydrate, 276 mg sodium, 121 mg cholesterol.

QUICK TIP

Quick-Cook Chicken Breasts
Boneless chicken breasts cook even faster if they are first flattened with a mallet, hammer or bottom of a heavy skillet.

Cheese Enchiladas with Bean and Corn Chili

Bake at 375° for 30 minutes.
Makes 5 servings.

Nutrient Value Per Serving:
522 calories, 26 g protein, 28 g
fat, 46 g carbohydrate, 982 mg
sodium, 54 mg cholesterol.

1   **cup chopped onion, fresh or frozen**
2   **cloves garlic, finely chopped**
3   **tablespoons vegetable oil**
1   **can (14 ounces) Italian-style plum tomatoes**
¾   **teaspoon ground cumin**
¼   **teaspoon salt**
⅛   **teaspoon black pepper**
⅛   **teaspoon red pepper flakes**
1   **can (19 ounces) kidney beans, *un*drained**
1   **can (12 ounces) corn niblets, drained**
1   **container (8 ounces) ricotta cheese**
2   **cups shredded Monterey Jack-style cheese with jalapeño pepper (8 ounces)**
1   **package (5.3 ounces) 5-inch corn tortillas**

1. Sauté the onion and the garlic in 1 tablespoon of the oil in a large skillet until soft, for about 5 minutes.
2. Add the tomatoes to the skillet. Stir in the cumin, salt, black pepper and red pepper flakes. Bring the mixture to boiling, breaking up the tomatoes with a wooden spoon. Add the kidney beans and the corn. Return the mixture to boiling. Lower the heat. Cover the skillet and simmer for 15 minutes, stirring.
3. Preheat the oven to moderate (375°). Lightly grease a 13 x 9 x 2-inch baking pan or casserole. Spoon the chili into the pan.
4. Combine the ricotta and 1½ cups of the Monterey Jack-style cheese in a small bowl.
5. Soften a corn tortilla briefly in ½ teaspoon of hot oil in a small skillet over medium-high heat, turning the tortilla once. Spoon 2 tablespoons of the cheese filling down the center of the tortilla. Roll up the tortilla. Place the tortilla on the chili. Repeat with the remaining tortillas and the filling; you should have about 10 enchiladas. Sprinkle the remaining Monterey Jack-style cheese over the enchiladas.
6. Bake the enchiladas and the chili in the preheated moderate oven (375°) for 30 minutes or until bubbly.

Menu Idea

Cheese Enchiladas with Bean and Corn Chili*

Nachos

Guacamole Salad with Tomato Wedges

Vanilla Ice Cream with Fudge Sauce

QUICK TIP

Nifty Nachos
For a snack or as an appetizer—nachos can't be beat! Two easy ways to make them: Just pop an uncovered jar of process cheese spread (they even come with jalapeño) into your microwave for 20 to 30 seconds on high; then pour over a platter of taco chips. Or, sprinkle grated sharp Cheddar cheese over chips on a cookie sheet and bake at 350° for about 3 to 5 minutes or until the cheese is melted and bubbly.

99

Pork, Veal & Lamb

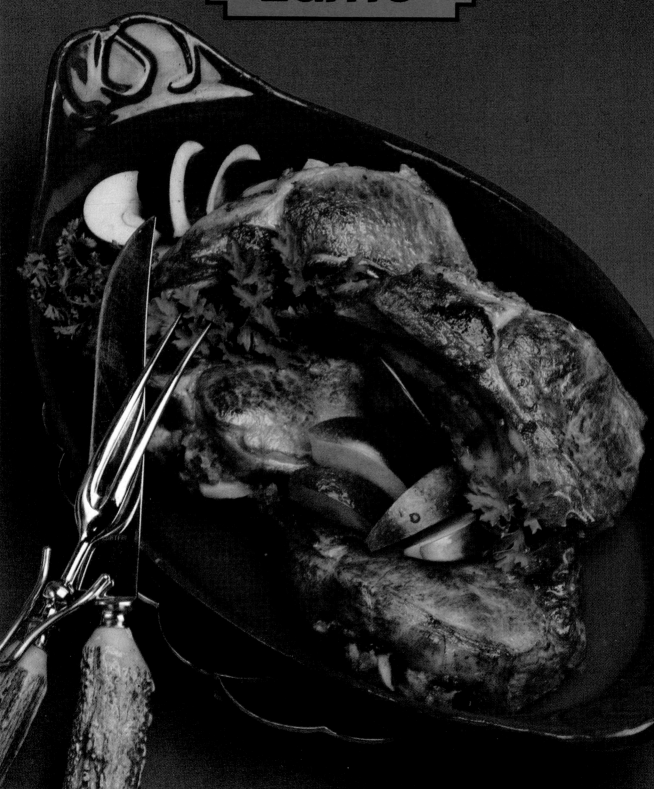

Braised Stuffed Pork Chops

Tart apples are used for this savory dressing. Good choices include Granny Smiths and Winesaps.

Makes 4 servings.

Nutrient Value Per Serving: 543 calories, 28 g protein, 35 g fat, 28 g carbohydrate, 557 mg sodium, 106 mg cholesterol.

4   **double-thick loin pork chops (about 6 ounces each)**
1   **small tart apple, peeled, cored and diced**
1   **small onion, finely chopped (¼ cup)**
2   **tablespoons butter or margarine**
1¾   **cups soft bread crumbs**
¼   **cup raisins, chopped**
½   **teaspoon salt**
¼   **teaspoon powdered sage**
⅛   **teaspoon pepper**
     All-purpose flour
2   **tablespoons vegetable oil**
¼   **cup chicken broth**
     Apple slices and parsley, for garnish

1. Cut a pocket in each chop. Set the chops aside.
2. Sauté the apple and the onion in the butter or margarine in a medium-size skillet until soft, for about 4 minutes. Mix in the bread crumbs, raisins, salt, sage and pepper. Spoon the stuffing into the chop pockets. Close the openings with wooden picks. Dredge the chops in the flour.
3. Brown the chops on both sides in the oil in a heavy skillet. Pour off the drippings. Add the broth to the skillet. Cover the skillet and cook over medium-low heat for about 45 minutes or until the chops are tender. Remove the wooden picks before serving. Garnish with the apple slices and the parsley.

Menu Idea

Braised Stuffed Pork Chops*

Sugar Snap Peas with Radish and Ginger* *(page 156)*

Coconut Cake

QUICK TIP

Stuffing — The Speedy Way
For stuffing in minutes to serve with any dish, keep an assortment of the packaged stuffing mixes from your supermarket shelf. For a distinctive touch, stir in 1 tablespoon of orange rind, ¼ cup of chopped walnuts, almonds or peanuts or 2 tablespoons of chopped celery leaves or parsley.

Braised Stuffed Pork Chops are filled with an apple raisin stuffing.

Potato, Pepper and Kielbasa Casserole

Menu Idea

Potato, Pepper and
  Kielbasa
  Casserole*
Broccoli
Semolina Bread
Apple Cake

This casserole takes less than 15 minutes to prepare before it's ready for the oven. It's an easy dish to divide for 2 or multiply for 6 or 8.

*Bake at 400° for 55 minutes.
Makes 4 servings.*

*Nutrient Value Per Serving:
615 calories, 16 g protein, 49 g fat, 28 g carbohydrate, 911 mg sodium, 100 mg cholesterol.*

2   large sweet peppers, red
       and/or green
2   medium-size onions
1   pound small red-skinned
       potatoes (about 8)
12   ounces kielbasa
¼   teaspoon salt
¼   teaspoon pepper
¼   cup olive oil
½   cup heavy cream
     Chopped parsley, for
       garnish (optional)

Wedges of sweet red pepper, slices of onion, potato and spicy sausage make up the special mix in Potato, Pepper and Kielbasa Casserole.

1. Preheat the oven to hot (400°).
2. Core and seed the peppers. Cut the peppers into 1½-inch pieces and place in a large bowl. Cut the onions into thin wedges and add to the bowl. Halve the potatoes and add to the bowl. Peel the casing from the kielbasa, if necessary. Cut the kielbasa into ½-inch-thick slices and add to the bowl. Sprinkle the potato mixture with the salt and the pepper. Add the oil and toss to mix well. Transfer the mixture to a shallow 1½-quart casserole dish. Cover with a lid or aluminum foil.
3. Bake the casserole in the preheated hot oven (400°) for 45 minutes. Stir the cream into the casserole. Cover and bake for 10 minutes more or until the mixture is bubbly and the cream and the oil have blended thoroughly. Garnish with chopped parsley, if you wish.

Microwave Instructions
(for a 650-watt variable power microwave oven)

Ingredient Changes: Reduce the cream to ¼ cup.
Directions: Combine the peppers, onion, potatoes, kielbasa, salt, pepper and oil as in Step 2 above in a microwave-safe 2-quart casserole. Cover the casserole. Microwave at full power for 15 minutes, stirring after 5 and 10 minutes. Mix in the cream. Cover. Microwave at full power for 2 minutes.

Sausage and Eggplant Ragoût

Makes 4 servings.

Nutrient Value Per Serving:
617 calories, 19 g protein, 45 g
fat, 39 g carbohydrate, 1,198 mg
sodium, 65 mg cholesterol.

2 **small dried hot red chili peppers, broken in half**
6 **tablespoons olive oil**
¾ **pound sweet Italian sausage**
1 **large eggplant (about 2 pounds), unpeeled, cut into ½-inch cubes, salted and drained on paper toweling for 1 hour**
2 **medium-size zucchini (12 ounces), trimmed and cut into ¾-inch cubes**
2 **red onions, quartered and thinly sliced (4 cups)**
1 **large sweet red pepper, halved, cored, seeded and cut into 1 x ¼-inch strips**
1 **large sweet green pepper, halved, cored, seeded and cut into 1 x ¼-inch strips**
2 **large cloves garlic, finely chopped**
½ **teaspoon salt**
¼ **teaspoon pepper**
1½ **teaspoons leaf thyme, crumbled**
1 **teaspoon leaf oregano, crumbled**
8 **small ripe plum tomatoes (about 1¼ pounds), peeled, quartered lengthwise and squeezed gently to seed**
2 **tablespoons finely chopped parsley**

1. Sauté 1 of the chili peppers in 2 tablespoons of the oil in a deep 12-inch skillet or Dutch oven until browned; discard the chili pepper. Add the sausage to the skillet and sauté just until browned on all sides. Transfer the sausage to a cutting surface. Slice crosswise into ½-inch-thick rounds and reserve.

2. Add 1 tablespoon of the oil to the same skillet. Add the eggplant cubes to the skillet and sauté over medium-low heat, stirring constantly, until the cubes are golden brown, for about 5 minutes. Transfer the eggplant cubes to a colander to drain.

3. Clean the skillet, if necessary. Add 1 tablespoon of the oil. Add the zucchini and sauté until golden, for about 3 minutes. Transfer the zucchini to a colander to drain.

4. Add 1 to 2 tablespoons of the oil, as necessary, to the skillet. Add the onion, red and green peppers, garlic, the remaining chili pepper, the salt and pepper and sauté until the vegetables are softened, for about 3 minutes. Lower the heat, partially cover the skillet and cook for 30 minutes.

5. Add the reserved eggplant, zucchini and sausage, the thyme and oregano. Cover the skillet and cook for 10 to 15 minutes or until the sausage is no longer pink.

6. Add the tomatoes and toss gently to heat through. Sprinkle the ragoût with the parsley and serve warm.

Menu Idea

Sausage and Eggplant Ragoût*
Orzo or Rice
Orange Slices with Vinaigrette
Breadsticks
Fresh Fruit Compote

103

Porcupine Balls

Menu Idea
Porcupine Balls*
Parslied Noodles
**String Bean
   Vinaigrette**
Cheesecake

Every cook during the 30's had a recipe for this easy and inexpensive entrée. Here is an updated version, but it still takes a vivid imagination to see a porcupine.

*Bake at 350° for 40 minutes.
Makes 4 servings.*

*Nutrient Value Per Serving:
455 calories, 23 g protein, 26 g
fat, 32 g carbohydrate, 841 mg
sodium, 84 mg cholesterol.*

8	ounces lean ground beef
8	ounces ground pork
½	cup fresh bread crumbs (1 slice)
1	medium-size onion, finely chopped (½ cup)
1	teaspoon salt
½	teaspoon pepper
½	cup uncooked long-grain rice
1	can (16 ounces) tomatoes, *un*drained and chopped
1	cup dry red wine
1	bay leaf
½	teaspoon leaf oregano, crumbled
1	large sweet green pepper, halved, seeded and cut into 1-inch squares

1. Preheat the oven to moderate (350°).
2. Combine the beef, pork, bread crumbs, onion, ½ teaspoon of the salt, ¼ teaspoon of the pepper and the rice in a medium-size bowl. Pat the mixture together with your hands until it is well blended. Divide the mixture into 12 equal portions and shape each portion into a ball. Set the meatballs aside.
3. Combine the tomatoes, wine, bay leaf, oregano, the remaining ½ teaspoon of salt and the remaining ¼ teaspoon of pepper in a 2-quart flameproof casserole. Bring the mixture to boiling on top of the stove. Drop the meatballs into the sauce and return to boiling. Cover the casserole.
4. Bake the casserole in the preheated moderate oven (350°) for 30 minutes. Stir in the green pepper. Cover and bake the casserole for 10 minutes longer.

QUICK TIP

**Pound For
Pound . . .**
To save time *and* money, buy meat and poultry in quantity when the price is right and the meat looks good; then date and freeze it. (Keep track of the "regular" prices so you can tell if you're really getting a bargain or not.)

Knockwurst Cheese Popover

Ham and Potato Bake with Cheese

Bake at 425° for 25 to 30 minutes.
Makes 4 servings.

Nutrient Value Per Serving: 360 calories, 19 g protein, 24 g fat, 17 g carbohydrate, 658 mg sodium, 260 mg cholesterol.

1   cup milk
3   eggs
½   cup *uns*ifted all-purpose flour
1   tablespoon Dijon-style mustard
1   knockwurst, halved lengthwise and sliced ⅛ inch thick (about 4 ounces)
4   ounces mild Cheddar cheese, shredded
1   green onion with some green top, finely chopped

1. Preheat the oven to hot (425°). Generously grease a 10-inch pie plate.
2. Combine the milk, eggs, flour and mustard in the container of a food processor or an electric blender. Cover and whirl until well mixed. Transfer the batter to a medium-size bowl. Stir in the knockwurst, Cheddar cheese and green onion. Pour the batter into the prepared pie plate.
3. Bake the popover in the preheated hot oven (425°) for 25 to 30 minutes or until puffed and browned. Cut the popover into wedges and serve immediately.

Bake at 425° for 45 minutes.
Makes 6 servings.

Nutrient Value Per Serving: 733 calories, 32 g protein, 42 g fat, 58 g carbohydrate, 1,610 mg sodium, 102 mg cholesterol.

1   cup chopped onion
1   cup chopped sweet green pepper
3   tablespoons butter
3   tablespoons flour
½   teaspoon salt
⅛   teaspoon pepper
3   cups milk
2   cups shredded Cheddar cheese (8 ounces)
1   tablespoon Dijon-style mustard
1   bag (2 pounds) frozen cottage fry-style potatoes
1   bag (1 pound) frozen baby carrots
1   pound canned ham, cut into ½-inch cubes

1. Preheat the oven to hot (425°). Butter six 2-cup casseroles.
2. Sauté the onion and the green pepper in the butter in a Dutch oven over medium heat until soft but not browned, for about 5 minutes. Stir in the flour, salt and pepper; add the milk. Simmer, stirring, until thickened, for about 2 minutes.
3. Stir in 1 cup of the Cheddar cheese and the mustard. Cook, stirring, until the cheese is melted; remove from the heat. Fold in the potatoes, carrots and ham. Pour into the casseroles and cover with foil.
4. Bake in the preheated hot oven (425°) for 30 minutes. Remove the foil. Sprinkle with the remaining Cheddar cheese. Bake, uncovered, for 15 minutes or until bubbly.

Menu Idea

Knockwurst Cheese Popover*
Grated Carrot Salad
Berries with Yogurt

Menu Idea

Ham and Potato Bake with Cheese*
Tomato Slices with Vinaigrette
Dinner Rolls
Chocolate Cake

105

Ham, Leek and Cheese Tart

Menu Idea

Ham, Leek and Cheese Tart*

Sautéed Cherry Tomatoes* *(page 151)*

Melon Ice

Bake the pie shell at 425° for 10 minutes; bake the tart at 375° for 30 minutes.
Makes 6 servings.

Nutrient Value Per Serving: 435 calories, 13 g protein, 33 g fat, 17 g carbohydrate, 939 mg sodium, 215 mg cholesterol.

1   **unbaked 9-inch pie shell**
1½   **cups finely diced cooked ham (8 ounces)**
1   **medium-size leek, finely chopped**
3   **tablespoons butter**
3   **eggs**
¾   **cup milk**
½   **cup heavy cream**
½   **cup shredded Swiss cheese**
⅛   **teaspoon salt**
     Pinch ground hot red pepper
     Pinch ground nutmeg

1. Preheat the oven to hot (425°).
2. Bake the empty pie shell in the preheated hot oven (425°) for 10 minutes. Remove the shell. Lower the oven temperature to moderate (375°).
3. Sauté the ham and the leek in 2 tablespoons of the butter in a large skillet until the leek is tender, for about 5 minutes. Spoon the ham and the leek over the bottom of the pie shell.
4. Beat the eggs lightly in a medium-size bowl. Beat in the milk and the cream. Stir in the Swiss cheese, salt, ground hot red pepper and nutmeg. Pour the egg mixture into the pie shell. Dot with the remaining butter. Place the tart on a baking sheet.
5. Bake the tart in the preheated moderate oven (375°) for 30 minutes or until the custard is set and the top is golden. Let the tart stand for 5 to 10 minutes before cutting.

QUICK TIP

Pastry Smarts
Whenever you're making pastry for pie, make 2 pie shells; use 1 and freeze the other for future use. Wrap unbaked pie shells in aluminum foil and freeze. To use, thaw the unbaked shell at room temperature for about 30 minutes and use in the recipe as directed. Always cool a baked pie shell before wrapping and freezing.

Chicken, Ham and Sausage Sauté

A quick and easy dish that can be made with leftover baked ham. Oregano and white wine give this dish its unique flavor.

Makes 8 servings.

Nutrient Value Per Serving:
419 calories, 40 g protein, 25 g fat, 8 g carbohydrate, 1,013 mg sodium, 121 mg cholesterol.

1   **broiler-fryer (3½ pounds), cut into 8 serving pieces**
1   **tablespoon olive oil**
2   **hot Italian sausages, sliced into fourths (5 ounces)**
2   **sweet Italian sausages, sliced into fourths (5 ounces)**
1   **large onion, chopped (1 cup)**
1   **medium-size sweet green pepper, coarsely chopped (⅔ cup)**
1   **medium-size sweet red pepper, coarsely chopped (⅔ cup)**
1   **clove garlic, finely chopped**
12 **large mushrooms, halved (10 ounces)**
2   **cups cubed cooked ham (⅔ pound)**
1   **can (14 ounces) Italian plum tomatoes, *un*drained and chopped**
½   **cup dry white wine**
½   **cup chicken broth**
1   **teaspoon leaf oregano, crumbled**
1   **teaspoon leaf marjoram, crumbled**
¼   **teaspoon salt**
¼   **teaspoon pepper**
    Chopped parsley, for garnish *(optional)*

1. Brown the chicken in batches in the oil in a large, heavy skillet for about 15 minutes per batch. As the chicken browns, transfer it to a plate.
2. Brown the sausages in the fat remaining in the skillet. Transfer the sausages to the plate.
3. Pour off all but 1 tablespoon of the fat from the skillet. Add the onion, green and red peppers and garlic and sauté until tender, for about 5 minutes. Add the mushrooms and sauté for 3 minutes.
4. Return the chicken and the sausages to the skillet, scattering the vegetables on top. Add the ham, tomatoes, wine, broth, oregano, marjoram, salt and pepper and stir to mix all the ingredients well. Cover the skillet. Simmer over low heat for 20 minutes or until the chicken is no longer pink near the bone. Sprinkle with parsley to garnish, if you wish.

Menu Idea

Chicken, Ham and Sausage Sauté*

Turmeric Rice

Shredded Romaine Lettuce Salad

Orange, Pineapple and Banana Sprinkled with Shredded Coconut

QUICK TIP

Perfect Rice, Right To The Edge
Serve hot cooked rice in a warmed serving bowl to avoid a gummy consistency around the edge.

107

Veal Scaloppine in Tomato Tarragon Sauce

Menu Idea

Veal Scaloppine
 in Tomato
 Tarragon Sauce*

Hot Cooked Rice

Snow Peas

Butter Pecan Ice
 Cream with
 Chocolate Sauce
 and Coconut

Makes 8 servings.

Nutrient Value Per Serving:
342 calories, 24 g protein, 24 g
fat, 7 g carbohydrate, 285 mg
sodium, 127 mg cholesterol.

2   **pounds veal round, sliced**
       ¼ inch thick and pounded
       thin as for scaloppine
½   **teaspoon salt**
⅛   **teaspoon black pepper**
⅛   **teaspoon ground hot red**
       pepper
       All-purpose flour
¼   **cup (½ stick) butter or**
       margarine

Tomato Tarragon Sauce:
1½   **tablespoons finely chopped**
        shallots OR: green onion
¾   **cup dry white wine**
1   **cup coarsely chopped**
       tomatoes (fresh or canned)
1½   **teaspoons lemon juice**
¾   **cup heavy cream**
2   **teaspoons chopped fresh**
       tarragon, or other fresh
       herb OR: ¾ teaspoon leaf
       tarragon, or other leaf
       herb
       Salt and pepper, to taste
       Fresh tarragon sprigs and
       orange wedges, for garnish
       (optional)

1. Sprinkle the veal with the salt, black pepper and ground hot red pepper. Dredge the veal lightly with the flour.
2. Heat the butter or margarine in a large skillet over medium-high heat. Add the coated veal slices, working in batches to not crowd the pan. Sauté for 3 minutes or until veal is golden. Turn veal and sauté the second side. Remove veal from skillet to a serving plate; keep warm.
3. Prepare the Tomato Tarragon Sauce: Add the shallots or green onion to the skillet and cook for 1 to 2 minutes or until softened. Add the wine, stirring to dissolve browned particles in bottom of skillet. Boil for 1 to 2 minutes to reduce slightly.
4. Add tomatoes and lemon juice to the skillet. Cook, stirring, for 3 minutes. Add the cream.
5. Bring mixture to boiling and cook until sauce is thick enough to coat the veal. Stir in tarragon or other herb. Season with salt and pepper. Pour the sauce over the veal.
6. Garnish with fresh tarragon and orange wedges, if you wish.

You can substitute boneless chicken breasts or flounder fillets for the veal in sautéed Veal Scaloppine in Tomato Tarragon Sauce.

Vegetable Lamb Casserole

Bake at 375° for 40 minutes.
Makes 4 servings.

Nutrient Value Per Serving:
434 calories, 15 g protein, 27 g
fat, 35 g carbohydrate, 319 mg
sodium, 53 mg cholesterol.

2 **tomatoes (about 12 ounces)**
2 **small zucchini (about**
   1 pound)
1 **medium-size onion, finely**
   chopped
½ **pound ground lamb**
¼ **teaspoon salt**
¼ **teaspoon pepper**
½ **cup long-grain white rice**
2 **tablespoons raisins**
2 **tablespoons olive oil**
1 **cup beef broth**
2 **tablespoons tomato paste**
½ **cup dairy sour cream**
2 **tablespoons chopped fresh**
   dill OR: mint

1. Preheat the oven to moderate (375°).
2. Thinly slice the tomatoes. Cut the zucchini into ¼-inch-thick slices. Spread one of the sliced tomatoes over the bottom of a 2-quart flameproof casserole. Top with half the zucchini slices and sprinkle with half the onion. Crumble the lamb on top and sprinkle with the salt and the pepper. Sprinkle the rice evenly over the top. Add the raisins and the remaining onion. Overlap the remaining tomato and zucchini slices over the top. Sprinkle lightly with a little additional salt and pepper. Drizzle the casserole with the oil. Combine the broth and the tomato paste in a small bowl and pour into the casserole.
3. Bring the casserole to a full boil on top of the stove. Cover the casserole tightly and bake in the preheated moderate oven (375°) for 40 minutes or until the rice is cooked.
4. Stir together the sour cream and the dill or mint in a small bowl and serve with the casserole.

Microwave Instructions
(for a 650-watt variable power microwave oven)

Directions: Assemble the recipe as in Step 2 above in a microwave-safe 2½-quart casserole, eliminating the olive oil. Cover the casserole. Microwave the casserole at full power for 15 minutes. Then microwave at half power for 15 minutes longer. Let the casserole stand for 10 minutes before serving.

Menu Idea

Vegetable Lamb
   Casserole*
Sugar Snap Peas
   with Radish and
   Ginger*
   (page 156)
Melon Sorbet

QUICK TIP

Casserole Temp
Most casseroles should be baked at moderate oven temperatures (350° to 375°) so that the meats do not toughen and the flavors of the ingredients have time to blend well.

109

Fish

Warm Deviled Crab and Asparagus Salad

Makes 2 servings.

Nutrient Value Per Serving: 466 calories, 27 g protein, 36 g fat, 9 g carbohydrate, 347 mg sodium, 114 mg cholesterol.

½   **pound trimmed asparagus, steamed and cooled to room temperature**
1   **tablespoon red wine vinegar**
1   **tablespoon vegetable oil**
    Pinch leaf thyme, crumbled
⅓   **cup chopped white onion**
⅓   **cup chopped celery**
⅓   **cup chopped sweet green pepper**
1   **clove garlic, finely chopped**
⅛   **teaspoon leaf thyme, crumbled**
¼   **cup vegetable oil**
½   **pound lump crabmeat, coarsely flaked**
2   **tablespoons chopped green onion**
    Large pinch ground hot red pepper
¼   **teaspoon Worcestershire sauce**
    Lemon juice, salt and pepper, to taste

1. Divide the asparagus between 2 individual serving plates. Drizzle the asparagus with the vinegar, the 1 tablespoon of oil and the pinch of leaf thyme. Let the asparagus stand.
2. Sauté the white onion, celery, green pepper, garlic and the ⅛ teaspoon of leaf thyme in the ¼ cup of oil in a large skillet over medium heat for 5 minutes or until the vegetables are tender but not brown.
3. Gently stir in the crabmeat, green onion, ground hot red pepper and Worcestershire sauce. Continue cooking, stirring very gently several times, for 8 to 10 minutes. Taste and add the lemon juice, salt and pepper. Spoon the crab over the asparagus and serve warm.

Menu Idea

Warm Deviled Crab and Asparagus Salad*
Boston Lettuce Salad
Crackers
Pineapple Pecan Foster* *(page 231)*

QUICK TIP

Celery, Chop Chop!
To make fast work of chopping celery, first make several parallel cuts down the length of the stalk. Then, holding the long pieces tightly together, cut across the stalk.

Sautéed crabmeat makes a delicious topping for steamed asparagus in Warm Deviled Crab and Asparagus Salad.

Shrimp with Dill Mayonnaise

Menu Idea
Shrimp with Dill
  Mayonnaise*
Melba Toast
Raspberry Granita*
  (page 263)

A cooling salad that will satisfy equally well for lunch or a light supper.

Makes 4 servings.

*Nutrient Value Per Serving:
163 calories, 13 g protein, 12 g
fat, 3 g carbohydrate, 346 mg
sodium, 119 mg cholesterol.*

8   ounces frozen, cooked,
    shelled and deveined
    shrimp, thawed

Dill Mayonnaise:
¼   cup mayonnaise
¼   cup chopped fresh dill
2   tablespoons fresh lemon
    juice
¼   teaspoon salt
⅛   teaspoon pepper
4   drops liquid red pepper
    seasoning

2   avocados, halved and pitted
8   romaine lettuce leaves
4   sprigs fresh dill, for garnish
4   lemon wedges, for garnish

1. Drain the thawed shrimp
   thoroughly between several
   layers of paper toweling in the
   refrigerator for at least 30
   minutes.
2. Prepare the Dill Mayonnaise:
   Combine the mayonnaise, dill,
   lemon juice, salt, pepper and
   liquid red pepper seasoning in
   a medium-size bowl. Add the
   shrimp and toss gently until all
   the ingredients are evenly
   coated.
3. Spoon the shrimp mixture into
   avocado halves on a platter
   lined with the romaine leaves.
   Garnish with the fresh dill
   sprigs and the lemon wedges.

Creole Shrimp

Makes 4 servings.

*Nutrient Value Per Serving:
195 calories, 25 g protein, 6 g
fat, 11 g carbohydrate, 657 mg
sodium, 173 mg cholesterol.*

1   **cup chopped onion, fresh or
    frozen**
2   **cloves garlic, chopped**
1   **tablespoon olive oil**
1   **can (14 ounces) Italian-style
    plum tomatoes**
½   **cup white wine**
½   **teaspoon leaf oregano,
    crumbled**
½   **teaspoon leaf basil,
    crumbled**
¼   **teaspoon salt**
⅛   **teaspoon ground black
    pepper**
½   **teaspoon liquid red pepper
    seasoning**
1   **can (4 ounces) chopped
    green chilies, drained**
1   **pound shelled and deveined
    shrimp**

1. Sauté the onion and the garlic in the oil in a large skillet over medium-high heat until the onion is soft, for about 5 minutes.
2. Stir the tomatoes, wine, oregano, basil, salt, black pepper, liquid red pepper seasoning and green chilies into the skillet. Bring the mixture to boiling, breaking up the tomatoes with a wooden spoon. Lower the heat and simmer the mixture over medium heat, uncovered, for 10 minutes to reduce.
3. Add the shrimp to the skillet, spooning a little of the sauce over the shrimp. Cover the skillet and simmer for 3 to 5 minutes or until the shrimp are firm and curled.

Menu Idea
Creole Shrimp*
Hot Cooked Rice
Okra
Corn Muffins
**Strawberries with
   Champagne**

QUICK TIP

Berry Best
Bright color is the best test for quality berries. Ripe berries should be stored in the refrigerator, covered, unwashed, and unstemmed. Use fresh berries as soon as possible (except for cranberries, which can be refrigerated for 1½ weeks).

Poached Swordfish with Lemon and Lime

Lemon Lime Poaching Liquid

Menu Idea

Poached Swordfish with Lemon and Lime*

Steamed Red Potatoes

String Bean Vinaigrette

Pound Cake with Raspberry Purée

For more information on how to poach fish, see page 70.

Makes 6 servings.

Nutrient Value Per Serving: 246 calories, 40 g protein, 8 g fat, 1 g carbohydrate, 365 mg sodium, 78 mg cholesterol.

Lemon Lime Poaching Liquid *(recipe at right)*
3   pounds swordfish steaks, 1 inch thick
Dill sprigs, for garnish

1. Prepare Lemon Lime Poaching Liquid. Place fish in a heavy skillet large enough to hold it in one layer. Pour poaching liquid over the fish just to cover.
2. Place skillet over medium-low heat, keeping liquid just below simmering point, for 8 minutes or until fish flakes when tested with fork. Place fish in a glass dish. Cool fish and poaching liquid separately, then pour liquid over the fish and chill.
3. Refrigerate fish until serving time. Garnish with dill sprigs.

2   quarts water
1   cup dry white wine
¼   cup lemon juice
¼   cup lime juice
1   medium-size onion, sliced
3   lemon slices
3   lime slices
1   teaspoon salt
5   whole peppercorns
1   carrot, peeled, sliced and cut into decorative shapes
Handful dill sprigs

1. Combine the water, wine, lemon and lime juices, onion, lemon and lime slices, salt and peppercorns in a medium-size saucepan. Bring to boiling over medium heat and boil the liquid for 20 minutes.
2. Add the carrot and the dill and simmer for 10 minutes longer before using.

The Fish Caper
Add chopped capers and a squeeze of lemon juice to mayonnaise for a tasty sauce for broiled or grilled fish.

Cooling warm weather fare — Poached Swordfish with Lemon and Lime.

Emerald Scallops

Zucchini and scallops are quickly stir-fried to make a dish that is equally tasty served hot or at room temperature.

Makes 8 servings.

**Nutrient Value Per Serving:
336 calories, 12 g protein, 28 g fat, 8 g carbohydrate, 768 mg sodium, 18 mg cholesterol.**

½ **pound scallops, halved widthwise**
1 **egg white**
2 **teaspoons cornstarch**
½ **teaspoon salt**
1½ **tablespoons dry sherry**
1½ **tablespoons soy sauce**
3 **tablespoons water**
1½ **teaspoons white wine vinegar**
1 **teaspoon sesame oil**
1½ **teaspoons cornstarch**
½ **cup peanut oil**
1 **slice gingerroot, peeled and finely chopped**
2 **cloves garlic, finely chopped**
2 **large zucchini, trimmed and sliced**
   Carrot slices cut in decorative shapes, for garnish (optional)

1. Combine the scallops with the egg white, the 2 teaspoons of cornstarch and the salt in a medium-size bowl. Mix until all the ingredients are well blended (your hands will do the best job). Cover the bowl with plastic wrap. Let stand in the refrigerator for at least 30 minutes or up to 8 hours.
2. Combine the sherry, soy sauce, 1 tablespoon of the water, the vinegar, sesame oil and the 1½ teaspoons of cornstarch in a 1-cup measure. Set the sauce mixture aside.
3. Heat the peanut oil in a wok or large skillet over medium heat. Add the scallops and stir-fry quickly so they don't stick together. Continue stir-frying until the scallops are almost cooked (not quite opaque through the center). Remove the scallops from the wok with a strainer or slotted spoon and set aside.
4. Pour off all but 2 tablespoons of the oil from the wok. Add the gingerroot and the garlic. Stir-fry for 10 seconds. Add the zucchini and stir-fry to coat the zucchini with the oil. Sprinkle the remaining 2 tablespoons of water over the zucchini. Cover the wok, lower the heat and let the zucchini steam for 4 minutes or until almost tender. Uncover the wok.
5. Return the scallops to the wok and stir-fry until the scallops are opaque; do not overcook.
6. Pour the reserved sauce mixture into the wok. Cook, stirring constantly, until the sauce thickens and bubbles, for about 1 minute. Serve the scallops hot or at room temperature. Garnish with carrot slices cut in decorative shapes, if you wish.

Menu Idea
Chilled Gazpacho*
  (page 169)
Emerald Scallops*
Hot Cooked Rice
Breadsticks
Plum Ice*
  (page 264)

QUICK TIP

**Sin Of Sins:
Overcooked Fish**
If you've overcooked fish, rescue it by serving with a compatible sauce over rice, pasta, toast points or pastry shells.

DO IT AHEAD
IF YOU CAN

Chapter 4 shows you how to prepare make-ahead dishes to save time during your busy week. Do-ahead cooking can be done a week ahead, two days before or earlier in the day. Whenever you do it, the goal is to lessen last-minute flurry at meal time.

It pays to take time on a weekend or slow day (if there is such a thing!) to prepare a dish for the refrigerator or freezer. Frozen Green and White Stuffed Shells *(page 131)* thaw overnight and bake for 40 minutes, fuss-free. Mexican Turkey Salad with Creamy Avocado Dressing *(page 126)*, like our other layered salads, is assembled a day before, then whisked out of the fridge for dinner.

There are many quick dishes where the main ingredient can be marinated earlier in the day, as in our Chicken Satay *(page 135),* then popped into the broiler or on the barbecue at dinnertime.

We even take care of your once-a-year, invite-all-your-friends party with a crowd-pleasing buffet *(page 139)* that offers all make-aheads so there's a minimum of cooking when the fun begins.

Remember, meal time doesn't have to be frenetic if you think do-ahead. Sure, there are days when it's out of the question—but when you *can* prepare beforehand, it can save you time (and sanity!) in the long run.

For fast, hot-weather dining, nothing beats our make-ahead main dish salads. Clockwise from top left: Wild Rice Turkey Salad (page 122) and fresh green beans; Picante Chicken Salad (Chapter 1, page 26) on crispy corn tortillas; Salmon Pasta Salad (page 120) with sour cream-cucumber dressing.

Main-Dish
Salads

Cioppino Salad

We've used scallops in this variation of the seafood stew. Assemble the salad early in the day and then just dress at serving time.

Makes 6 servings.

Nutrient Value Per Serving:
319 calories, 25 g protein, 16 g
fat, 20 g carbohydrate, 932 mg
sodium, 95 mg cholesterol.

1½	cups sliced celery
2	cups chopped sweet green pepper
2	large onions, chopped (2 cups)
2	large cloves garlic, finely chopped
½	cup olive oil
4	cups vegetable juice cocktail
2	cups chicken broth
1	cup dry red wine
1	cup dry white wine
¼	cup tomato paste
1	large bay leaf
1	teaspoon leaf basil, crumbled
2	dried red chilies, seeded and chopped
½	teaspoon sugar
1	pound bay scallops or sea scallops, halved
1	pound shrimp, shelled and deveined
18	cherrystone clams, scrubbed
1	cup chopped tomato
9	cups shredded iceberg lettuce
	Lemon slices, for garnish (optional)

1. Sauté 1 cup of the celery, 1 cup of the green pepper and the onion and garlic in the oil in a large, deep saucepan over medium heat until the vegetables are tender.
2. Add the vegetable juice, broth, red and white wines, tomato paste, bay leaf, basil, chilies and sugar. Bring the mixture to boiling over medium heat. Lower the heat and simmer for 30 minutes.
3. Add the scallops and the shrimp to the tomato mixture. Cover and simmer for 5 minutes; do not overcook. Add the clams. Cover and cook just until the shells open. Remove the seafood with a slotted spoon from the tomato mixture to a bowl. Cover and refrigerate.
4. Stir the remaining celery and green pepper and the chopped tomato into the tomato mixture. Cover and refrigerate.
5. At serving time, line 6 individual salad plates or bowls with the shredded lettuce. Divide the seafood among the plates. Spoon part of the reserved tomato mixture over the seafood. Garnish with lemon slices, if you wish.

Menu Idea
Cioppino Salad*
Breadsticks
Chilled Peach and Blueberry Compote with Yogurt Sauce* *(page 251)*

A seafood lover's delight, Cioppino Salad is prepared ahead.

119

Salmon Pasta Salad

Menu Idea

Salmon Pasta
    Salad*

Red and Yellow
    Pepper
    Vinaigrette

Lemon Sorbet

This sea-worthy Salmon Pasta Salad is tossed in a sour cream-cucumber dressing.

Cook the fresh salmon ahead of time, or use canned salmon. Then assemble and dress the salad early in the day.

> **Bake fresh salmon at 350° for 12 to 15 minutes.**
> **Makes 4 servings.**

> **Nutrient Value Per Serving:**
> **605 calories, 29 g protein, 32 g fat, 49 g carbohydrate, 378 mg sodium, 60 mg cholesterol.**

¾ pound fresh salmon fillet OR: 1-pound canned salmon (pink or red)
1 teaspoon lemon juice**
⅛ teaspoon salt**

Cucumber Dressing:
2 medium-size cucumbers, peeled and seeded
¾ cup dairy sour cream
¼ cup mayonnaise
2 tablespoons snipped fresh dill OR: 1 teaspoon dillweed, crumbled
1 tablespoon finely chopped shallots OR: finely chopped green onion, white part only
1 tablespoon distilled white vinegar
¼ teaspoon salt
⅛ teaspoon white pepper

8 ounces rotelle or other spiral-shaped pasta
8 leaves romaine lettuce
    Cucumber slices, for garnish (*optional*)
    Dill sprigs, for garnish

1. Preheat the oven to moderate (350°) if using fresh salmon. If using canned salmon, proceed to Step 5 below.
2. Place the fresh salmon fillet, skin side down, in a small baking pan about 10 x 6¼ inches. Sprinkle the salmon with the lemon juice and the ⅛ teaspoon of salt. Cover the salmon with a buttered sheet of wax paper, buttered side down.
3. Bake the salmon in the preheated moderate oven (350°) for 12 to 15 minutes or until the fish flakes easily when tested with a fork. Cool the salmon in the pan at room temperature for 20 to 30 minutes without removing the buttered wax paper. Refrigerate the salmon, covered, until well chilled, for about 2 hours.
4. Remove the skin and bones, if any, from the salmon. Break the fish into ½-inch pieces. Refrigerate the salmon.
5. If using canned salmon, drain the salmon and remove all the skin and bones. Break the salmon into ½-inch pieces. Set the salmon aside in the refrigerator.
6. Prepare the Cucumber Dressing: Grate the cucumbers, place in a fine sieve and drain for at least 30 minutes at room temperature.
7. Combine the drained cucumber with the sour cream, mayonnaise, dill, shallots or green onion, vinegar, salt and white pepper in a small bowl.
8. Cook the pasta following the package directions until *al dente*, firm but tender. Drain the pasta in a colander and rinse briefly under cold running water. Drain the pasta well.
9. Place the pasta in a large bowl and add the dressing. Toss until the pasta is well coated. Gently fold in the salmon.
10. Arrange the lettuce leaves on a serving platter. Spoon the salad over the leaves. Garnish the salad with cucumber slices and dill sprigs, if you wish. Serve the salad immediately.

**Note: *Use the lemon juice and the ⅛ teaspoon of salt only if using fresh salmon instead of canned salmon.*

Cucumber Dressing Serving Suggestions: Make extra dressing and mix with cooked pasta, ham or any fish, including canned tuna.

QUICK TIP

The Cutting Edge
When using fresh herbs, such as dill, chives and parsley, hold the sprigs or bunches closely together and snip with kitchen scissors. You'll find the herbs will be light and fluffy, not bruised and wet as they often are when you chop them with a knife. And snipping is faster.

121

Wild Rice Turkey Salad

Menu Idea

Wild Rice Turkey Salad*

Sesame Seed Breadsticks

Chocolate Layer Cake

4 ounces wild rice (about ⅔ cup)
1½ cups water
½ teaspoon salt
⅓ cup white rice

Basil Mustard Vinaigrette:
⅓ cup vegetable oil
¼ cup red wine vinegar
1½ teaspoons Dijon-style mustard
½ teaspoon leaf basil, crumbled
1 clove garlic, crushed
¼ teaspoon pepper

¾ pound green beans, trimmed
¾ pound cooked turkey breast, cut into ½-inch pieces
¼ pound mushrooms, sliced thin
1 cup thinly sliced carrots
¼ cup chopped parsley
8 leaves green leaf lettuce
Parsley sprigs, for garnish

Wild Rice Turkey Salad can be prepared early in the day so the flavors have a chance to blend.

1. Pick over the wild rice and discard any dark bits. Rinse the rice in cold water. Combine the wild rice with the 1½ cups of water and the salt in a medium-size saucepan. Bring to boiling. Lower the heat and simmer the rice, covered, for 25 minutes. Add the white rice. Simmer the rice, covered, for 20 minutes or until all the water is absorbed. Spoon into a large bowl. Let the rice stand for 30 minutes.
2. Prepare the Basil Mustard Vinaigrette: In a jar with a tight-fitting lid, combine the oil, vinegar, mustard, basil, garlic and pepper. Cover; shake to mix the vinaigrette. Set aside.
3. Cook the green beans in enough boiling salted water to cover the beans in a large pot for 3 to 5 minutes or until crisp-tender. Drain the beans in a colander. Run the beans under cold running water. Drain the beans well. Place in a medium-size bowl. Add 2 tablespoons of the dressing and toss to coat the beans. (If preparing the salad ahead, don't dress the beans until just before serving.) Set the beans aside.
4. Combine the rice, turkey, mushrooms, carrot, chopped parsley and the remaining dressing in a large bowl.
5. Arrange the lettuce leaves on a serving platter; spoon the salad on top. Garnish with green beans and parsley sprigs.

Basil Mustard Vinaigrette Serving Suggestions: Make extra vinaigrette and use it to dress most rice, pasta or green salads. This vinaigrette is also good with lightly cooked green beans, broccoli or other vegetables for a summer side dish.

Creole Shrimp Salad

A little spicy heat usually characterizes Louisiana cooking. Marinate the shrimp for 12 to 24 hours.

Makes 4 servings.

Nutrient Value Per Serving: 253 calories, 23 g protein, 4 g fat, 32 g carbohydrate, 718 mg sodium, 131 mg cholesterol.

1   **can (14 ounces) stewed tomatoes, drained and chopped**
1   **medium-size sweet green pepper, halved, seeded and chopped**
¼   **cup finely chopped celery**
¼   **cup finely chopped onion**
3   **tablespoons red wine vinegar**
2   **teaspoons chopped fresh thyme OR: ½ teaspoon leaf thyme, crumbled**
¼   **to ½ teaspoon liquid red pepper seasoning**
¼   **teaspoon salt**
⅛   **teaspoon pepper**
1   **pound medium-size shrimp, peeled and deveined**
1½ **cups cooked white rice**
¼   **cup chopped parsley**
8   **Boston lettuce leaves Celery leaves, for garnish (optional)**

1. Combine the tomatoes, green pepper, celery, onion, vinegar, thyme, liquid red pepper seasoning, salt and pepper in a medium-size bowl.
2. Bring 3 quarts of salted water to boiling in a large pot. Add the shrimp and cook for 1½ to 2 minutes or until the shrimp are pink and opaque throughout. Drain the shrimp thoroughly.
3. Place the shrimp in a clean bowl. Pour the tomato mixture over the shrimp. Cover the bowl and refrigerate the shrimp for 12 to 24 hours.
4. Just before serving, mix the tomato and shrimp mixture with the cooked rice and the parsley.
5. Arrange the lettuce leaves on a serving platter. Spoon the shrimp salad over the leaves. Garnish with celery leaves, if you wish.

Menu Idea
Creole Shrimp Salad*
Cornbread
Sliced Jerusalem Artichoke
Pralines

Keep It Fresh
Keep salads, cold meat plates and hors d'oeuvres fresh on your buffet table by covering them with damp paper toweling until your guests arrive.

Beef and Potato Platter

Menu Idea

Beef and Potato Platter*
Coleslaw
Rye Bread
Coconut Cake

The potatoes can be mixed with the dressing the day before.

Makes 4 servings.

*Nutrient Value Per Serving:
497 calories, 30 g protein, 26 g fat, 39 g carbohydrate, 350 mg sodium, 69 mg cholesterol.*

1¼ **pounds all-purpose potatoes**
1 **tablespoon red wine vinegar**
2 **medium-size ears corn OR: 1½ cups cooked corn kernels**

Mustard Dressing:
⅓ **cup vegetable oil**
3 **tablespoons red wine vinegar**
1 **tablespoon Dijon-style mustard**
1 **clove garlic, crushed**
¼ **teaspoon salt**
¼ **teaspoon pepper**
1 **cup sliced green onions**

6 **cups spinach leaves (about 5 ounces), washed**
¾ **pound thinly sliced roast beef (leftover or deli)**
⅓ **cup sliced red radish (about 4 or 5), for garnish**

1. Cover the potatoes with cold water in a pan big enough to hold the potatoes in one layer; bring to a boil. Cook the potatoes until tender, for about 20 minutes. Remove the potatoes from the water and cool for 30 minutes. Peel the potatoes and cut into ½-inch pieces. Place the pieces in a medium-size bowl and sprinkle the 1 tablespoon of vinegar over the potatoes while they are still warm. Cover the bowl and refrigerate until well chilled.
2. If using ears of corn, bring 2 quarts of salted water to boiling. Add the ears of corn and boil for 2 to 4 minutes or until the corn is tender. Remove the ears from the water; cool. Scrape the kernels off the cobs with a sharp knife; set aside.
3. Prepare the Mustard Dressing: Combine the oil, the 3 tablespoons of vinegar, the mustard, garlic, salt and pepper in a small bowl and mix well. Stir in the green onion and the corn. Reserve ½ cup of the dressing for the beef. Toss the remaining dressing with the potatoes until well coated.
4. Arrange the spinach leaves on a platter. Fan the sliced roast beef down the middle of the plate. Arrange the potato salad around the beef. Spoon the reserved dressing over the beef. Garnish with the sliced radish.

Mustard Dressing Serving Suggestions: Make extra dressing and add to any potato, chicken or green salad. Try the dressing on cold cooked vegetables.

QUICK TIP

Quick Potato Salad
Here's another use for that good old egg slicer. When you want to make a large bowl of potato salad, use the slicer to dice the potatoes. It works like a charm and saves time. It also works well for mushrooms.

Salami, Pepper and Rice Salad

Our make-ahead main-dish salad tastes even better the next day because the rice absorbs more flavor after several hours of refrigeration.

Makes 4 servings.

Nutrient Value Per Serving: 656 calories, 17 g protein, 45 g fat, 46 g carbohydrate, 954 mg sodium, 48 mg cholesterol.

¼ cup finely chopped onion
1 medium-size clove garlic, finely chopped
½ cup olive oil
1 medium-size sweet red pepper
2 medium-size sweet green peppers OR: 1 sweet green pepper and 1 sweet yellow pepper
6 ounces sliced Genoa salami
2 teaspoons lemon juice
½ teaspoon Dijon-style mustard
½ teaspoon pepper
1 recipe Cooked Rice *(recipe follows)*
½ cup grated Parmesan cheese
    Oil-cured Italian or Greek olives, for garnish

1. Sauté the onion and the garlic in ¼ cup of the oil in a medium-size skillet until the onion is softened, for about 5 minutes.
2. Cut the peppers in half lengthwise; remove the stems, seeds and ribs. Slice the peppers into 2 x ¼-inch strips.
3. Cut the salami into ½-inch-wide strips.
4. Combine the remaining ¼ cup of oil, the lemon juice, mustard and pepper in a small bowl.
5. Combine the Cooked Rice, Parmesan cheese, onion mixture, peppers, salami and dressing in a large bowl. Toss all the ingredients together to mix well. Refrigerate the salad, covered, for several hours or overnight. Garnish the salad with the olives.

Cooked Rice: Bring 2½ cups of water to boiling in a medium-size saucepan. Add 1 cup of long-grain white rice. Lower the heat. Cover the saucepan and simmer the rice for 20 minutes. Remove the saucepan from the heat and let the saucepan stand until all the water is absorbed by the rice. Let the rice cool slightly before using. *Makes about 4 cups.*

Menu Idea

Salami, Pepper and Rice Salad*
Dark Rye Bread
Mixed Salad Greens
Cherry Cheese Tart*
(page 259)

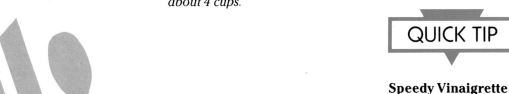

QUICK TIP

Speedy Vinaigrette For a very fast vinaigrette, combine 2 parts oil with 1 part vinegar or citrus juice in a food processor or blender. To jazz up your dressing, add chopped fresh herbs, mustard, garlic or honey. Whirl all ingredients until they are well mixed.

Mexican Turkey Salad

Menu Idea

Mexican Turkey
Salad*

Orange and
Watercress Salad

Sangria* (page 299)

Raspberry Mousse*
(page 258)

A turkey salad gone Mexican! And it can be prepared up to a day ahead.

Makes 6 servings.

Nutrient Value Per Serving:
615 calories, 29 g protein, 38 g
fat, 44 g carbohydrate, 1,049 mg
sodium, 69 mg cholesterol.

Creamy Avocado Dressing:
- 1   large clove garlic
- 2   green onions, trimmed and quartered
- 2   ripe avocados
- ¼   cup mayonnaise
- ¼   cup dairy sour cream
- ¼   cup fresh lime juice
- 1   tablespoon bottled chili sauce
- 1   teaspoon salt
- ½   teaspoon crushed red pepper flakes
- ⅛   teaspoon black pepper

Salad:
- ½   head romaine lettuce, shredded (about 4 cups)
- 1   can (8 ounces) whole kernel corn, drained
- ½   head iceberg lettuce, quartered, cored and shredded (about 4 cups)
- 1   sweet red pepper, halved, cored, seeded and chopped (about 1 cup)
- 1   can (16 ounces) chick-peas, drained
- 2   cups cooked shredded turkey (about ½ pound)
- ½   pound Monterey Jack cheese, shredded (2 cups)
- ½   of 7½-ounce package taco-flavored tortilla chips, broken

1. Prepare the Creamy Avocado Dressing: Drop the garlic through the feed tube of a food processor with the motor running and process until the garlic is finely chopped. Turn the motor off. Add the green onion and process until the green onion is finely chopped.

2. Halve and pit the avocados. Spoon the flesh into the processor bowl. Add the mayonnaise, sour cream, lime juice, chili sauce, salt, red pepper flakes and black pepper. Process with on-and-off pulses until the mixture is smooth and well blended.

3. Assemble the Salad: Place the romaine in the bottom of a 4-quart glass or crystal bowl. Add a layer of the corn. Top with the iceberg lettuce. Add layers of the red pepper, chick-peas and turkey. Spread the dressing over the top. Sprinkle with the Monterey Jack cheese. Cover the bowl with plastic wrap. Refrigerate the salad until serving time, for up to 1 day.

4. If serving this dish to company, sprinkle the salad with the tortilla chips and present the salad to your guests. Then toss the salad to coat all the ingredients well.

Layered Ham Salad

A hearty salad made with deli ham. To make it easy on yourself at meal time, prepare the salad a day ahead.

Makes 8 servings.

Nutrient Value Per Serving: 288 calories, 18 g protein, 19 g fat, 10 g carbohydrate, 847 mg sodium, 43 mg cholesterol.

Creamy Herb Dressing Parmesan:
- 1 **clove garlic**
- ¼ **cup mayonnaise**
- ½ **cup plain yogurt**
- ¼ **cup grated Parmesan cheese**
- 1 **tablespoon capers, drained**
- 1 **tablespoon reserved marinade from artichoke hearts** *(see Salad, below)*
- ½ **teaspoon mixed Italian herbs, crumbled**

Salad:
- 1 **medium-size head romaine lettuce, shredded (10 cups)**
- 1 **can (6 ounces) marinated artichoke hearts, drained (reserve 1 tablespoon of marinade) and each heart cut into thirds**
- 6 **cherry tomatoes, sliced**
- ½ **medium-size red onion, thinly sliced (about ¾ cup)**
- 1 **bunch watercress, stems removed**
- ½ **pound cooked deli ham, sliced and cut into thin strips**
- ½ **pound Provolone, cut into ½-inch cubes**
- 4 **sesame seed breadsticks, broken up**

1. Prepare the Creamy Herb Dressing Parmesan: Drop the garlic through the feed tube of a food processor with the motor running and process until the garlic is finely chopped. Turn off the motor. Add the mayonnaise, yogurt, Parmesan cheese, capers, reserved marinade and the Italian herbs. Process the mixture with on-and-off pulses until the mixture is smooth and creamy. Taste the dressing and adjust the seasonings, if necessary.
2. Assemble the Salad: Place the romaine in a 4-quart glass or crystal bowl. Top with layers of the artichoke hearts, tomatoes and onion. Layer on top half the watercress, the ham and the remaining watercress. Spread the dressing over the top. Sprinkle with the Provolone. Cover the bowl with plastic wrap. Refrigerate the salad until serving time, for up to 1 day.
3. Just before serving, sprinkle the broken breadsticks over the top. If serving this dish to company, present the salad to your guests first, then toss the salad to coat all the ingredients well.

Menu Idea

Red Pepper Soup* *(page 167)*

Layered Ham Salad*

Breadsticks

Lemon Swirl Cheesecake* *(page 245)*

QUICK TIP

Layered Salads
When it's time to eat, whisk a beautiful, layered main-dish salad from the refrigerator and your guests will be amazed—you've spent no time in the kitchen. Here's the trick: The day before, you've assembled the salad layers in a clear glass bowl and spread the salad dressing over the top. Now there's nothing left to do except present the salad, toss and enjoy!

127

Chicken Oriental Salad

Menu Idea
Chicken Oriental Salad*

Radish Vinaigrette Salad

Sesame Seed Breadsticks

Plum Ice*
(page 264)

It can all be prepared the day before.

Makes 6 servings.

Nutrient Value Per Serving: 375 calories, 17 g protein, 27 g fat, 19 g carbohydrate, 359 mg sodium, 50 mg cholesterol.

Creamy Sesame Dressing:
- ¾ cup mayonnaise
- ¼ cup plain yogurt
- 1½ teaspoons grated fresh gingerroot
- ½ teaspoon finely chopped garlic
- 2 green onions, finely chopped
- 2 teaspoons soy sauce
- 1½ teaspoons Oriental sesame oil**
- 1½ teaspoons honey
- ⅛ teaspoon ground hot red pepper

Salad:
- 4 cups shredded Chinese cabbage (about 1 pound)
- 2 cups shredded red cabbage (about ½ pound)
- 1 cup thinly sliced celery (about 2 medium-size stalks)
- 2 cups cooked shredded chicken (about ½ pound)
- 1 small head broccoli, cut into flowerets and steamed until crisp-tender (reserve steamed stems)
- 1 can (8 ounces) water chestnuts, drained and slivered
- ¼ pound snow peas, trimmed and cooked until crisp-tender
- 1 tablespoon sesame seeds, toasted

1. Prepare the Creamy Sesame Dressing: Combine the mayonnaise, yogurt, gingerroot, garlic, green onion, soy sauce, Oriental sesame oil, honey and ground hot red pepper in a small bowl until well blended.
2. Assemble the Salad: Layer the Chinese cabbage, then the red cabbage in a 4-quart glass or crystal bowl. Top with the celery. Scatter the chicken over the top. Slice the reserved broccoli stems into ½-inch pieces. Arrange the flowerets around the edge of the bowl; fill the center with the stem pieces. Top with the water chestnuts. Spread the dressing over the top. Arrange the snow peas over the dressing. Sprinkle with the sesame seeds. Cover the bowl with plastic wrap. Refrigerate the salad until serving time, for up to 1 day.
3. If serving this dish to company, present the salad to your guests first, then toss the salad to coat all the ingredients well.

***Note:** Oriental sesame oil has more flavor and is darker in color than regular sesame oil. It can be found in the Oriental food section of many supermarkets or in Oriental specialty food stores.*

New England Lobster Salad

The lobster mixture can be prepared early in the day.

Makes 4 servings.

Nutrient Value Per Serving: 419 calories, 20 g protein, 34 g fat, 13 g carbohydrate, 376 mg sodium, 84 mg cholesterol.

2 **live lobsters (about 1½ pounds each) OR: 12 ounces imitation lobster, thawed if frozen**

Chive Mayonnaise Dressing:
⅓ **cup mayonnaise**
4 **tablespoons chopped chives**
4 **teaspoons fresh lemon juice**
  Pinch white pepper

½ **cup finely chopped celery**
2 **medium-size ripe avocados****
1 **pint cherry tomatoes, halved**
2 **tablespoons chopped parsley**
2 **teaspoons red wine vinegar**
2 **teaspoons vegetable oil**
⅛ **teaspoon pepper**
  Pinch salt
8 **Boston lettuce leaves**
1 **small bunch watercress, trimmed, for garnish**
  Lemon twists, for garnish (optional)

1. If using live lobsters, pour water in a large pot to a depth of 2 to 4 inches; bring to a boil. Add the lobsters and cook, covered, for 12 minutes. Remove the lobsters from the pot with tongs and cool for 30 minutes at room temperature. Refrigerate until well chilled, for 2 to 4 hours.
2. Pull off the claws at the joint to the main body. Leave the small legs attached. Cut the lobsters in half lengthwise with a sharp knife or poultry shears. Remove the meat from the tail and the lower body. Discard the sac with the stomach and the intestine. Remove the tomalley and the coral, if any, and reserve the coral, if you wish. Rinse the shell halves with cold water and drain on paper toweling. Crack the claws and the claw joints with a nutcracker or the back of a heavy knife or meat mallet. Remove the meat. Cut the lobster meat into ½-inch pieces; add the coral, if you wish.
3. Prepare the Chive Mayonnaise Dressing: Combine the mayonnaise, chives, lemon juice and white pepper in a medium-size bowl. Add the lobster meat and the celery to the dressing and toss well.
4. Spoon the lobster salad back into the shells, or if using imitation lobster meat, use 4 avocado halves. (Remove the pit and peel; rub the cut surfaces with lemon juice to prevent discoloration.)
5. Toss the cherry tomatoes with the parsley, vinegar, oil, pepper and salt in a medium-size bowl.
6. For each serving, place 2 lettuce leaves on a plate. Place half a lobster shell, or half an avocado, filled with the salad on the leaves. Spoon the cherry tomatoes on the side. Garnish with watercress and a lemon twist, if you wish.

**Note: *Use the avocado only if using imitation lobster meat instead of live lobsters.*

Chive Mayonnaise Dressing Serving Suggestions: Serve with fish, chicken and pasta salads.

Menu Idea
New England Lobster Salad*
Lightly Steamed Broccoli Flowerets
Blueberry Pie

129

Other Main
Dishes

Green and White Stuffed Shells

Prepare these shells ahead and freeze for up to 1 week. Then just defrost in the refrigerator overnight and bake before serving.

Bake, covered, at 425° for 30 minutes, then uncovered for 10 minutes.
Makes 12 servings.

Nutrient Value Per Serving: 376 calories, 20 g protein, 17 g fat, 38 g carbohydrate, 928 mg sodium, 62 mg cholesterol.

Sauce:
- 1 cup finely chopped onion
- 2 tablespoons olive oil
- 2 cloves garlic, finely chopped
- 2 cans (2 pounds, 3 ounces each) Italian-style plum tomatoes, *un*drained
- 1 can (16 ounces) tomato sauce
- 2 teaspoons sugar
- 1 teaspoon salt
- 1 teaspoon leaf oregano, crumbled
- ½ teaspoon leaf basil, crumbled
- ¼ teaspoon pepper
- ¼ teaspoon fennel seeds
- 2 tablespoons chopped flat-leaf Italian parsley

Ricotta Filling:
- 2 containers (15 ounces each) ricotta cheese
- 1 package (8 ounces) mozzarella cheese, cut into ¼-inch pieces
- ½ cup grated Parmesan cheese
- 1 egg
- ¼ teaspoon pepper
- 2 tablespoons chopped flat-leaf Italian parsley
- 1 package (10 ounces) frozen chopped spinach, thawed

- 1 box (12 ounces) jumbo pasta shells
- 2 tablespoons olive oil

1. Prepare the Sauce: Sauté the onion in 2 tablespoons of the oil in a large saucepan over medium heat until tender, for about 5 minutes. Add the garlic and sauté for 1 minute longer.
2. Add the tomatoes, breaking them up with a wooden spoon, tomato sauce, sugar, salt, oregano, basil, ¼ teaspoon of pepper and the fennel seeds. Cover the saucepan and cook, stirring occasionally, over low heat for 1 hour. Uncover and cook for 1 hour and 20 minutes longer to thicken the sauce, stirring ocassionally. Remove the saucepan from the heat and stir in the 2 tablespoons of parsley.
3. Prepare the Ricotta Filling: Combine the ricotta, mozzarella and Parmesan cheeses, the egg, ¼ teaspoon of pepper and 2 tablespoons of parsley in a large bowl.

(Recipe continues next page.)

Menu Idea
Green and White Stuffed Shells*
String Bean Vinaigrette
Frozen Blueberry Yogurt*
(page 265)

Green and White Stuffed Shells are a make-ahead-and-freeze main dish.

131

Green and White Stuffed Shells —continued

4. Remove 1¾ cups of the filling to a medium-size bowl. Drain the spinach well; press the spinach between layers of paper toweling to remove excess moisture. Stir the spinach into the 1¾ cups of filling.

5. Cook the pasta shells, following the package directions. You should have about 48 shells.

6. Meanwhile, divide the sauce between two 13 x 9 x 2-inch glass baking dishes, spreading the sauce evenly over the bottoms.

7. Spoon the ricotta filling without the spinach into a pastry bag fitted with a very large (⅜- to ½- inch) plain tip. Pipe about 1 tablespoon of the filling into each of 24 cooked shells. Arrange the filled shells on the sauce, dividing between the 2 dishes.

8. Spoon the spinach filling into the same bag. Pipe the spinach filling into the remaining shells and arrange the shells on the sauce, dividing between the dishes. Brush the shells with the remaining 2 tablespoons of oil. Cover the dishes with aluminum foil and refrigerate until 1 hour before serving. Or freeze the shells for up to 1 week; thaw the shells in the refrigerator for 8 hours or overnight before baking.

9. When ready to bake the shells, preheat the oven to hot (425°).

10. Bake the shells, covered, in the preheated hot oven (425°) for 30 minutes. Uncover the dishes and bake for 10 minutes longer or until the shells are heated through and the sauce is bubbly.

Note: For the photo on page 130, we used a smaller baking dish than the one called for in this recipe.

QUICK TIP

Dish Headed For The Freezer?
If you are planning to freeze a pasta dish or casserole, line the container with aluminum foil. Place the cooked dish in the container, cool and freeze. When the dish is frozen solid, remove the contents *in the foil* and overwrap with more foil. Store in the freezer for 2 to 3 months—and you have the use of the container in the meantime.

Spinach Roll Lasagne

For an attractive presentation, arrange these lasagne roll-ups so that they are standing up on end on a serving platter. Assemble the rolls up to 4 hours ahead and refrigerate.

Bake at 375° for 45 to 50 minutes.
Makes 4 servings.

Nutrient Value Per Serving: 678 calories, 29 g protein, 42 g fat, 50 g carbohydrate, 214 mg sodium, 128 mg cholesterol.

8   curly-edge lasagne noodles
3   cups loosely packed shredded Fontina cheese (½ pound)
4   packages (10 ounces each) chopped frozen spinach, thawed and squeezed dry
½   cup (1 stick) unsalted butter, melted

1. Preheat the oven to moderate (375°). Grease a 9 x 9 x 2-inch-square baking dish.
2. Cook the lasagne noodles following the package directions. Rinse the noodles and drain on paper toweling.
3. Reserve ½ cup of the Fontina cheese. Mix together the remaining Fontina cheese and the spinach in a medium-size bowl.
4. Lay out the noodles separately on a sheet of wax paper on a flat surface. Spread about ⅔ cup of the spinach filling evenly over each strip. Starting at a short end, roll up each noodle jelly-roll fashion. Place the rolls in the prepared baking dish, seam sides down. Generously brush the melted butter over the curly edges of the noodles. Pour the remaining butter over the tops of the rolls. Cover the baking dish tightly with aluminum foil. Prepare the rolls up to this point and refrigerate for up to 4 hours.
5. Bake the rolls in the preheated moderate oven (375°) for 45 to 50 minutes or until the rolls are heated through. Just before serving, sprinkle the top of the rolls with the reserved ½ cup of Fontina cheese.

Microwave Instructions
(for a 650-watt variable power microwave oven)

Ingredient Changes: Reduce the butter to 2 tablespoons.
Directions: Cook the lasagne noodles and fill as directed in the above recipe. Place the rolls, seam sides down, in a 9 x 9 x 2-inch-square microwave-safe baking dish. Place the 2 tablespoons of butter in a microwave-safe 1-cup measure. Microwave the butter, uncovered, at full power for 1 minute or until melted. Brush the melted butter over the rolls. Cover the dish. Microwave at full power for 7 minutes, rotating the dish one quarter turn after 4 minutes. Let the rolls stand for 3 minutes before serving. *Nutrient Value Per Serving: 526 calories, 29 g protein, 25 g fat, 50 g carbohydrate, 212 mg sodium, 81 mg cholesterol.*

Menu Idea
Spinach Roll Lasagne*
Ginger Orange Salad* *(page 181)*
Striped Fruit Pops* *(page 260)*

133

Honey Mustard Pork Skewers

Menu Idea
Honey Mustard Pork Skewers*
Hot Cooked Rice with Almonds
Sugar Snap Peas with Radish and Ginger*
(page 156)
Watermelon Ice*
(page 263)

Zucchini, carrot and potato sticks garnish the thyme-accented pork skewers. The pork can be marinated earlier in the day.

Broil for 2 to 4 minutes.
Makes 4 servings.

Nutrient Value Per Serving:
297 calories, 30 g protein, 10 g fat, 21 g carbohydrate, 97 mg sodium, 81 mg cholesterol.

1   **pound boneless pork loin, fat trimmed**
2   **tablespoons dry mustard**
2   **tablespoons water**
2   **tablespoons honey**
⅛   **teaspoon leaf thyme, crumbled**
1   **can (10 ounces) low-sodium chicken broth, refrigerated and then fat removed from top**
1   **cup potato sticks, 3 x ¼-inch (6 ounces)**
1   **cup zucchini sticks, 3 x ¼-inch (2 small)**
1   **cup carrot sticks, 3 x ¼-inch (2 medium-size)**

1. Cut the pork loin crosswise into 8 equal slices. Divide each slice into 4 equal pieces to yield 32 pieces, each about ¾ to 1 inch. Reserve the pieces.
2. Stir together the mustard and the water in a 11¾ x 7½ x 1¾-inch glass baking dish until smooth. Stir in the honey and the thyme. Add the reserved pork and toss well to coat the pork with the marinade. Cover the dish and refrigerate for at least 4 hours, turning the pork once.
3. Preheat the oven to broil. Bring the broth to boiling in a medium-size saucepan.
4. Meanwhile, thread 8 pork pieces on each of 4 skewers.
5. Broil the skewers 5 inches from the heat, turning the skewers often and brushing them with the marinade, for 2 to 4 minutes or until the centers are no longer pink. Arrange one skewer on each of 4 plates and keep warm.
6. Add the potatoes to the boiling broth and cook for 2 minutes. Add the zucchini and the carrots and cook for 2 to 3 minutes longer or until the potatoes are tender. Remove the vegetables with a slotted spoon and divide them among the 4 plates.

QUICK TIP

Pretty Potatoes
To prevent potatoes from turning dark after peeling, completely immerse them in a bowl of cold water until ready to use.

Chicken Satay

An elegant, sliced chicken thigh dish with a peanutty marinade. The chicken can be marinated earlier in the day.

Broil for 5 to 6 minutes.
Makes 6 servings.

Nutrient Value Per Serving:
255 calories, 21 g protein, 6 g fat, 30 g carbohydrate, 170 mg sodium, 63 mg cholesterol.

¼   **cup shelled raw peanuts (1 ounce)****
¼   **cup white wine vinegar**
2   **tablespoons water**
2   **tablespoons reduced-sodium soy sauce**
1   **tablespoon lemon juice**
2   **cloves garlic**
10   **sprigs cilantro** *(optional)*
    Pinch crushed red pepper flakes
1   **pound boneless, skinned chicken thighs, fat trimmed**
    Nonstick vegetable cooking spray
    Hot cooked rice
1   **pound trimmed asparagus, steamed (about 1½ pounds untrimmed)**

1. Combine the peanuts, vinegar, water, soy sauce, lemon juice, garlic, cilantro if you wish, and the red pepper flakes in the container of an electric blender or a food processor. Cover and whirl until the peanuts are finely chopped. Turn the mixture into a 13½ x 8½ x 2-inch glass baking dish.
2. Add the chicken thighs to the marinade and press the thighs out flat. Cover the dish and refrigerate for at least 1½ hours, turning the chicken occasionally.
3. Preheat the oven to broil. Spray a cold broiler pan rack with nonstick vegetable cooking spray. Remove the chicken from the marinade and arrange on the broiler pan, boned side down. Discard the marinade.
4. Broil the thighs 6 inches from the source of the heat for 2 to 3 minutes on one side or until crisp. Turn the thighs and broil for 3 minutes longer or until the meat is no longer pink. (Cover the top of the chicken with a sheet of aluminum foil during the last minutes of cooking if the coating browns too fast.)
5. Slice the chicken on the diagonal and arrange the slices fan-shaped over the rice. Serve the chicken with the asparagus.

**Note: *Shelled raw peanuts can be found in health food stores. If unavailable, substitute dry-roasted unsalted peanuts.*

Menu Idea
Chicken Satay*
Hot Cooked Rice
Steamed Asparagus
Nectarine Sorbet*
  (page 261)

Chicken and Wild Rice Salad

Menu Idea

Chicken and Wild Rice Salad*

Sliced Tomatoes with Basil

Lime Cheesecake*
(page 247)

Make this salad early in the day so the flavors will have a chance to develop properly. To save even more time, cook the chicken and rice the day before and refrigerate overnight.

Makes 12 servings.

Nutrient Value Per Serving: 249 calories, 22 g protein, 11 g fat, 17 g carbohydrate, 195 mg sodium, 44 mg cholesterol.

6   **boneless, skinned chicken breast halves (2 pounds)**
1   **can (13¾ ounces) chicken broth**
2   **cups water**
1   **package (8 ounces) wild rice**
⅓   **cup olive oil**
¼   **cup lemon juice (2 lemons)**
⅛   **teaspoon pepper**
1   **medium-size sweet green pepper, cored and seeded**
½   **cup chopped red onion**
¼   **cup chopped flat-leaf Italian parsley**
3   **ounces pine nuts (about ⅔ cup)**

1. Combine the chicken and the broth in a medium-size saucepan. Bring the broth to boiling over medium-high heat. Reduce the heat to low and simmer, covered, for 10 minutes or until the chicken is firm to the touch. Remove the chicken to a plate. Cover and refrigerate until the chicken is chilled, for several hours.

2. Strain the chicken cooking liquid through a double thickness of cheesecloth into a 4-cup measure. Add the water to make 3½ cups of liquid. Pour the liquid back into the saucepan. Bring to boiling over high heat. Add the rice. Return to boiling, stirring. Reduce the heat to low. Cover the saucepan and cook the rice, stirring occasionally, for 45 minutes or until the rice is puffed open and tender, but not mushy. Pour the rice into a large bowl and refrigerate, covered with plastic wrap, for several hours.

3. Whisk together the oil, lemon juice and pepper in a small bowl.

4. When the chicken is chilled, cut it into 1-inch pieces.** Cut the green pepper lengthwise into ¼-inch-wide strips and cut the strips in half.

5. Add the chicken, green pepper, onion, parsley and pine nuts to the rice in the large bowl. Toss gently to combine all the ingredients. Pour the dressing over the salad and toss to combine all the ingredients. Arrange the salad on a platter. Refrigerate, covered, for several hours to develop the flavors.

Note: *For the photo, we cut the chicken diagonally into 1-inch-thick slices. We then arranged the chicken on the rice after it was tossed with the dressing and other ingredients.*

Chicken and Wild Rice Salad can be prepared early in the day so the flavors have a chance to blend.

Jamaican Chicken Calypso

Bake at 375° for 40 to 45 minutes.
Makes 4 servings.

Nutrient Value Per Serving:
421 calories, 40 g protein, 17 g fat, 28 g carbohydrate, 638 mg sodium, 116 mg cholesterol.

1   can (8 ounces) pineapple chunks in juice
½   cup rum
3   tablespoons lime juice
2   tablespoons soy sauce
1   tablespoon dark brown sugar
2   teaspoons curry powder
2   cloves garlic, finely chopped
½   teaspoon ground ginger
¼   teaspoon ground cloves
¼   teaspoon crushed red pepper flakes
4   chicken breast halves with bones (about 2 pounds)
1   can (11 ounces) mandarin oranges, drained
1   lime, cut into wedges, for garnish *(optional)*

1. Drain juice from pineapple chunks into a shallow, nonmetal dish large enough to hold the chicken. Cover; refrigerate fruit for use later. To pineapple juice, add the rum, lime juice, soy sauce, brown sugar, curry powder, garlic, ginger, cloves and red pepper flakes. Stir to blend well.
2. Add chicken to marinade, turning to coat well. Leave chicken skin side down. Cover dish and marinate in the refrigerator for 3 to 6 hours.
3. When you are ready to cook the chicken, preheat oven to 375°.
4. Drain marinade from chicken; reserve. Place skin side up in a shallow roasting pan.

5. Bake, uncovered, in the preheated oven (375°), basting chicken often with pan juices and leftover marinade, for 35 minutes. Add reserved pineapple chunks and mandarin oranges to pan. Bake for 5 to 10 minutes longer or until chicken is no longer pink near bone.
6. To serve, arrange chicken with pineapple and oranges on a platter. Skim fat from pan juices and pour juices over chicken. Garnish with lime wedges, if you wish.

Microwave Instructions
(for a 650-watt variable power microwave oven)

Ingredient Changes: Use only ¼ cup of the juice drained from the pineapple, reduce rum to 2 tablespoons, reduce lime juice to 2 tablespoons, reduce curry powder to 1 teaspoon, reduce ginger to ¼ teaspoon, reduce cloves to ⅛ teaspoon.

Directions: Combine the pineapple juice, rum, lime juice, soy sauce, brown sugar, curry powder, garlic, ginger, cloves and red pepper flakes in a medium-size bowl. Place chicken in the marinade, turning to coat all sides. Cover and marinate in refrigerator for 3 hours, turning chicken once. Arrange chicken in a 10-inch microwave-safe pie plate, placing thicker parts toward outside of plate. Pour half of marinade over chicken. Cover with wax paper. Microwave at full power for 6 minutes. Add remaining marinade, pineapple chunks and oranges. Microwave, uncovered, at full power for 3 to 5 minutes longer or until chicken is tender.

Menu Idea
Jamaican Chicken Calypso*
Buttered Sweet Potatoes
Ginger Melon*
(page 246)

137

Two Make-Ahead
Meal Menus

Leek Soup

Prepare the soup a day ahead, then reheat it just before serving.

Makes about 16 servings (8 cups).

Nutrient Value Per Serving: 78 calories, 2 g protein, 6 g fat, 6 g carbohydrate, 508 mg sodium, 8 mg cholesterol.

¼ cup (½ stick) unsalted butter
2 tablespoons vegetable oil
2 pounds leeks OR: green onions, trimmed, well rinsed and thinly sliced
2 cloves garlic, finely chopped
3 tablespoons all-purpose flour
2 quarts chicken stock, preferably homemade, heated
Ground white pepper, to taste
Salt, to taste

1. Heat the butter and the oil together in a large casserole or Dutch oven. Add the leeks or green onions and stir to coat with the butter mixture. Cover the casserole. Cook over low heat for 15 minutes; the leeks should be very soft.
2. Add the garlic to the casserole and cook over medium heat, uncovered, stirring frequently, until the leeks are lightly browned, for about 15 to 20 minutes.
3. Sprinkle the flour over the leeks and stir to combine. Cook the leek mixture, stirring, for about 2 to 3 minutes.
4. Slowly stir in the hot chicken stock. Simmer the soup, partially covered, for about 30 minutes or until the flavor develops.
5. Season the soup with the white pepper and the salt. Serve the soup in mugs with your favorite crackers.

Crowd-Pleasing Buffet (from right to left): Leek Soup, Pecan Chicken with Yogurt Mustard Sauce (page 141), Beet and Cucumber Salad with Orange-Honey Dressing (page 143), Pumpkin Muffins (page 144), Basmati Rice with Red Pepper and Green Onion (page 142), Sausage Cranberry Baked Apples (page 140) and cheese toasts. Keep dessert simple — fruit compote and coffee or tea.

Menu Idea Dinner Buffet For 24 Guests

Cheese Toasts

Leek Soup*

Pecan Chicken with Yogurt Mustard Sauce*

Beet and Cucumber Salad with Orange-Honey Dressing*

Pumpkin Muffins*

Basmati Rice with Red Pepper and Green Onion*

Sausage Cranberry Baked Apples*

Vegetable Medley*

Fruit Compote

Coffee or Tea

QUICK TIP

Speedy Soups
Vegetable soups can all be prepared in 30 minutes or less — and they're ideal for cleaning out leftover vegetables from the refrigerator. First, cook the cut-up vegetables in water or stock or a combination. Strain, reserving the cooking liquid. Purée the solids in a blender, food processor or food mill. Add enough of the strained liquid to reach the consistency you like. For extra richness, stir in a little milk, cream or butter.

Sausage Cranberry Baked Apples

Prepare the sausage stuffing ahead.

Bake at 375° for 30 minutes.
Makes 8 servings.

Nutrient Value Per Serving:
438 calories, 15 g protein, 22 g
fat, 48 g carbohydrate, 555 mg
sodium, 97 mg cholesterol.

1	**pound sweet Italian sausage**
2	**medium-size onions,** **chopped (1½ cups)**
2	**tablespoons butter**
¼	**cup white wine**
3	**cups cranberries (12** **ounces), coarsely chopped**
1	**egg, slightly beaten**
2	**tablespoons chopped** **parsley**
2	**tablespoons brown sugar**
1½	**cups shredded white** **Vermont Cheddar cheese** **(6 ounces)**
8	**large baking apples, such as** **Rome Beauty or Granny** **Smith (8 to 10 ounces** **each)**
1	**tablespoon lemon juice**
¼	**cup bourbon**
¼	**cup water**
16	**whole cranberries, for** **garnish**

1. Remove and discard the casing from the sausage. Crumble the sausage into a large skillet. Cook the sausage over medium heat until the sausage is no longer pink, stirring occasionally. Remove the sausage with a slotted spoon to paper toweling to drain.
2. Wipe out the skillet. Sauté the onion in the butter in the skillet until softened, for 3 to 4 minutes. Add the wine and cook, scraping up any browned bits with a wooden spoon, until the wine is slightly reduced. Pour the liquid into a medium-size bowl.
3. Add the sausage, chopped cranberries, egg, parsley, brown sugar and 1 cup of the Vermont Cheddar cheese to the bowl and mix well.
4. Slice off 1 inch from the top of each apple and core with a melon baller. Scoop out the remaining flesh, leaving a ¼-inch shell. Place the apple flesh in a heavy, medium-size saucepan. Add the lemon juice, bourbon and water to the saucepan. Simmer the apple mixture, partially covered, until thick, for about 30 minutes.
5. Preheat the oven to moderate (375°).
6. Spoon about ¾ cup of the sausage filling into each apple. Sprinkle the tops with the remaining ½ cup of Vermont Cheddar cheese, dividing equally. Place 2 whole cranberries on the top of each apple for garnish. Place the apples in a large baking dish.
7. Bake the apples in the preheated moderate oven (375°) for 30 minutes. Let the apples stand for 10 minutes. Serve with the applesauce.

QUICK TIP

Wine To Dine On
When you have leftover wine, cork it tightly and store it in the refrigerator to be used in cooking within a week or two. Any wine that has turned to vinegar is great for marinades and salad dressings, so don't throw it out.

Pecan Chicken with Yogurt Mustard Sauce

The chicken breasts can be coated and refrigerated for up to 4 hours before serving time.

Bake at 375° for 15 to 20 minutes.
Makes 8 servings.

Nutrient Value Per Serving:
607 calories, 55 g protein, 37 g fat, 16 g carbohydrate, 401 mg sodium, 127 mg cholesterol.

8   skinned, boneless chicken breast halves (6 to 8 ounces each)
1   container (16 ounces) lowfat plain yogurt
½   cup coarse-grained mustard
2   cans (6 ounces each) pecans

Yogurt Mustard Sauce:
1   container (8 ounces) lowfat plain yogurt
½   cup dairy sour cream
3   tablespoons coarse-grained mustard

1. Trim the chicken breasts of any fat. Combine one container of the yogurt and the ½ cup of mustard in a bowl. Place the pecans in the container of a food processor or, working in batches, of an electric blender. Cover and whirl until the nuts are coarsely ground. Spread the pecans evenly on a sheet of wax paper.
2. Using your hands, coat the chicken with the yogurt mixture. Roll the chicken in the pecans to coat evenly all over. Place the chicken on a wax paper-lined cookie sheet. Cover the chicken with a sheet of wax paper. Refrigerate the chicken for up to 4 hours.
3. When ready to bake the chicken, preheat the oven to moderate (375°).
4. Place the chicken on a baking sheet. Bake the chicken in the preheated moderate oven (375°) for 15 to 20 minutes or until the chicken is no longer pink in the center.
5. Prepare the Yogurt Mustard Sauce: Combine the remaining container of yogurt, the sour cream and the 3 tablespoons of mustard in a heavy saucepan. Heat the sauce over low heat, stirring, until heated through.
6. Arrange the chicken on a large platter. Spoon the sauce over the chicken or pass the sauce separately. Garnish the platter with greens, if you wish.

QUICK TIP

Pickin' Chicken
When buying chicken, look for chicken that has moist skin without any dry spots. Avoid packages where blood or juice has accumulated in the bottom—a sign that the chicken has been out for too long. Chicken should smell fresh. This can mean no smell at all or a pleasant chicken aroma. If when you open the package at home you smell a slight chicken odor, rinse the chicken under cold water and rub with a lemon half or dip briefly in a mixture of vinegar and water.

141

Vegetable Medley

Steam the vegetables ahead, then sauté just before serving.

Makes 10 servings.

*Nutrient Value Per Serving:
78 calories, 1 g protein, 5 g fat,
8 g carbohydrate, 159 mg
sodium, 9 mg cholesterol.*

½ pound green beans, trimmed
3 large carrots, trimmed and peeled
1 medium-size yellow squash, trimmed and scrubbed
1 medium-size zucchini, trimmed and scrubbed
1 small jicama**, quartered and peeled OR: 2 medium-size turnips (10 ounces), peeled
3 tablespoons butter
1 tablespoon vegetable oil
½ teaspoon salt
¼ teaspoon pepper

1. Cut the green beans into 3-inch lengths. Cut the carrots, squash, zucchini and jicama or turnips into 3 x ¼-inch sticks.
2. Steam the carrots for 4 minutes or until firm-tender; steam the green beans for 3 minutes or until firm-tender; steam the turnips, if using, for 1 minute. Do not precook the jicama, if using. Rinse the vegetables in a colander under cold running water. Place all the vegetables in a plastic bag and refrigerate until ready to serve.
3. To serve, sauté the vegetables in the butter and the oil in a large skillet until heated through, for about 4 minutes. Season with the salt and pepper.

Note: *Jicama is a turnip-shaped tuber.*

Basmati Rice with Red Pepper and Green Onion

Basmati rice is a North Indian aromatic grain.

Makes 10 to 12 servings.

*Nutrient Value Per Serving:
186 calories, 4 g protein, 3 g fat,
35 g carbohydrate, 519 mg
sodium, 6 mg cholesterol.*

2½ cups basmati rice (about 1 pound) OR: converted white rice
4⅓ cups chicken broth OR: water
2 bay leaves
½ teaspoon salt
6 green onions, trimmed and thinly sliced, both green and white parts (about 1 cup)
1 sweet red pepper, cored, seeded and diced (about 1 cup)
2 tablespoons butter

1. If using the basmati rice, pick the rice over and remove any brown grains and dark bits. Rinse the rice with cold water.
2. Cook the basmati or converted white rice in a large pot with the broth or water, the bay leaves and salt following the package directions.
3. Meanwhile, sauté the green onion and the red pepper in the butter in a medium-size skillet until the vegetables are slightly softened, for 2 to 3 minutes. Reserve the vegetable mixture in the skillet off the heat.
4. When the rice is firm-tender and has absorbed all the liquid, stir the vegetable mixture into the rice. Transfer the rice to a large serving bowl.

Beet and Cucumber Salad with Orange-Honey Dressing

Prepare the salad and dressing separately, ahead of time.

Makes 10 servings.

Nutrient Value Per Serving: 163 calories, 2 g protein, 15 g fat, 7 g carbohydrate, 121 mg sodium, 0 mg cholesterol.

1   head leafy green lettuce
1   head romaine lettuce
1   long European-variety
    cucumber
1   fresh beet (about 8 ounces)

Orange-Honey Dressing:
3   tablespoons orange juice
1   tablespoon lemon juice
1   tablespoon honey
2   teaspoons Dijon-style
    mustard
2   teaspoons grated orange
    rind
¼   to ½ teaspoon salt
⅔   cup vegetable oil

1. Separate the head of green leafy lettuce into individual leaves. Wash the leaves and blot dry with paper toweling. Gather half the leaves together and cut crosswise into 1-inch-wide strips. Repeat the same process with the romaine.
2. Alternate the whole lettuce leaves and the whole romaine leaves around the inside edge of a large salad bowl. Fill the center with the shredded lettuce and the shredded romaine. Cover the greens with damp paper toweling. Refrigerate the bowl until serving time.
3. Scrub and cut the cucumber in half lengthwise. Cut the halves crosswise into thin half-moons. Place the cucumber slices in a plastic bag and refrigerate.
4. Peel the beet; be careful since the beet juice will stain (you may want to cover the work surface with wax paper). Coarsely shred the beet. Place the shredded beet in a plastic bag and refrigerate.
5. Prepare the Orange-Honey Dressing: Combine the orange juice, lemon juice, honey, mustard, orange rind and salt in a small bowl. Whisk in the oil until the dressing is well blended. Refrigerate, covered, until ready to use.
6. To serve the salad, pour about half the dressing over the lettuce strips in the bowl. Toss the strips to coat well with the dressing. Arrange the cucumber slices in a circle in the center of the salad. Arrange the shredded beet in a ring around the cucumber. Serve the salad with the remaining dressing on the side.

QUICK TIP

Double-Duty Salad Dressings
Put your prepared or homemade salad dressings to work: they make quick seasonings for marinades, basting sauces and for fish and vegetables cooked in aluminum-foil packets. Test your favorite combinations with regular and low-calorie dressings.

143

Pumpkin Muffins

Bake at 400° for 20 to 25 minutes.
Makes 10 muffins or 12 small savarins (ring molds).

Nutrient Value Per Muffin:
168 calories, 4 g protein, 6 g fat, 25 g carbohydrate, 213 mg sodium, 42 mg cholesterol.

1¾ cups *uns*ifted all-purpose flour
¼   cup sugar
2   teaspoons baking powder
½   teaspoon ground cinnamon
½   teaspoon ground nutmeg
½   teaspoon salt
1   egg, slightly beaten
1   cup solid-pack pumpkin purée
¾   cup milk
¼   cup (½ stick) unsalted butter, melted

1. Preheat the oven to hot (400°). Butter ten 2½-inch muffin-pan cups or twelve ½-cup savarin molds.
2. Stir together the flour, sugar, baking powder, cinnamon, nutmeg and salt in a medium-size bowl.
3. Whisk together the egg, pumpkin purée, milk and butter in another medium-size bowl until the mixture is well blended.
4. Add the dry ingredients all at once to the pumpkin mixture. Stir just until the dry ingredients are moistened; do not overstir.
5. Scoop a scant ¼ cup of the batter into each of the prepared muffin-pan cups or savarin molds. Gently press the batter down with your fingertip.
6. Bake the muffins or savarins in the preheated hot oven (400°) for 20 to 25 minutes or until a wooden pick inserted in the centers comes out clean. Run a knife around the muffins or savarins to loosen. Turn out the muffins or savarins onto a wire rack and cool slightly.

QUICK TIPS

Muffin Magic
Some important tips for making muffins:
• Add the beaten liquid to the combined dry ingredients with a few quick stirring strokes to just moisten the dry ingredients.
• The batter should be lumpy: if it pours smoothly from the spoon, you are guilty of overbeating.
• You can recognize overbeaten muffins by the coarse texture and the tunneling throughout.
• Fill muffin-pan cups quickly and easily— just use an ice cream scoop or small soup ladle.

144

Garden Vegetable Soup

Prepare the soup 1 to 2 days ahead.

Makes 8 servings.

Nutrient Value Per Serving:
170 calories, 6 g protein, 7 g fat, 24 g carbohydrate, 994 mg sodium, 0 mg cholesterol.

4   cups shredded Savoy or green cabbage (1 medium-size)
4   carrots, sliced (1½ cups)
3   ribs celery, sliced (1 cup)
2   parsnips, peeled and diced (1 cup)
3   tablespoons vegetable oil
4   cans (13¾ ounces each) chicken broth
3   medium-size all-purpose potatoes, peeled and diced
2   zucchini, sliced (2 cups)
2   cups cauliflower flowerets
1   small sweet red pepper, halved, seeded and diced
2   tomatoes, cored, seeded and diced
¼   teaspoon salt
1   teaspoon leaf thyme, crumbled
2   teaspoons Worcestershire sauce
¼ to ½ teaspoon pepper
¼   cup chopped parsley

1. Sauté the cabbage, carrot, celery and parsnips in the oil in a large kettle or Dutch oven over medium heat until the cabbage is wilted, for 10 to 15 minutes.
2. Meanwhile, place the broth in a medium-size saucepan. Bring the broth to boiling. Add the broth to the kettle. Add the potatoes, zucchini, cauliflower, red pepper, tomatoes, salt, thyme, Worcestershire sauce and pepper. Bring the mixture to boiling. Cover the kettle and lower the heat. Simmer for 15 to 20 minutes or until the vegetables are just tender. Uncover the kettle and cool, stirring occasionally. Cover and refrigerate for 1 to 2 days or until ready to serve.
3. To reheat the soup and serve, slowly bring the soup just to boiling, stirring often. Stir in the parsley. Ladle the soup into large, shallow soup bowls.

**Menu Idea
Sunday
Afternoon Lunch
Serves 6**
Garden Vegetable Soup*
Curried Beef Piroshki*
Ham and Lentil Loaves*
Carrot Cake or Gingerbread
Coffee or Tea
Milk

QUICK TIP

Souper Freezing
To save time in the kitchen, freeze homemade soup in family-size portions in a bowl. When they are frozen, remove the rounds and place them in plastic bags. When it is time to reheat the soup, the frozen rounds fit perfectly into the big soup kettle.

Curried Beef Piroshki

Bake at 375° for 30 minutes.
Reheat at 325° for 10 to 15
minutes.
Makes 6 servings (12 piroshki).

Nutrient Value Per Piroshki:
589 calories, 26 g protein, 26 g
fat, 62 g carbohydrate, 424 mg
sodium, 120 mg cholesterol.

1½   cups whole-wheat flour
1   envelope active dry yeast
¼   teaspoon salt
1¼   cups very warm water
1   tablespoon vegetable oil
1   egg, slightly beaten
2   to 2½ cups *un*sifted all-
       purpose flour
½   cup chopped onion
       (1 medium-size)
1   clove garlic, finely chopped
3   tablespoons butter
1   pound ground beef chuck
2   to 2½ teaspoons curry
       powder
½   teaspoon salt
1   container (8 ounces) plain
       yogurt
     Melted butter *(optional)*

1. Combine the whole-wheat flour, yeast and the ¼ teaspoon of salt in a medium-size bowl; stir to blend. Add the water and oil all at once. ("Very warm water" should feel comfortably warm when dropped on your wrist.) Beat the mixture for 2 minutes, scraping down sides of the bowl. Stir in the egg and ½ cup all-purpose flour. Beat mixture for 2 minutes. Stir in enough of remaining all-purpose flour to make a soft dough that leaves the side of the bowl clean.

2. Turn dough out onto a lightly floured board. Knead until smooth and elastic, 5 to 10 minutes. Shape dough into a ball. Place in a greased bowl and turn dough to coat with the oil on all sides. Cover bowl. Let dough rise in a warm place away from drafts for 1 hour or until doubled in bulk.

3. While dough is rising, prepare filling. Sauté the onion and garlic in butter until softened, for about 5 minutes. Stir in the beef and cook, stirring often, until meat is no longer pink. Stir in the curry powder and ½ teaspoon of salt and cook for 2 minutes. Blend in yogurt. Cover skillet; lower heat. Simmer for 10 to 15 minutes. Set aside.

4. After dough has risen, punch it down. Divide into quarters. Cut each into 3 equal pieces. Cover with plastic wrap.

5. Working in batches of three, roll out pieces of dough into circles with 4-inch diameters. Place 2 tablespoons of filling in each center. Lightly moisten edges of circles with water. Fold circles over to make half-moons. Press edges together to seal. Transfer to a greased cookie sheet; cover. Repeat with remaining dough and filling. Let rise in a warm place away from drafts for 1 hour.

6. Preheat the oven to 375°.

7. Bake the piroshki in the oven (375°) for 30 minutes or until golden. Brush tops with melted butter, if you wish. Cool piroshki on wire racks. Wrap and refrigerate for 1 to 2 days.

8. To reheat, place on a cookie sheet in a preheated oven (325°) for 10 to 15 minutes.

QUICK TIPS

Peel Out!
● To quickly peel onions: Cut off the bottom, then the top. Cut a slash in the side and remove the first outer peel, including the skin.
● To quickly peel garlic: With the palm of your hand, crush the entire head of garlic so that the cloves fall apart. Select one clove and place the fat side of a large knife over it; hit the knife gently with your hand. The clove skin will come off immediately.

146

Ham and Lentil Loaves

Prepare and bake these loaves on a weekend. Slice into individual servings, wrap and then freeze. When ready to serve, thaw and reheat in a moderate oven (350°) or in a microwave oven.

Bake at 350° for 1 hour. Makes 2 loaves (6 servings each).

Nutrient Value Per Serving: 214 calories, 16 g protein, 4 g fat, 30 g carbohydrate, 612 mg sodium, 78 mg cholesterol.

1	**pound dried lentils, picked over and rinsed**
1	**pound smoked ham hocks**
1	**small carrot, trimmed and halved**
1	**celery stalk, halved**
1	**small handful celery leaves**
6	**cups water**
1	**large onion, halved**
4	**whole cloves**
1	**chopped onion (1 large)**
1	**cup chopped celery**
1	**tablespoon butter or margarine**
4	**slices whole-wheat bread**
3	**eggs**
1	**cup shredded carrot**
2	**teaspoons salt**
¾	**teaspoon pepper**

1. Combine the lentils, ham hocks, halved carrot and celery stalk, celery leaves and water in a large saucepan. Stud the onion halves with the cloves and add the onion to the saucepan. Bring the mixture to boiling. Lower the heat; cover the saucepan and simmer for 45 minutes. Uncover the saucepan and simmer for 15 minutes or until both the lentils and ham are very tender. Let the mixture cool.

2. Meanwhile, sauté the chopped onion and the celery in the butter in a large skillet until tender, about 5 minutes. Cool slightly.

3. Preheat the oven to moderate (350°). Grease two 9 x 5 x 3-inch loaf pans very well. Line the long sides and the bottom of the pans with aluminum foil cut large enough to make a 4-inch overhang on each side. Grease the foil very well.

4. Remove the cloves from onion and return the onion halves to the lentil mixture. Cut the meat from the ham hocks and add to the lentil mixture.

5. Place the bread slices in the container of the food processor; process to make crumbs. Transfer the crumbs to a large bowl.

6. Working in batches, place the lentil mixture in the workbowl of a food processor. Pulse with on-and-off motions to chop the vegetables and the ham. Add the lentil mixture to the bread crumbs with the eggs, sautéed onion mixture, shredded carrot and salt and pepper. Mix gently to combine.

7. Spoon the mixture into prepared pans and smooth the tops. Fold the aluminum foil overhang over the top of the loaves.

8. Bake the loaves in the preheated moderate oven (350°) for 1 hour or until firm and set around edges. Cool the pans on a wire rack for 10 minutes. Invert the loaves onto a plate. Remove the foil. Serve hot, at room temperature or chilled.

WHAT TO SERVE
WITH THE
MAIN COURSE

Chapter 5 offers an eclectic mix of side dishes. How long it takes you to whip up the main course will help you decide the go-withs. Preparation time for these dishes ranges from three minutes to make-ahead.

Speedy entrées call for speedy side dishes: Sugar Snap Peas with radish and ginger *(page 156)* is ready for the table in less than 10 minutes, and Sautéed Cherry Tomatoes with sage and lemon *(page 151)* is done in less than 5 minutes. If you have a dish baking in the oven, pop in Acorn Squash and Onion Marinara *(page 155)*, or make it earlier in the day and serve it at room temperature. And of course there are salads. If you wash the greens ahead, wrap them in paper toweling and refrigerate them in a plastic bag, you'll cut salad prep-time to practically zero. Use these greens for Ginger Orange Salad *(page 181)* or Spinach Salad with Curried Orange and Maple Dressing *(page 173)*.

Finally, we offer three more step-by-step primers: the first explains how to cook perfect corn on the cob. (Plus, there's a selection of flavored butters to enjoy!) Another shows you how to make quick skillet gravy from a variety of sautéed dishes, and the third illustrates—from beginning to end—how to make chicken stock and freeze it. We found that chicken stock is the busy cook's instant flavor enhancer for practically anything—except, of course, desserts!

A bevy of salads to serve with the main course. Counterclockwise, from top: Curried Rice Salad (page 177), Orzo and Feta Cheese Salad (page 178), Herbed New Potato Salad (page 176), Fusilli with Broccoli and Garlic (page 180) and Mexican Brown Rice Salad (page 179).

Vegetables

Sautéed Cherry Tomatoes

This recipe even works well with supermarket variety cherry tomatoes "out of season," and is ready to go in less than 5 minutes. If there are any leftovers, try them as a chilled salad with shredded romaine, or shredded cooked ham for a heartier version.

Makes 4 servings.

Nutrient Value Per Serving: 66 calories, 1 g protein, 6 g fat, 3 g carbohydrate, 168 mg sodium, 8 mg cholesterol.

1   tablespoon butter
1   tablespoon olive oil
1   pint cherry tomatoes, stems removed and tomatoes rinsed
¼   teaspoon salt
¼   teaspoon pepper
2   tablespoons chopped fresh sage or other fresh herb OR: 2 teaspoons leaf sage or other leaf herb, crumbled
1   teaspoon grated lemon rind (do not include any of the bitter white pith)

1. Heat the butter and the oil in a large skillet.
2. Add the tomatoes, salt and pepper. Gently sauté the tomatoes over medium heat for 3 to 4 minutes or until the tomatoes are heated through and slightly softened. Be careful not to break the tomato skins. Remove the skillet from the heat.
3. Sprinkle the tomatoes with the sage or other herb and the lemon rind. Serve the tomatoes immediately.

QUICK TIP

Veggie Magic
Corn and other fresh vegetables can be steamed, blanched or microwaved in a very short amount of time, and they need nothing more than a sprinkle of salt and pepper, a pinch of basil or tarragon, and a pat of butter if you really want to splurge.

Rice Custard à la Greque

This hearty Greek-style casserole is assembled quickly and cuts nicely into squares for serving.

Bake at 400° for 55 minutes. Makes 9 servings.

Nutrient Value Per Serving: 228 calories, 12 g protein, 10 g fat, 22 g carbohydrate, 386 mg sodium, 174 mg cholesterol.

2	cups canned tomatoes with liquid
½	cup long-grain rice
1	jar (6 ounces) marinated artichoke hearts, drained and coarsely chopped
1	package (9 ounces) frozen French-cut green beans, slightly thawed
1	jar (7 ounces) roasted red peppers, drained and coarsely chopped
2	cups milk
5	eggs
⅓	cup *un*sifted all-purpose flour
1½	cups grated Romano cheese
¼	teaspoon salt
¼	teaspoon pepper

1. Preheat the oven to hot (400°).
2. Drain the tomatoes, reserving the liquid. Chop the tomatoes coarsely. Sprinkle the rice evenly over the bottom of a 9 x 9 x 2½-inch-square baking dish. Space the artichoke hearts and the chopped tomatoes evenly over the rice. Pour on the tomato liquid. Separate the green beans and arrange evenly over the tomatoes. Top with the red peppers.
3. Combine the milk, eggs, flour, 1¼ cups of the Romano cheese, the salt and pepper in the container of an electric blender. Cover and whirl until the mixture is well blended. Pour the custard over the contents of the casserole. Sprinkle the top with the remaining ¼ cup of Romano cheese.
4. Bake the casserole in the preheated hot oven (400°) for 55 minutes or until the top is browned and a knife inserted in the center comes out clean. Let the casserole stand for about 15 minutes before cutting into squares.

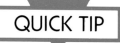

QUICK TIP

Eggs-actly!
If you're in doubt about an egg's freshness, break it into a saucer. A super-fresh egg has a cloudy white and a high-standing yolk. Older eggs will have less cloudy whites and flatter yolks. A "bad" egg will have a definite odor or chemical smell when sniffed.

Bourbon Ginger Sweet Potatoes

The potato purée can be made the day before, then piped and baked 30 minutes before you're ready to eat.

Bake at 350° for 30 minutes.
Makes 8 servings.

Nutrient Value Per Serving:
151 calories, 2 g protein, 2 g fat,
32 g carbohydrate, 397 mg
sodium, 4 mg cholesterol.

3 **pounds (6 to 8 medium-size) sweet potatoes, scrubbed**
¼ **cup bourbon**
1 **tablespoon butter or margarine, melted**
1 **tablespoon light brown sugar**
1 **tablespoon finely chopped, peeled fresh gingerroot**
1 **teaspoon salt**
8 **walnut or pecan halves (optional)**

1. Cook the potatoes in enough boiling salted water to cover the potatoes in a large saucepot or Dutch oven for 30 minutes or until the potatoes are tender. Drain the potatoes in a colander. When the potatoes are cool enough to handle, peel and place half the potatoes in the container of a food processor or, working in batches, of an electric blender. Cover and whirl until the potatoes are puréed. Transfer the potatoes to a large bowl. Repeat with the remaining potatoes.
2. Preheat the oven to moderate (350°).
3. Stir the bourbon, butter or margarine, brown sugar, gingerroot and salt into the puréed potatoes.
4. Spoon the potato mixture into a pastry bag fitted with a large star tip. Pipe the mixture into 8 large swirls in a shallow, round 1½-quart baking dish.
5. Bake the potatoes in the preheated moderate oven (350°) for 30 minutes or until hot. Garnish each swirl with a walnut or pecan half, if you wish.

QUICK TIP

Don't Go Nuts!
When a recipe calls for nuts, don't spend your valuable time shelling and chopping them. Nuts are available in almost any form — halves, quartered, chopped — they may cost a bit more but, when you're trying to beat the clock, they're worth it.

153

Lemon Dilled Brussels Sprouts

It takes less than 20 minutes to prepare this side-dish.

Makes 10 to 12 servings.

Nutrient Value Per Serving:
67 calories, 2 g protein, 4 g fat,
7 g carbohydrate, 197 mg
sodium, 10 mg cholesterol.

1½ **cups water**
¾ **teaspoon salt**
3 **containers (10 ounces each) Brussels sprouts, trimmed OR: 3 packages (10 ounces each) frozen Brussels sprouts**
¼ **cup (½ stick) butter or margarine**
2 **tablespoons snipped fresh dill OR: ½ teaspoon dried dillweed**
1 **tablespoon fresh lemon juice**
1 **can (8 ounces) sliced water chestnuts, drained**

1. Bring the water and the salt to boiling in a large saucepan. If using fresh Brussels sprouts, cut an X in the stem ends. Add the sprouts to the saucepan. Cover the saucepan and return the water to boiling. Lower the heat and simmer, covered, for about 12 to 15 minutes or until the sprouts are tender. Drain the sprouts and return them to the saucepan.
2. Meanwhile, melt the butter or margarine in a small saucepan. Add the dill, lemon juice and water chestnuts. Set the saucepan aside.
3. To serve, pour the butter dill mixture over the Brussels sprouts and toss together until the sprouts are well coated with the butter mixture. Serve immediately.

Lemon Dilled Brussels Sprouts go well with poultry or fish.

Acorn Squash and Onion Marinara

This vegetable dish is delicious served either hot, directly from the oven, or an hour or two later at room temperature.

Bake at 425° for 45 minutes. Makes 12 servings.

Nutrient Value Per Serving: 66 calories, 2 g protein, 0 g fat, 16 g carbohydrate, 149 mg sodium, 0 mg cholesterol.

1   can (14 ounces) Italian-style plum tomatoes
2   teaspoons leaf oregano, crumbled
½   teaspoon salt
⅛   teaspoon pepper
4   acorn squash (4 pounds)
3   medium-size yellow onions (1 pound)
2   tablespoons olive oil

1. Preheat the oven to hot (425°).
2. Pour the tomatoes into a shallow, 4-quart oven-to-table casserole. Mash the tomatoes with a wooden spoon to break them up. Sprinkle 1 teaspoon of the oregano, the salt and pepper over the tomatoes. Stir to combine the ingredients.
3. Wash the squash well. Cut the squash in half lengthwise; remove and discard the seeds. Cut the squash halves crosswise into ⅓-inch-thick slices.
4. Peel the onions and slice into ¼-inch-thick rounds. Arrange the squash and the onions, overlapping, over the tomatoes in the casserole. Brush the tops with the oil and sprinkle the remaining teaspoon of oregano over all. Cover the casserole tightly with aluminum foil.
5. Bake the casserole in the preheated hot oven (425°) for 45 minutes or until the onion and the squash are tender when pricked with a fork. Serve the casserole hot or at room temperature.

Note: You may assemble this casserole ahead and store it, tightly covered, in the refrigerator for several hours. Then bake as directed in Step 5.

QUICK TIP

Red-Dot Protection
If you are saving a particular item or items for a planned-ahead meal, mark them with a red, self-adhesive dot. Then inform your family that a red dot means off limits. You'll never be left without an important ingredient again!

155

Sugar Snap Peas with Radish and Ginger

This quick, easy stir-fry preserves the delicate flavor of the pea, whether you use the short, rounded sugar snap pea or the flatter, thinner snow pea. In the off season, this recipe works equally well with the frozen variety. With either fresh or frozen, this is a 10-minute dish.

Makes 4 servings.

Nutrient Value Per Serving: 143 calories, 3 g protein, 10 g fat, 10 g carbohydrate, 9 mg sodium, 0 mg cholesterol.

1	pound trimmed sugar snap peas OR: snow peas
2	tablespoons olive oil
2	green onions, chopped (2 tablespoons)
2	teaspoons chopped, peeled fresh gingerroot
½	cup slivered red radish (about 6 small radishes)
1	tablespoon lemon juice
1	tablespoon Oriental sesame oil*

1. If using the sugar snap peas, first blanch the sugar snaps in a large saucepan of boiling water for about 2 minutes or until the peas are slightly softened. Drain the peas in a colander and rinse under cold running water to stop the cooking. Drain the peas well.
2. Heat a wok or large skillet. Add the olive oil and swirl to coat the pan. When the oil is hot, add the green onion and the gingerroot. Stir-fry for about 10 seconds or until fragrant.
3. Add the peas and stir-fry for 3 to 4 minutes or until the peas are heated through. Add a little more oil to prevent sticking, if necessary.
4. Add the radish to the wok and stir-fry for 1 minute. Remove the wok from the heat.
5. Drizzle the lemon juice and the Oriental sesame oil over the peas. Toss the peas to coat and serve immediately.

Note: Oriental sesame oil is richer in flavor and darker in color than regular sesame oil. It can be found in the Oriental food section of many supermarkets or in Oriental specialty food stores.

QUICK TIP

What To Do With Overcooked Vegetables?
Purée and serve as the side vegetable, or add the purée to casseroles and/or cream soups.

Crisp Zucchini Pancakes

Once the zucchini drains, these fritters take no time at all.

Makes 14 pancakes.

Nutrient Value Per Pancake:
93 calories, 2 g protein, 8 g fat,
3 g carbohydrate, 129 mg
sodium, 41 mg cholesterol.

3	medium-size zucchini, trimmed and shredded (about 1 pound)
¾	teaspoon salt
1	medium-size onion, finely chopped (½ cup)
1	tablespoon unsalted butter
2	eggs, slightly beaten
¼	cup *un*sifted all-purpose flour
⅛	teaspoon pepper Vegetable oil for frying

1. Place the zucchini in a colander and sprinkle with ½ teaspoon of the salt. Set the colander aside for 30 minutes.
2. Squeeze as much liquid as possible from the zucchini with your hands. Reserve the zucchini.
3. Sauté the onion in the butter in a medium-size skillet over medium-high heat until softened, for about 3 minutes.
4. Transfer the reserved zucchini and the onion to a large bowl. Stir in the eggs, flour, the remaining ¼ teaspoon of salt and the pepper.
5. Pour the oil into a clean skillet to a depth of ⅛ inch and heat. Drop slightly rounded tablespoonfuls of the zucchini batter into the oil and flatten to a 3-inch diameter with the back of a spoon. Cook the pancakes, turning once, for 1 minute on each side or until golden.
6. Remove the pancakes from the skillet with a slotted spoon to drain on paper toweling. Keep the pancakes hot until all the pancakes are cooked. Serve the pancakes immediately.

Need to use up all the extra zucchini from your garden? Try our golden Crisp Zucchini Pancakes.

157

Busy Cook's Primer: How to Cook Perfect Corn on the Cob

How to Clean Corn

1. Remove the husks and the silk from the ears of corn just before cooking.
2. To get rid of stubborn strands of silk, hold each ear under cold running water and lightly run a vegetable brush along the rows between the kernels, moving the brush toward the stem.

How to Grill Corn

In the Husks

1. Pull the husks back from each ear, leaving the husks attached at the stem. Remove the silk and butter the ears.
2. Re-cover the ears with the husks. Tie the ends of the husks securely with string or a long strip of husk. Soak the husks in cold water for 10 minutes.
3. Grill the corn over medium to hot coals for 15 to 20 minutes, turning every 3 to 4 minutes. The husks will char.
4. Carefully remove the hot husks from the ears, using oven mitts.

In Aluminum Foil
(not pictured here)

1. Butter the cleaned ears.
2. Loosely wrap each ear in heavy-duty aluminum foil.
3. Grill the ears over hot coals for 15 to 20 minutes, turning the ears every 5 to 6 minutes.

How to Microwave Corn
(650-watt oven)

1. Place each cleaned ear of corn on a separate piece of wax paper. Brush the ear with melted butter and wrap in the paper, twisting the ends closed.
2. Microwave one ear at full power for 2½ to 3½ minutes, two ears for 5½ to 6½ minutes.

How to Boil Corn

Hot Water Method

1. Bring a large pot of water to boiling. You may add a little sugar and milk, but no salt—it toughens the corn.
2. Slide the cleaned ears of corn into the boiling water; don't overcrowd the pot. Cover the pot. When the water returns to boiling, cook the corn for 2 to 3 minutes. Drain the corn and serve with butter.

Cold Water Method

1. Place the cleaned ears in a large, deep skillet or flameproof baking pan without overcrowding. Add cold water to cover the ears.
2. Cover the skillet. Bring the water to boiling over medium-high heat. Remove the skillet from the heat. Drain the corn and serve with butter.

Flavored Butters

Keep a few of these "logs" in your freezer and you'll always be able to add a special touch to corn on the cob or other vegetables. You can also try flavored butters on burgers, grilled meats and fish.

Each makes about ½ cup.

Nutrient Value Per Tablespoon: 102 calories, 0 g protein, 11 g fat, 0 g carbohydrate, 2 mg sodium, 31 mg cholesterol.

Chive Butter:
- ½ cup (1 stick) unsalted butter, softened
- 2 tablespoons chopped fresh chives OR: green onions, green part only
- 1 tablespoon lemon juice

Coriander Butter:
- ½ cup (1 stick) unsalted butter, softened
- ¼ teaspoon ground coriander
- ¼ teaspoon turmeric

Lime Butter:
- ½ cup (1 stick) unsalted butter, softened
- 1 tablespoon lime juice
- ½ teaspoon grated lime rind

Sweet Red Pepper Butter:
- ½ cup (1 stick) unsalted butter, softened
- 2 tablespoons finely chopped bottled roasted red peppers

1. Cut the butter into small pieces and place in the container of a small food processor or in a small mixer bowl. Add the other ingredients. Process, beat the butter with a mixer or mash with a wooden spoon until the butter is smooth and all the ingredients are well blended.
2. Scrape the butter onto a piece of wax paper. Shape the butter into a log 6 to 8 inches long, rolling up the wax paper. Twist the ends of the paper to seal.
3. Wrap the paper-wrapped butter tightly in aluminum foil. Refrigerate the butter for 1 day for the flavors to develop, or freeze for longer storage.
4. Slice off pats of the butter as needed to spread on corn, burgers, steak, fish, cooked vegetables, etc.

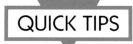

QUICK TIPS

Buying Basics For Corn On The Cob
To make sure you bring home young ears of corn just at their peak, follow these shopping tips:
- Look for ears with fresh, green husks.
- Pull back the husks to be certain the corn is worm-free.
- Choose corn with plump, glossy kernels in rows that are close together.
- For the best flavor, cook corn the same day you buy or pick it. Some new, sweeter corn hybrids, however, may be wrapped and refrigerated for up to 1 week.

Soups

Strawberry "Gazpacho"

A refreshingly different fruit version of the Spanish classic that you can make a day ahead.

Makes 10 servings.

Nutrient Value Per Serving:
157 calories, 1 g protein, 0 g fat,
40 g carbohydrate, 8 mg
sodium, 0 mg cholesterol.

8	tablespoons strawberry or red currant jelly
¾	cup water
6	cups frozen unsweetened strawberries (1½ twenty-ounce packages), partially thawed
1	can (6 ounces) frozen strawberry daiquiri mix, thawed
1½	cups white grape juice
	Sugar, to taste
2	to 3 tablespoons kirsch (*optional*)
3	ripe kiwis, peeled
1	papaya, peeled, seeded and cut into ¼- to ⅓-inch dice, for garnish
	Toasted sliced almonds
	Crunchy granola cereal

1. Heat the jelly and the water in a small saucepan until melted. Cool. Place the strawberries in the container of a food processor or an electric blender. Cover and whirl until the strawberries are a smooth purée. (You should have about 3 cups of purée.) Stir in the daiquiri mix, jelly mixture and grape juice. Pour the soup into a bowl or plastic storage container. Cover and chill the soup for at least 4 hours or overnight. Taste the soup and add sugar, if necessary. Stir in the kirsch, if you wish.

2. To serve, choose a 2- to 2½-quart glass bowl. Cut enough thin slices of kiwi to press against the inside of the bowl to make a complete circle around the bowl. Dice the remaining kiwi. Carefully ladle the soup into the prepared bowl. Garnish the soup with the diced kiwi and papaya. Serve the soup in glass soup bowls or stemmed glasses. Serve the almonds and the cereal on the side as crunchy toppings.

QUICK TIP

Nutty Advice
To toast nuts easily, spread shelled nuts in a shallow baking pan and bake in a preheated moderate oven (350) for 10 minutes. Remove from the pan and cool.

Cold Strawberry "Gazpacho," served with diced fruit, nuts and cereal for garnishes.

Tomato Soup with Lima Beans

A little pasta thickens this shortcut version of an all-time favorite.

Makes 6 servings.

Nutrient Value Per Serving:
103 calories, 7 g protein, 1 g fat,
18 g carbohydrate, 541 mg
sodium, 1 mg cholesterol.

1   **can (16 ounces) Italian-style tomatoes, *un*drained**
1   **can (10½ ounces) condensed beef broth**
1⅓ **cups water**
1   **package (10 ounces) frozen lima beans**
3   **tablespoons small pasta, such as orzo or pastina**
2   **tablespoons grated Parmesan cheese**

1. Place the tomatoes with their liquid in the container of an electric blender or a food processor. Cover and whirl until the tomatoes are puréed. Pour the tomato purée into a medium-size saucepan. Add the broth, water, frozen lima beans and pasta to the saucepan. Bring the soup to boiling. Lower the heat and simmer the soup, uncovered, for 15 minutes.
2. Ladle the soup into 6 warmed soup bowls. Sprinkle each serving with 1 teaspoon of the Parmesan cheese and serve.

Green Pea and Onion Soup

Makes 4 servings.

Nutrient Value Per Serving:
162 calories, 6 g protein, 7 g fat,
17 g carbohydrate, 739 mg
sodium, 20 mg cholesterol.

1   **can (10½ ounces) condensed French onion soup**
1⅓ **cups water**
1   **package (10 ounces) frozen green peas**
½   **teaspoon leaf tarragon, crumbled**
½   **cup light cream OR: half-and-half**
¼   **cup sliced green onion, for garnish**

1. Combine the onion soup, water, frozen green peas and tarragon in a medium-size saucepan. Bring the mixture to boiling. Lower the heat and simmer, uncovered, for 15 minutes.
2. Pour the soup mixture into the container of an electric blender or a food processor, working in batches if necessary. Cover and whirl until the soup is smooth. Pour the soup back into the saucepan. Stir in the cream or half-and-half. Gently heat the soup until heated through, but do not boil.
3. Ladle the soup into 4 warmed soup bowls. Garnish the soup with the green onion and serve.

QUICK TIP

The Stock Market
Don't throw away any fresh bones or trimmings. Freeze them until you have enough for a hearty pot of beef or chicken stock. (Dark-colored bones should not be used.)

Tomato Egg Soup

Sometimes called egg drop soup, the "petals" of egg in the broth are said to resemble the petals of a flower. For less sodium, use a light soy sauce or eliminate it.

Makes 4 servings.

Nutrient Value Per Serving: 155 calories, 5 g protein, 9 g fat, 10 g carbohydrate, 1,536 mg sodium, 69 mg cholesterol.

2   medium-size tomatoes (about ¾ pound)
5   cups chicken broth
2   tablespoons cornstarch
1   tablespoon Oriental sesame oil*
1   egg
1   teaspoon vegetable oil
1   tablespoon dry sherry (optional)
1   tablespoon soy sauce
2   small green onions, finely chopped, for garnish

1. Peel the tomatoes and cut them in half crosswise. Squeeze out the seeds and remove the cores; discard the seeds and cores. Cut the tomatoes into ½-inch chunks and reserve.
2. Measure ¼ cup of the broth into a small dish. Stir in the cornstarch and the Oriental sesame oil until well blended.
3. Whisk together the egg and the vegetable oil in a small bowl until smooth.
4. Pour the remaining 4¾ cups of broth into a medium-size saucepan. Add the sherry, if you wish, and the soy sauce. Bring the mixture to boiling over medium heat. Add the reserved tomatoes. Gradually stir in the cornstarch mixture. Return the mixture to boiling and cook, stirring, until the mixture is thickened and translucent, for about 1 minute. Remove the saucepan from the heat.
5. While stirring the soup constantly in a circular motion, add the beaten egg mixture in a thin stream; the egg will lightly cook in thin shreds. Sprinkle the top with the chopped green onion. Serve immediately.

Note: Oriental sesame oil is richer in flavor and darker in color than regular sesame oil. It can be found in the Oriental food section of many supermarkets or in Oriental specialty food stores.

QUICK TIP

"Souper" Taste!
Try these garnishes to dress up simple soups (chicken, beef, vegetable or fish) or to "disguise" leftovers.
Fresh Herbs — parsley, tarragon, dill, rosemary, basil, chives, mint or coriander, or a mixture.
Shredded Greens — finely shredded arugula, spinach, bok choy, romaine, endive or sorrel.
Citrus Rind — thin strips of or finely grated lemon, lime or orange rind.
Sliced Mushrooms — simmer thinly sliced mushrooms in the soup for a few minutes.
Pasta or Rice — simmer small or broken-up pieces of noodles, pasta, macaroni, rice or pastina until tender.
Grated Cheese — sprinkle with grated Parmesan or Romano or float thin shavings of hard cheese on top.
Mixed Vegetables — simmer thin slivers or matchstick pieces of carrot, turnip, sweet pepper, celery, green onion or whole peas to add color and crunch.

163

Corn and Pepper Soup

When fresh corn isn't available, use canned or frozen corn to make this delicious chilled soup, which can be made the day before.

Makes 4 servings.

Nutrient Value Per Serving:
328 calories, 12 g protein, 15 g fat, 43 g carbohydrate, 115 mg sodium, 26 mg cholesterol.

4	cups fresh, thawed frozen or drained canned corn kernels
3	cups milk
1	cup chopped onion (1 large)
2	tablespoons corn oil
1	cup chopped sweet red pepper
¼	cup finely chopped, seeded jalapeño pepper
	Salt and pepper, to taste

1. Combine the corn and the milk in the top of a double boiler placed over simmering water. Cover and cook for 10 minutes, stirring occasionally, until the corn is tender.
2. Meanwhile, sauté the onion in the oil in a skillet over medium heat, stirring, for 5 minutes or until softened. Add the red and jalapeño peppers and sauté for 5 minutes longer.
3. Reserve 1 cup of the corn kernels. Place the remaining corn kernels, part at a time, in the container of a food processor or an electric blender. Cover and whirl until puréed. Transfer the purée to a bowl. Stir in the sautéed onion mixture and the reserved corn kernels. Cover the bowl and refrigerate.
4. Taste and adjust the seasonings. Garnish with additional sautéed red and jalapeño peppers, if you wish.

QUICK TIP

Jalapeño Hotline
Avoid touching your face, eyes, nose, mouth or any other sensitive areas when you're working with jalapeño peppers. The juice from these peppers will sting and burn, even several hours later. Remember to wash your hands thoroughly after you've finished handling them.

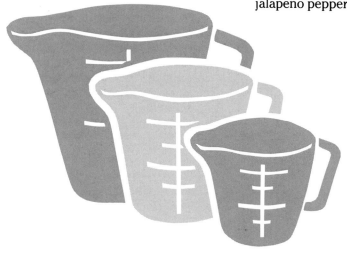

Avocado and Lemon Soup

Prepare early in the day or the night before.

Makes 8 servings.

Nutrient Value Per Serving: 220 calories, 5 g protein, 13 g fat, 25 g carbohydrate, 555 mg sodium, 1 mg cholesterol.

1	medium-size onion, chopped (½ cup)
2	leeks, trimmed, halved, well washed and chopped (white part only)
2	tablespoons vegetable oil
1	quart chicken broth
4	boiling potatoes (about 2 pounds), peeled and diced
1	cup buttermilk
2	ripe avocados, peeled, seeded and sliced
	Juice of 2 lemons
½	teaspoon liquid red pepper seasoning
	Salt and pepper, to taste
	Lemon slices, for garnish *(optional)*

Lemon adds a sprightly touch to this smooth and velvety chilled Avocado and Lemon Soup.

1. Sauté the onion and the leeks in the oil in a medium-size stockpot over medium heat until soft but not brown. Add the broth and bring to boiling. Add the potatoes. Lower the heat and simmer, stirring ocassionally, for 20 to 30 minutes or until the potatoes are very tender. Let mixture cool.
2. Place part of the potato mixture in the container of an electric blender or a food processor. Add part of the buttermilk, avocado and lemon juice. Cover and whirl until puréed. Transfer the purée to a large bowl. Repeat the puréeing with the remaining potato mixture, buttermilk, avocado and lemon juice and transfer to the bowl. Stir in the liquid red pepper seasoning, salt and pepper.
3. Cover the bowl and refrigerate the soup until well chilled. Taste and adjust the seasonings, if necessary. Garnish each serving with a lemon slice, if you wish.

QUICK TIP

Avocado Advice
Hold an avocado in your hands and gently press the ends. If it yields to gentle pressure, it's ripe and ready. (Most avocados, however, are not allowed to mature on the tree and will consequently be hard.) It's best to plan ahead and buy several underripe avocados and let them stand at room temperature to ripen. Enclosing them in a brown paper bag will hasten the ripening. Avocados have a high fat content, most of which is unsaturated. Half of an 8-ounce avocado has 150 calories and provides vitamin C, riboflavin, magnesium and potassium. When the flesh of the avocado is cut, it discolors rapidly. Brush the cut surfaces with citrus juice, diluted vinegar or an ascorbic-acid mixture to reduce the discoloration. If you have half an avocado left over, keep it unpeeled, with the pit still in, wrap it in aluminum foil and refrigerate.

Tortilla Soup

Nutrient Value Per Serving:
130 calories, 5 g protein, 6 g fat,
17 g carbohydrate, 1,301 mg
sodium, 0 mg cholesterol.

6   **corn tortillas, for garnish**
1   **tablespoon corn oil**
3   **ripe tomatoes, chopped**
1   **medium-size onion,**
      chopped (¾ cup)
1   **small jalapeño pepper,**
      seeded and chopped (use
      less if a milder flavor is
      desired)
4   **cloves garlic, chopped**
1   **tablespoon ground cumin**
2½ **quarts (10 cups) chicken**
      stock
      Salt and pepper, to taste
      Diced avocado, chopped
        cilantro and shredded
        Cheddar cheese, for
        garnish

1. Cut the tortillas into julienne strips, then in half. Halve the strips again, if necessary, to make bite-size pieces. Cook the tortilla strips in hot oil in a large saucepan until crisp. Reserve the tortilla strips for garnish.
2. Add the tomatoes, onion, jalapeño pepper, garlic and cumin to the saucepan and cook for 10 minutes.
3. Add the chicken stock to the saucepan and simmer over low heat for 30 minutes.
4. Transfer the soup to the container of an electric blender or a food processor, working in batches if necessary. Whirl until puréed. Taste and add the salt and pepper, if necessary. (If ripe tomatoes are unavailable, you may want to improve the color of the soup by adding 1 teaspoon of tomato paste at this point.)
5. Strain the soup through a piece of cheesecloth back into the saucepan and discard the solids.
6. Garnish the soup with the julienned fried tortillas, diced avocado, chopped cilantro and shredded Cheddar cheese.

QUICK TIP

Fiesta From The Freezer
For a cook's night off, pop frozen burritos, enchiladas or tacos into the oven or the microwave, then add your own garnish of shredded lettuce, chopped onion, tomato and sweet red pepper — and for the daring, a whole jalapeño pepper!

Red Pepper Soup

No-cook Red Pepper Soup is as tasty as it is colorful.

Canned pimientos are the base of this soup.

Makes 4 servings.

Nutrient Value Per Serving: 92 calories, 3 g protein, 0 g fat, 21 g carbohydrate, 663 mg sodium, 0 mg cholesterol.

1   **can (28 ounces) whole tomatoes in thick purée**
1½ **cups tomato juice**
2   **jars (4⅔ ounces each) whole sweet pimientos, drained**
1   **tablespoon finely chopped onion**
2   **tablespoons chopped fresh basil OR: 1½ tablespoons leaf basil, soaked in 1 tablespoon water**
2   **tablespoons chopped fresh parsley**
    Salt and pepper, to taste
    Dairy sour cream OR: plain yogurt, for garnish

1. Drain the tomatoes, reserving the purée separately. Place the tomatoes in the container of a food processor. Cover and pulse on and off until the tomatoes are coarsely chopped. Transfer the mixture to a medium-size bowl.
2. Combine the reserved purée, the tomato juice, pimientos, onion, basil and parsley in the food processor container. Cover and process on high speed until smooth. Add the puréed mixture to the chopped tomatoes in the bowl. Stir to blend well. Taste and adjust the seasonings.
3. Cover the soup and refrigerate until chilled. Taste the soup once more and adjust the seasonings, if necessary.
4. At serving time, garnish the soup with dollops of the sour cream or plain yogurt.

Tomato Orange Soup

A soup that's equally good served hot or cold.

Makes 4 servings.

Nutrient Value Per Serving:
141 calories, 3 g protein, 7 g fat,
18 g carbohydrate, 234 mg
sodium, 0 mg cholesterol.

2   large onions, chopped
      (about 2 cups)
1   clove garlic, finely chopped
2   tablespoons olive oil
1   cup tomato juice
½   cup freshly squeezed
      orange juice
4   large ripe tomatoes, peeled,
      seeded and chopped
      Salt and pepper, to taste
      Lemon juice, to taste
      Orange zest cut into thin
      strips, for garnish**

1. Cook the onion and the garlic in the oil in a large saucepan over medium heat for 1 minute. Cover the pan, lower the heat and cook for 10 minutes. Uncover the pan. Add the tomato and orange juices.
2. Bring the mixture to a simmer. Add the chopped tomatoes. Cover the pan and simmer for 10 to 15 minutes or until the mixture thickens.
3. If you wish, force the soup through a food mill or purée, part at a time, in a food processor or blender. Chill.
4. Taste the soup and add the salt, pepper and lemon juice. Garnish the servings with the julienned orange zest.

**Note: *For best flavor, orange zest should be carefully stripped so no bitter white pith is removed with it. Boil the zest in water for 1 minute. Drain and simmer in a second pot of boiling water if the zest is very strong. Cool; cut into julienne strips.*

QUICK TIP

Grate Idea
Lemons, limes and oranges should be grated before squeezing when a recipe calls for both grated rind and juice. The same applies when zest is called for in a recipe. Carefully remove the zest using a very sharp paring knife or a vegetable parer — then squeeze for the juice.

Chilled Gazpacho

Makes 6 servings.

Nutrient Value Per Serving:
49 calories, 2 g protein, 0 g fat,
11 g carbohydrate, 25 mg
sodium, 0 mg cholesterol.

1   **can (16 ounces) no-salt-added whole tomatoes with liquid**
2   **cans (12 ounces each) no-salt-added tomato juice**
1   **medium-size sweet red pepper, halved, cored, seeded and finely chopped**
½   **cup finely chopped seeded, unpeeled cucumber (½ medium-size)**
¼   **cup finely chopped onion**
¼   **cup finely chopped cilantro OR: parsley**
3   **tablespoons fresh lime juice**
1   **tablespoon red wine vinegar**
2   **cloves garlic, finely chopped**
½   **of fresh jalapeño pepper, seeded and finely chopped**

1. Drain the liquid from the tomatoes into a soup tureen. Transfer the tomatoes to a cutting board and coarsely chop the tomatoes, discarding as many of the seeds as possible. Add the tomatoes to the liquid in the tureen.
2. Stir the tomato juice, red pepper, cucumber, onion, cilantro or parsley, lime juice, vinegar, garlic and jalapeño pepper into the soup tureen. Cover the tureen and refrigerate the soup for several hours or overnight to chill and to blend the flavors. Serve the soup cold.

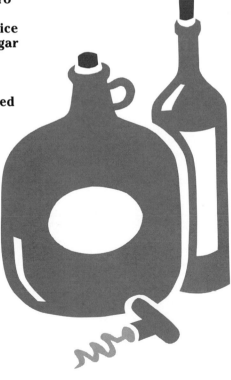

QUICK TIP

Herb Alert!
If you don't have ¼ cup fresh cilantro or parsley on hand, substitute 4 teaspoons dried herbs. Here's the formula to figure out other fresh herb substitutions: One tablespoon of fresh herbs = 1 teaspoon dried herbs.

169

Salads

Tomato Walnut Salad with Blue Cheese Dressing

You can prepare the dressing a day or two ahead.

Makes 4 servings.

Nutrient Value Per Serving: 286 calories, 11 g protein, 22 g fat, 14 g carbohydrate, 330 mg sodium, 30 mg cholesterol.

½ cup blue cheese (about 3 ounces)
½ cup dairy sour cream
½ cup plain yogurt
½ cup coarsely broken walnuts, toasted
¼ teaspoon pepper
3 large ripe tomatoes, preferably beefsteaks (about 1½ pounds), sliced ¼ inch thick
1 medium-size onion, Bermuda or Spanish, thinly sliced

1. Crumble the blue cheese into a small bowl. Set aside 2 tablespoons of the blue cheese for a garnish. Stir in the sour cream, yogurt, all but 2 tablespoons of the walnuts and the pepper until well blended. Cover the bowl and refrigerate until ready to use.
2. Arrange the tomato and onion slices, overlapping, on a large platter or 4 individual salad plates. Ladle the dressing over the top and sprinkle with the reserved blue cheese and walnuts.

Use the ripest tomatoes you can find for this Tomato Walnut Salad with Blue Cheese Dressing.

Green Beans and Radishes in Sour Cream Vinaigrette

Prepare this side-dish early in the day.

Makes 6 servings.

Nutrient Value Per Serving: 130 calories, 2 g protein, 11 g fat, 7 g carbohydrate, 19 mg sodium, 4 mg cholesterol.

1 pound green beans, trimmed
¼ cup olive oil
3 tablespoons red wine vinegar
¼ cup dairy sour cream
2 cups thinly sliced radishes (about 2 bunches red and/or white)
½ cup finely chopped green onion

1. Cook the green beans in enough boiling salted water to cover the beans in a saucepan until they are crisp-tender, for 6 to 7 minutes. Drain the beans in a colander and rinse with cold water. Drain the beans well. Transfer the beans to a serving bowl.
2. Sprinkle the beans with 2 tablespoons of the oil and 1 tablespoon of the vinegar and toss the beans gently to mix. Reserve the beans.
3. Whisk together the sour cream, the remaining 2 tablespoons of oil and the remaining 2 tablespoons of vinegar in a small bowl until the mixture is smooth.
4. Add the dressing, radishes and green onion to the green beans and toss gently to mix well. Marinate the beans for at least 2 hours. Serve the beans at room temperature or slightly chilled.

QUICK TIP

Getting A Jump On The Salad
If you're making your own salad dressing, prepare ahead and refrigerate.

Antipasto Platter

This zesty beginning to your meal may be made ahead and then assembled just before you are about to serve.

Makes 12 servings.

Nutrient Value Per Serving:
117 calories, 3 g protein, 10 g fat, 5 g carbohydrate, 142 mg sodium, 4 mg cholesterol.

3	large sweet red peppers
2	cans (2 ounces each) anchovy fillets
½	cup olive oil
3	tablespoons lemon juice
2	tablespoons chopped flat-leaf Italian parsley
1	clove garlic, finely chopped
¼	teaspoon salt
⅛	teaspoon pepper
1	pound medium-size mushrooms, trimmed, washed and halved
1	small head chicory or green-leaf lettuce
1	fennel bulb, trimmed and cut lengthwise into ¼-inch-thick slices, then each slice halved lengthwise

1. Preheat the broiler. Lay the peppers in a single layer on the broiler pan. Broil the peppers 2 inches from the source of the heat, turning the peppers frequently, until they are blackened all over, for about 15 minutes.
2. Cool each red pepper under cold running water. Remove the blackened skin with a sharp knife and discard. Core and seed the peppers. Cut the peppers into ¾- to 1-inch-wide strips. Pat the strips dry on paper toweling. Place the strips in a large bowl.
3. Mash 3 of the anchovy fillets in a small bowl. Add the oil, lemon juice, parsley, garlic, salt and pepper. Whisk briskly to combine.
4. Add the mushrooms and the dressing to the red peppers. Toss lightly to coat the mushrooms and the red peppers. Cover the bowl and refrigerate for several hours or overnight.
5. To serve, arrange the lettuce leaves on a platter. Spoon out the mushrooms and mound off-center on the platter. Arrange the red peppers and the fennel in alternating piles around the mushrooms. Roll up the remaining anchovy fillets and arrange them on the platter. Drizzle any remaining dressing over the platter.

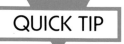

QUICK TIP

It Takes 4 People To Make A Salad:
A spendthrift for the oil, a miser for the vinegar, a wise man for the salt and a madman to toss.

Spinach Salad with Curried Orange and Maple Dressing

A dressing that is as delicious as it is exotic. And it takes 2 minutes or less to prepare.

Makes 6 servings.

Nutrient Value Per Serving:
208 calories, 6 g protein, 1 g fat,
47 g carbohydrate, 356 mg
sodium, 0 mg cholesterol.

3   **pounds bulk spinach**
1½ **cups frozen concentrate for orange juice or apple juice**
½   **cup distilled white vinegar**
⅓   **cup maple syrup**
3   **tablespoons Dijon-style mustard**
    Juice of 1 lemon
3   **cloves garlic**
½   **teaspoon curry powder**
    Pinch black pepper
1   **chili pepper, seeded and chopped** *(optional)*
    Orange zest and orange sections, for garnish *(optional)*

1. Trim the spinach of all coarse stems and bruised leaves. Rinse the spinach well in several changes of water to remove all traces of dirt and sand. Drain the spinach well on paper toweling. Place the spinach in a serving bowl.
2. Place the orange or apple juice concentrate in the container of an electric blender. Add the vinegar, maple syrup, mustard, lemon juice, garlic, curry powder and black pepper. Cover and whirl until blended.
3. If you are using the chili pepper, add it to the blended mixture and whirl on high speed until the chili is puréed.
4. Pour the dressing over the spinach and toss to coat the spinach. Garnish with orange zest and orange sections, if you wish.

QUICK TIP

Salad Days
Don't add the dressing to the salad until the last minute. Otherwise you'll have wilted and discolored greens. To crisp salad greens, wash them, roll them gently in a terry-cloth towel and put them in the crisper drawer of your refrigerator.

Pesto Red Potatoes

Makes 8 servings.

*Nutrient Value Per Serving:
178 calories, 5 g protein, 3 g fat,
35 g carbohydrate, 16 mg
sodium, 0 mg cholesterol.*

Pesto Dressing:

½ cup low-sodium chicken
     broth, refrigerated and
     then fat removed from top
1   tablespoon olive oil
2   teaspoons fresh lemon juice
2   tablespoons pine nuts
     (pignoli)
2   to 3 large cloves garlic
2   cups well-packed fresh basil
     leaves
¼ cup parsley leaves
¼ teaspoon pepper

3   pounds unpeeled red-
     skinned potatoes
1   tablespoon distilled white
     vinegar
½ cup coarsely chopped sweet
     red pepper

*Pesto Red Potatoes sparkle with sweet
red pepper.*

1. Prepare the Pesto Dressing: Combine the broth, oil, lemon juice, pine nuts, garlic, basil, parsley and pepper in the container of an electric blender or a food processor. Cover and whirl until the pine nuts and the garlic are finely chopped. Transfer the dressing to a bowl. Cover the bowl and refrigerate until the dressing is needed.

2. Cook the potatoes in enough boiling unsalted water to cover in a large saucepan for 15 to 20 minutes or just until the potatoes are tender. Drain the potatoes. When the potatoes are cool enough to handle, cut the potatoes crosswise into ½-inch-thick slices. Place the potatoes in a large serving bowl. Sprinkle with the vinegar and toss gently to coat the potatoes.

3. Add the red pepper to the potatoes. Spoon the reserved Pesto Dressing over the potatoes. Toss the potatoes carefully to coat well.

New Potato Salad with Rosemary Mayonnaise

This recipe can be prepared a day ahead.

Bake at 450 for 25 to 30 minutes.
Makes 12 servings.

Nutrient Value Per Serving:
357 calories, 4 g protein, 26 g
fat, 30 g carbohydrate, 618 mg
sodium, 7 mg cholesterol.

24 new red potatoes, scrubbed
½   to 1 cup corn oil
    Salt and freshly ground
      pepper, to taste
2   cups julienned zucchini
2   cups sliced Kalamata olives
    Rosemary Mayonnaise
      (recipe at right)

1. Preheat the oven to very hot (450).
2. Rub the potatoes with the oil, salt and pepper. Place the potatoes on a cookie sheet or jelly-roll pan.
3. Bake the potatoes in the preheated very hot oven (450) for 25 to 30 minutes or until the potatoes are cooked through but not mushy. Remove the potatoes from the oven and cool on the cookie sheet on a wire rack.
4. Cut each potato into ½-inch-thick slices and place the slices in a large bowl. Add the zucchini, olives and Rosemary Mayonnaise. Toss gently to mix all the ingredients. Taste and season with salt and pepper. Transfer the salad to a serving bowl and refrigerate, covered. To serve, let the salad come to room temperature.

Rosemary Mayonnaise

This herb and tomato-flavored mayonnaise would also be delicious with pieces of just-cooked lamb in bite-size sandwiches.

Makes about 3 cups.

Nutrient Value Per Tablespoon:
99 calories, 0 g protein, 11 g fat,
1 g carbohydrate, 54 mg
sodium, 5 mg cholesterol.

12 ripe plum tomatoes,
      chopped
¾   cup olive oil
½   cup dry white wine
2   bunches fresh parsley,
      finely chopped
2   bunches fresh rosemary OR:
      2 tablespoons leaf
      rosemary, crumbled
½   bunch fresh sage OR: 1
      teaspoon leaf sage,
      crumbled
2   cups mayonnaise

1. Sauté the tomatoes in ½ cup of the oil in a medium-size saucepan over medium heat until very soft, stirring often.
2. Add the wine. Bring the mixture to boiling. Lower the heat and simmer for 5 minutes. Strain the mixture through a fine sieve into a large bowl. Stir in the parsley.
3. Pick the rosemary and sage leaves from the stems. Sauté the leaves in the remaining ¼ cup of oil in a small skillet until lightly browned. Remove the herbs to a cutting board and coarsely chop. Add to the tomato mixture.
4. Stir the mayonnaise into the tomato mixture until well blended. Cover and refrigerate the mayonnaise for up to 3 or 4 days.

Herbed New Potato Salad

A perfect dish for any picnic or barbecue — this tasty salad becomes even more flavorful if you make it the day before.

Makes 6 servings.

Nutrient Value Per Serving: 239 calories, 4 g protein, 12 g fat, 28 g carbohydrate, 178 mg sodium, 0 mg cholesterol.

2   **pounds small new potatoes, scrubbed**
    About 1½ quarts chicken broth
¼   **cup French Sauterne wine**
    OR: other sweet white wine
    Salt and freshly ground pepper, to taste
¼   **cup mixed chopped herbs, such as parsley, chives, chervil, basil**
¼   **cup white wine vinegar**
⅓   **cup olive oil**

1. Halve the potatoes; place them in a large saucepan. Pour in enough broth to cover the potatoes.
2. Bring the broth to boiling over medium heat. Cook until the potatoes are tender but still firm. Drain the potatoes, reserving the broth for another use. Place the potatoes in a medium-size serving bowl.
3. Add the wine to the potatoes and toss carefully to mix. Season the potatoes with the salt and pepper, then add the herbs, vinegar and oil. Toss again to mix. Cover and let stand for at least 1 hour to allow the flavors to blend.

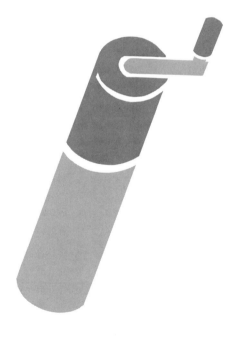

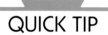
QUICK TIP

Cent-sible Sauterne
There's no need to buy pricey cooking wine for your gourmet recipes — regular jug wine adds the same flavor for less money. Use white wine for chicken and fish dishes; red wine can pep up bland tomato sauces or can be used as a marinade for less tender cuts of meat.

Lime Honey Sweet Potato Salad

Lime juice enhances the sweet potato's flavor. You can mix everything together the day before.

Makes 6 servings.

Nutrient Value Per Serving: 205 calories, 2 g protein, 12 g fat, 22 g carbohydrate, 36 mg sodium, 0 mg cholesterol.

3   medium-size sweet potatoes, peeled
⅓   cup plus 1 tablespoon freshly squeezed lime juice
1   cup frozen green peas, thawed OR: 1 pound fresh peas, shelled and blanched
2   teaspoons honey
½   teaspoon grated lime rind
⅛   teaspoon ground nutmeg
⅓   cup vegetable oil

1. Slice the potatoes in half, lengthwise, then in half lengthwise again. Slice the quarters crosswise into ½-inch-thick slices, dropping the slices into cold water as you cut them. Add the 1 tablespoon of lime juice to prevent discoloration.
2. Drain the potato slices and add them to a pot of boiling salted water over medium heat. Cook for 1 minute or just until tender. Drain and place under cold running water. Drain again very well. Place in a serving bowl. Add the peas.
3. Beat together the remaining ⅓ cup of lime juice, the honey, lime rind and nutmeg in a small bowl. Slowly beat in the oil in a thin stream using a wire whisk. Pour the dressing over the potatoes and toss gently to coat. Cover the salad and chill. Let the salad come to room temperature before serving.

Curried Rice Salad

This spicy salad is perfect with grilled meat, such as pork or beef.

Makes 6 servings.

Nutrient Value Per Serving: 598 calories, 7 g protein, 31 g fat, 74 g carbohydrate, 86 mg sodium, 0 mg cholesterol.

2   pieces fresh gingerroot, peeled and finely chopped
2   cloves garlic, finely chopped
¾   cup olive or vegetable oil
1   cup sliced onion
1   bunch carrots, peeled and julienne sliced
1   sweet green pepper, cored, seeded and diced
⅓   cup cashews
⅓   cup raisins
1½ to 2 tablespoons curry powder
    Juice of 1 orange
2   tablespoons mango chutney, chopped
6   cups cooked rice

1. Sauté the gingerroot and the garlic in the olive or vegetable oil in a very large skillet or saucepan over medium heat for 2 minutes. Add the onion and sauté, stirring often, for 5 minutes longer or until the onion is golden.
2. Add the carrot and the green pepper and sauté for 1 minute. Stir in the cashews, raisins and curry powder. Sauté, stirring constantly, for 1 minute. Add the orange juice and chutney.
3. Place the cooked rice in a large bowl. Pour the curry mixture over the rice; toss gently to combine. Transfer to a serving bowl, cover and chill. Let the salad come to room temperature before serving.

QUICK TIP

A Little Extra Grain Never Hurt
When you cook a grain such as barley, rice or kasha, cook a little extra. Refrigerate and use later in the week for soups, stuffings, stews or casseroles.

177

Orzo and Feta Cheese Salad

Because orzo is a tiny, rice-shaped pasta, it needs only a minimum of cooking. You can prepare the salad the day before, but save the tomato garnish until serving time.

Makes 6 servings.

Nutrient Value Per Serving: 279 calories, 6 g protein, 15 g fat, 30 g carbohydrate, 127 mg sodium, 10 mg cholesterol.

½ **pound orzo, cooked according to package directions and drained**
½ **cup chopped green onion**
½ **cup crumbled feta cheese**
⅓ **cup olive oil**
3 **tablespoons freshly squeezed lemon juice**
1 **tablespoon snipped fresh dill**
¼ **teaspoon leaf oregano, crumbled**
   Salt and freshly ground pepper, to taste
   Cherry tomatoes

1. Combine the orzo, green onion and feta cheese in a medium-size serving bowl.
2. Beat together the oil, lemon juice, dill and oregano in a small bowl until the mixture is well blended. Add the salt and pepper.
3. Pour the dressing over the orzo mixture. Gently toss with a fork to coat the orzo evenly. Refrigerate the salad to chill. To serve, let the salad come to room temperature. Top the salad with a ring of quartered cherry tomatoes.

Sweet 'N Sour Cucumber Relish

Marinate the cucumbers in a plastic food-storage bag the day before.

Makes 8 to 10 servings (4 cups).

Nutrient Value Per ½ Cup: 40 calories, 1 g protein, 0 g fat, 11 g carbohydrate, 141 mg sodium, 0 mg cholesterol.

1 **cup apple cider vinegar**
¼ **cup sugar**
2 **tablespoons snipped fresh dill**
2 **tablespoons chopped fresh parsley**
½ **teaspoon salt**
½ **teaspoon pepper**
2 **large or 3 medium-size cucumbers, scored and thinly sliced (about 6 cups)**
½ **cup thinly sliced radishes**

1. Combine the vinegar, sugar, dill, parsley, salt and pepper in a bowl and stir to dissolve the sugar. Add the cucumbers. Cover the bowl and refrigerate for several hours, stirring once or twice, or refrigerate overnight and stir once or twice in the morning.
2. Just before serving, stir the radish into the relish.

QUICK TIP

Rice The Second Time Around
Use leftover cooked rice in meatloaves, rice pudding, waffle or pancake batter, stuffing for eggplant or zucchini or in soups and stews.

Mexican Brown Rice Salad

Add some South-of-the-Border zest to your table with this spicy salad. Sautéed green onion, green chilies, garlic and red pepper are combined with brown rice in a cumin vinaigrette. The flavors improve if the salad is made a day ahead.

Makes 6 servings.

Nutrient Value Per Serving: 377 calories, 4 g protein, 24 g fat, 38 g carbohydrate, 5 mg sodium, 0 mg cholesterol.

½   **cup plus 2 tablespoons olive oil**
1   **bunch green onions, trimmed and sliced**
1   **large sweet red pepper, halved, cored, seeded and diced**
2   **green chili peppers, seeded and chopped (wear gloves when handling)**
2   **cloves garlic, finely chopped**
¼   **cup white wine vinegar**
1½   **teaspoons ground cumin**
½   **teaspoon ground hot red pepper**
½   **teaspoon sugar**
4   **cups cooked brown rice**

1. Heat the 2 tablespoons of oil in a large, nonstick skillet over medium heat. Add the green onion, red and green chili peppers and garlic. Sauté, stirring often, until the onion is tender but not brown. Stir in the remaining ½ cup of oil, the vinegar, cumin, ground hot red pepper and sugar.
2. Place the cooked brown rice in a large serving bowl. Add the sautéed vegetable mixture and toss gently to coat all the ingredients evenly. Cover the bowl and refrigerate. To serve, let the salad come to room temperature.

QUICK TIP

Marinating: Bag It!
For one less dish to clean, marinate meat, poultry or salads in plastic food-storage bags. This is also useful when you are marinating a salad for a picnic. A self-locking plastic bag takes up less space in your basket and is less likely to break than other types of containers.

179

Fusilli with Broccoli and Garlic

Gently sautéing sliced garlic until it is golden brings out a sweet, nutty flavor.

Makes 6 servings.

Nutrient Value Per Serving: 272 calories, 7 g protein, 13 g fat, 34 g carbohydrate, 22 mg sodium, 0 mg cholesterol.

1	bunch broccoli
½	pound cooked and drained fusilli (twists)
1	sweet red pepper, halved, seeded and cut into strips
⅓	cup olive oil
4	cloves garlic, thinly sliced*
	Salt and freshly ground pepper, to taste

1. Trim the broccoli. Cut off and break up the flowerets. Slice the stems into ½-inch-thick pieces.
2. Cook the stem pieces in a heatproof sieve in boiling salted water until barely tender. Immediately remove the sieve from the water and place the stem pieces under cold running water. Drain well. Repeat with the floweret pieces. Place the broccoli pieces in a large, portable bowl. Add the pasta and the red pepper.
3. Sauté the garlic in the oil in a small skillet over medium heat until the garlic turns golden. Pour over the pasta mixture. Toss gently to coat all the ingredients evenly. Add the salt and pepper. Cover and refrigerate.

Note: For a more pronounced garlic taste, chop the garlic instead of slicing it.

Snow Peas and Sprout Salad

Make the dressing in advance, but spoon over the salad just before tossing.

Makes 6 servings.

Nutrient Value Per Serving: 148 calories, 3 g protein, 13 g fat, 7 g carbohydrate, 188 mg sodium, 0 mg cholesterol.

1	clove garlic, finely chopped
½	teaspoon salt
1½	tablespoons lemon juice
1½	teaspoons dry mustard
2	tablespoons dry sherry
⅓	cup peanut, corn or olive oil
⅛	teaspoon crushed dried hot red peppers
½	pound snow peas, trimmed
½	pound Chinese (mung bean) sprouts (3 cups)
2	green onions, white bulbs and green tops, finely chopped
2	tablespoons finely diced sweet red pepper
1	tablespoon toasted sesame seeds

1. With the back of a spoon, mash the garlic with the salt in a small bowl to form a paste. Stir in the lemon juice, mustard and sherry. Whisk in the oil and the hot red pepper. Set the dressing aside.
2. Cook the peas in a large pot of boiling salted water for 30 seconds. Drain the peas in a colander and rinse under cold running water. Drain the peas again.
3. Arrange the sprouts in the bottom of a large serving bowl. Place the peas in the center and sprinkle with the green onion, red pepper and sesame seeds. Pour on the dressing and toss the salad well.

Broccoli and Artichoke Salad

Ginger Orange Salad

Use the marinade from prepared artichoke hearts to dress the broccoli.

Makes 6 servings.

Nutrient Value Per Serving: 112 calories, 4 g protein, 13 g fat, 34 g carbohydrate, 22 mg sodium, 0 mg cholesterol.

1   head broccoli, trimmed and cut into 1-inch pieces OR: 1 package (1 pound) frozen broccoli
2   jars (6 ounces each) marinated artichoke hearts
1   cup pimiento strips

1. Cook the broccoli pieces in boiling salted water to cover in a large saucepan over medium heat until tender but still crisp. Or prepare the frozen broccoli, following the package directions. Drain the cooked broccoli and immediately place under cold running water to stop the cooking. Drain the broccoli well, then place in a large serving bowl.
2. Drain the artichoke hearts, reserving the marinade.
3. Toss the broccoli with the artichoke hearts and the pimiento strips. Add the reserved marinade to taste and toss the salad to mix it well.

A spinach and orange salad sparked with ginger and vinegar. The pungent dressing can be prepared a day ahead.

Makes 4 servings.

Nutrient Value Per Serving: 92 calories, 3 g protein, 3 g fat, 15 g carbohydrate, 28 mg sodium, 2 mg cholesterol.

1   piece fresh gingerroot, peeled (about 3 inches x 1 inch)
4   teaspoons white wine vinegar
1   tablespoon frozen undiluted orange juice concentrate
2   teaspoons olive oil
    Pinch dry mustard
½   cup lowfat plain yogurt
2   large navel oranges, peeled and sliced crosswise into 6 rounds
12 spinach leaves
¼   cup chopped red onion, for garnish

1. Grate the gingerroot onto wax paper. Squeeze the ginger over a 2-cup glass measure. Reserve about 2 teaspoons of the ginger juice. Whisk the vinegar, orange juice concentrate, oil and mustard into the 2 teaspoons of ginger juice. Gradually whisk in the yogurt. Cover the dressing and refrigerate for at least 2 hours. Or for a really intense ginger flavor, chill the dressing overnight.
2. To serve the salad, arrange the orange slices and the spinach leaves on 4 individual salad plates. Stir the dressing and drizzle over the top. Garnish the salad with the red onion.

QUICK TIP

Clean Greens
Get a jump on salad making. Once or twice a week, wash the greens you'll need for the next few days, dry them well, wrap them in paper toweling and store them in plastic bags in the crisper section of the refrigerator.

181

Stock, Gravy & Sauces

Fresh 'N Easy Tomato Sauce

This sauce goes well with chicken, fish, veal cutlets or pork. Make it ahead and refrigerate or freeze.

Makes about 3 cups.

Nutrient Value Per ¼ Cup: 53 calories, 1 g protein, 3 g fat, 6 g carbohydrate, 122 mg sodium, 0 mg cholesterol.

2½ **pounds ripe plum tomatoes (about 15)**
1 **large onion, chopped (1 cup)**
2 **to 3 tablespoons olive or vegetable oil**
2 **cloves garlic, finely chopped**
1 **cup dry white wine OR: chicken broth**
2 **tablespoons tomato paste**
½ **bay leaf**
1 **teaspoon sugar**
½ **teaspoon salt**
½ **teaspoon leaf basil, crumbled**
¼ **teaspoon fennel or anise seeds**
   Pinch pepper
1 **to 2 teaspoons lemon juice, or to taste**

1. Peel the tomatoes. Cut the tomatoes in half crosswise. Gently squeeze out the seeds, remove the cores and discard the seeds and cores. Cut the tomatoes into 1-inch pieces.
2. Sauté the onion in the olive or vegetable oil in a medium-size saucepan until soft and translucent, for about 5 minutes. Add the garlic and sauté for 1 minute. Add the wine or broth, the tomato paste, bay leaf, sugar, salt, basil, fennel or anise and half the tomato pieces to the saucepan. Lower the heat and simmer the tomato sauce, uncovered, until thick and rich, for about 30 minutes. Add the remaining tomato pieces and the pepper to the saucepan. Bring the sauce to boiling. Immediately remove the saucepan from the heat. Stir the lemon juice into the sauce. Remove the bay leaf. Serve the sauce hot.

Just 45 minutes — that's all it takes to go from tomatoes to Fresh 'N Easy Tomato Sauce.

Busy Cook's Primer: Homemade Chicken Stock

Makes about 3 quarts.

Nutrient Value Per Cup:
48 calories, 1 g protein, 2 g fat,
7 g carbohydrate, 8 mg sodium,
cholesterol unavailable.

4   to 5 pounds frozen or
thawed chicken parts, such
as carcasses, backs, necks,
gizzards (no livers), wings
Cold water, as needed

Bouquet Garni:
8   sprigs parsley
1   teaspoon leaf thyme,
coarsely crumbled
1   bay leaf

2   large onions, with skins on,
quartered
2   large carrots, trimmed,
unpeeled and cut into
chunks
2   stalks celery with leaves, cut
into chunks
Coarse (kosher) salt
(optional)
6   whole white or black
peppercorns

1. Rinse the chicken parts in cold water. Place the parts in a heavy, nonaluminum 8½- to 10-quart stockpot just large enough to hold all the ingredients. Cover the chicken with lukewarm water. Bring the water to boiling. Immediately drain the chicken in a colander and rinse the chicken with cold water. Clean the stockpot.
2. Return the chicken to the stockpot. Add just enough cold water to the pot to cover the chicken by 1½ inches. Place a heavy, heatproof plate on top of the chicken to keep it submerged.
3. Heat the water very slowly over medium-low heat to boiling; this should take 30 to 60 minutes.
4. When the broth reaches boiling, skim off any scum and foam from the top with a ladle, skimmer or soup spoon.
5. Add 1 cup of cold water to the pot to release more cloud-forming particles. Return the water to boiling. Allow the foam to collect again and skim off.
6. Prepare the Bouquet Garni, or flavoring package, for the stock: Wrap the parsley, thyme and bay leaf in a double thickness of cheesecloth. Tie the cheesecloth neatly in a bundle with kitchen twine.
7. Add the onion, carrot, celery and Bouquet Garni to the pot. *Lightly* salt, if you wish. If you plan to reduce the stock, salt the stock only at the end.

8. Lower the heat so the stock simmers. (Only an occasional bubble should break the surface; the French call this "smiling.") If the liquid keeps returning to a boil, place a metal flame-tamer under the pot. Simmer the stock, partially covered.

9. Check the pot from time to time. Add hot water to the pot as needed to keep the solids covered. Maintain the simmer; boiling will cause the stock to cloud. Skim any foam from the top of the stock.

10. Simmer the broth for 3 to 4 hours or until the flavor is fully developed. Add hot water to the pot as needed. Near the end of the simmering time, add the peppercorns.

11. Line a large colander with a triple thickness of dampened cheesecloth. Place the colander over a large bowl to hold all the stock, or use several smaller bowls. (Stainless steel bowls will cool faster.) Carefully pour the stock into the colander. Gently press the solids with a spoon to extract the excess liquid from the solids. Discard the solids.

12. Cool the stock thoroughly before refrigerating. Place the bowl(s) in a sinkful of cold water. Stir the stock with a spoon, aerating the stock as you stir to cool the stock. Cover the bowl(s) tightly with plastic wrap and refrigerate overnight.

13. Remove the congealed fat from the top of the stock with a metal spoon or skimmer. Gently blot any remaining fat from the surface of the stock with white paper toweling. Wipe the side of the bowl(s) to remove any fat.

To Store and Use Stock

The stock may be refrigerated or frozen after Step 13, or it may be reduced to concentrate flavor and take up less storage room. To reduce: Pour the stock into a saucepan or pot. Boil the stock over medium-high heat until reduced by half. Remove any foam from the top as it accumulates. Cool the stock as in Step 12. Add salt, if you wish. To store the stock in the refrigerator: Place the stock in a tightly covered container and refrigerate for up to 3 days. To store the stock in the freezer: Pour the stock into ice cube trays. Freeze the stock. Remove the stock cubes from the trays and place in freezer storage bags. For larger quantities, place freezer bags in straight sided, plastic 1-pint or 1-quart containers. Pour the stock in the bags. Seal the bags, squeezing out as much air as possible. Freeze the stock. Remove the bags from the plastic containers and freeze for up to 6 months. To use: If using a large quantity of frozen stock, thaw the plastic bags in a bowl of warm water or under warm running water. Use the stock for soup and stew bases or in any recipe calling for chicken stock or broth. Use the ice cube size for making sauces and cooking vegetables or in any recipe where a little extra flavor won't hurt.

Add a Stewing Chicken for Even Richer Flavor

For a tasty bonus, you can add a whole 4- to 6-pound stewing chicken (or two 3-pound broiler-fryers) to the stock ingredients. When you're done, you'll have enough succulent poached chicken for a whole range of tasty dishes. Rinse the whole bird in cold water. Add along with the chicken parts in Step 1. After the first hour of simmering, check the whole chicken. When the thigh feels tender when pierced with a thin knife or skewer, remove the whole bird from the stock. A young bird should be done in about 1 hour, a stewing chicken in 1½ to 2 hours. When the chicken is cool enough to handle, remove the skin and discard. Remove the meat from the bones and reserve for other recipes, such as chicken hash, chicken curry, chicken potpie or chicken salad. (A 5-pound stewing chicken will yield about 5 cups of cooked meat.) Continue with the rest of the stock recipe.

Stock Tips

● Ask your butcher for chicken parts (backs, necks, etc.), or freeze chicken parts every time you prepare chicken for dinner, until you have enough parts to make the stock.
● Always blanch the chicken parts to remove the albumin protein particles that can cloud the broth. And be sure to clean the stockpot before going on to the next step.
● Adding cold water helps release more cloud-forming particles so they can be skimmed from the top of the stock.

Busy Cook's Primer: Quick Gravy for Sautéed Beef or Chicken

Makes about 1¾ cups.

2 cups hot liquid, combination of chicken or beef stock, and/or water
¼ cup bourbon, scotch, brandy or dry white or red wine *(optional)**
  Instant Thickener *(recipe at right)*

1. Sauté the chicken or beef in a skillet using your favorite recipe. Remove the meat to a heated platter and keep warm while preparing the skillet gravy.
2. Pour off any fat from the skillet, leaving only juices.
3. Return the skillet to high heat. Add 1 cup of the hot liquid, and the liquor or wine if you wish, stirring and scraping up any browned bits from the bottom of the skillet.
4. Add the remaining cup of hot liquid. Cook over high heat until the liquid is reduced to about 1¾ cups.
5. Add about 1 tablespoon of the Instant Thickener, bit by bit, to the liquid, boiling gently and stirring after each addition for 1 minute. Keep adding the Instant Thickener, if necessary, bit by bit, until the gravy reaches the desired consistency. Pour the gravy over or around the sautéed meat.

*Note: If adding liquor or wine to the skillet, be sure to boil the liquid in the skillet to evaporate the alcohol.

Instant Thickener

This is a quickly made thickening agent, known as *beurre manié*, which can be added to any liquid to turn it into a gravy. Freeze small amounts to have on hand.

Makes enough to thicken 4 to 6 cups very thin liquid.

¼ cup (½ stick) unsalted butter, softened
¼ cup all-purpose flour

1. Mix together the butter and the flour in a small bowl to form a smooth paste.
2. To freeze extra Instant Thickener: Scoop the butter mixture with a measuring tablespoon and spatula onto a wax paper-lined cookie sheet. Place the cookie sheet in the freezer until the butter mixture is hard. Remove the frozen mounds to a freezer bag. Store the Instant Thickener in the freezer for up to 3 months. One tablespoon is enough to thicken 1 to 2 cups of liquid.

QUICK TIP

Slow Down, You Cook Too Fast
To prevent sauces from burning or cooking too fast, place a heat diffuser on the burner. It evens out and reduces the heat.

187

easy ENTERTAINING

Chapter 6 is the party chapter. But can busy cooks throw parties? Of course they can. The secret is what they serve. And we highly recommend our easy, frazzle-free formula for entertaining: The classic cocktail party, updated. Serve make-ahead finger foods, and you'll enjoy your party as much as your guests do.

Make your selections from our appetizing assortment, from the very elegant Curried Crab Appetizers *(page 202)* to "down home" party snacks such as Pizza Popcorn *(page 193)* or Tangy Cheese Ball *(page 201)*.

For heartier munchies, our Picadillo Bread *(page 196)* is stuffed with ground beef, Jack cheese, black olives and raisins. We've even devised a Do-Ahead Hors d'Oeuvres menu, complete with recipes *(page 211)*. If you'd prefer a do-ahead buffet, see Chapter 4, page 139.

When you're planning your party, include beverages that offer something for everyone. If your guests prefer non-alcoholic drinks, there's Berry Punch *(page 219)*, while an elegant affair may call for champagne-laced Peach Blossom Sunrise *(page 221)*. We even supply you with our instant bartender planner *(page 225)* for all your needs, from tonic water to corkscrew. Cheers!

Serve these goodies at your next party! Italian Melba Bites (page 194) are topped with zucchini, tomato paste and tangy cheeses; sweet red pepper wedges are filled with Hummus (page 193); Pizza Popcorn (page 193), is flavored with tomato sauce and cheese; and Frozen Blueberry Yogurt in an Almond Crêpe Cup (Chapter 7, pages 265 and 266) is a sweet finale.

Bites & Things

Goat Cheese Biscuits

Tandoori Nuts

The biscuits may be topped while still warm from the oven. Or let them cool completely before adding the goat cheese.

Bake at 350° for 7 to 10 minutes. Makes 6 servings.

Nutrient Value Per Serving: 119 calories, 4 g protein, 7 g fat, 11 g carbohydrate, 410 mg sodium, cholesterol not available.

1 package (10 ounces) refrigerated buttermilk flaky biscuits
1 log (about 7 ounces) goat cheese
   Cracked pepper
   Sweet paprika
   Marinated sun-dried tomatoes, for garnish
   Fresh herbs, such as thyme or dill, for garnish

1. Preheat the oven to moderate (350°).
2. Separate the biscuits into thirds and place 2 inches apart on ungreased cookie sheets.
3. Bake the biscuits in the preheated moderate oven (350°) for 7 to 10 minutes or until golden.
4. Meanwhile, cut the goat cheese in half, lengthwise. Roll one half in the cracked pepper to taste (it is very spicy!), the other in the paprika.
5. Cut the goat cheese crosswise into ½-inch thick pieces. Place the cheese on the biscuit rounds. Garnish with the sun-dried tomatoes and the herbs.

Bake at 275° for 1 hour. Makes 4¾ cups.

Nutrient Value Per ¼ Cup: 188 calories, 3 g protein, 18 g fat, 6 g carbohydrate, 263 mg sodium, 7 mg cholesterol.

½ cup lowfat plain yogurt
¼ cup (½ stick) butter or margarine, melted
3 tablespoons ground curry powder
2 tablespoons ground cumin
2 teaspoons salt
1½ teaspoons ground cardamom
¾ teaspoon ground hot red pepper
½ teaspoon sugar
½ pound pecan halves
½ pound walnut halves

1. Preheat the oven to very slow (275°).
2. Combine the yogurt, butter or margarine, curry powder, cumin, salt, cardamom, ground hot red pepper and sugar in a large bowl. Add the pecans and the walnuts and toss to mix so the nuts are well coated with the spice mixture. Spread the nuts out in a large, shallow baking pan.
3. Bake the nuts, uncovered, in the preheated very slow oven (275°), stirring occasionally, for 1 hour or until the nuts are golden.
4. Cool the nuts completely. Store in a tightly covered container.

Goat Cheese Biscuits are made easy with refrigerated biscuit dough.

191

Endive with Red Pepper Pesto

Makes 24 servings.

Nutrient Value Per Serving:
19 calories, 1 g protein, 1 g fat,
2 g carbohydrate, 72 mg
sodium, 1 mg cholesterol.

Red Pepper Pesto:
1   cup water
3   large sweet red peppers
        (about 1⅓ pounds),
        coarsely chopped
2   cloves garlic, chopped
1   teaspoon leaf basil,
        crumbled
½   teaspoon salt
¼   teaspoon pepper
½   cup fresh bread crumbs
        (1½ slices)
⅓   cup grated Parmesan cheese
2   tablespoons finely ground
        pine nuts (pignoli)

2   large heads Belgian endive
        (about 4½ ounces each),
        separated into 24
        individual leaves

1. Prepare the Red Pepper Pesto: Bring the water to boiling in a 10-inch skillet. Add the red peppers and the garlic and return to boiling. Lower the heat, cover the skillet and simmer the mixture for 10 minutes or until the peppers are tender. Drain the peppers and garlic.

2. Place the cooked peppers and garlic in the container of an electric blender or a food processor. Cover and whirl until the peppers are puréed. Return the purée to the same skillet along with the basil, salt and pepper. Bring the mixture to boiling. Reduce the heat to low and simmer for 10 minutes or until the mixture thickens and most of the liquid is evaporated. Stir in the bread crumbs, Parmesan cheese and pine nuts. Cool the pesto slightly. Transfer the pesto to a bowl, cover and refrigerate for several hours or until completely cooled.

3. When ready to serve, spoon the pesto into a pastry bag fitted with a decorative tip. Pipe out about 1 scant tablespoon of pesto into the center of each endive leaf. Or spoon the pesto into the endive leaves.

QUICK TIP

**Instant
Entertainment**
Keep jars of pickled onions, olives, marinated roasted red peppers, marinated artichoke hearts, pickled hot peppers, Mexican salsa, corn chips, different flavored mustards, capers and canned smoked fish in your pantry or refrigerator and you'll be the busy cook who is ready for any unexpected guests.

Hummus

The hummus will keep in the refrigerator for 3 to 4 days.

Makes about 1⅔ cups.

Nutrient Value Per Tablespoon:
44 calories, 1 g protein, 3 g fat,
4 g carbohydrate, 75 mg
sodium, 0 mg cholesterol.

1   can (19 ounces) chick-peas
1   clove garlic, coarsely
      chopped
¼   cup olive oil
2   tablespoons lemon juice
½   cup parsley leaves
¼   teaspoon pepper
      Sweet red pepper strips
      (optional)
      Parsley sprigs, for garnish
      (optional)

Drain the chick-peas into a strainer; rinse them with cold water. Drain the chick-peas well. Place the chick-peas, garlic, oil, lemon juice, parsley and pepper in the container of a food processor or, working in batches, of an electric blender. Cover and whirl until the mixture is puréed. Transfer the purée to a small bowl. Refrigerate the purée, covered, until chilled. Scoop the hummus into red pepper strips, if you wish. Garnish with parsley sprigs, if you wish.

Pizza Popcorn

Makes about 2 quarts.

Nutrient Value Per ½ Cup:
44 calories, 2 g protein, 3 g fat,
3 g carbohydrate, 74 mg
sodium, 4 mg cholesterol.

1   tablespoon olive oil
1   tablespoon tomato paste
1   tablespoon grated
      Parmesan cheese
¼   teaspoon leaf oregano,
      crumbled
⅛   teaspoon garlic salt
2   quarts popped popcorn
⅓   cup shredded mozzarella
      cheese

Stir together the oil, tomato paste, Parmesan cheese, oregano and garlic salt in a cup. Combine the hot popcorn and the mozzarella cheese in a large bowl. Drizzle the oil mixture over the popcorn. Stir gently to mix all the ingredients well.

Microwave Instructions
(for a 650-watt variable power microwave oven)

Ingredients: Use 3½-ounce bags of microwave popping corn, which each yield 1 quart.
Directions: Pop the corn in the microwave oven, following the package directions. Meanwhile, combine the oil, tomato paste, Parmesan cheese, oregano, garlic salt and mozzarella cheese in a cup. Empty the hot popcorn into a large bowl and add the oil mixture. Mix the popcorn gently with a spoon to combine all the ingredients and serve.

QUICK TIP

Tiny Toast Cups
To make your own toast cups, cut out 2-inch rounds from thin-sliced white bread. Press the rounds with a rolling pin to compact them slightly. Brush both sides with melted butter. Press the rounds firmly into miniature muffin-pan cups. Toast in a preheated moderate oven (350°) for 15 minutes. Cool on wire racks. Fill the toast cups with chicken salad, ham salad, seasoned liverwurst and any other favorite savory hors d'oeuvre mixture.

Italian Melba Bites

Bake in a toaster oven for 3 to 5 minutes.
Makes 12 "bites" (4 servings).

Nutrient Value Per Serving:
73 calories, 3 g protein, 3 g fat,
8 g carbohydrate, 82 mg
sodium, 7 mg cholesterol.

1   tablespoon tomato paste
12   melba toast rounds
⅓   cup thinly sliced zucchini
½   teaspoon olive oil
¼   cup shredded mozzarella
       cheese
1   tablespoon grated
       Parmesan cheese
⅛   teaspoon leaf oregano,
       crumbled
       Sliced stuffed green olives,
       for garnish (optional)

1. Lightly spread the tomato paste on the melba rounds. Top the rounds with the zucchini slices. Brush the tops with the oil. Combine the mozzarella and Parmesan cheeses and the oregano in a small bowl. Sprinkle the cheese mixture over the zucchini. Place the rounds on a toaster oven tray.

2. Bake the rounds in the toaster oven set at 350° for 3 to 5 minutes or until the cheese melts. Garnish the bites with slices of stuffed green olives, if you wish.

Microwave Instructions
(for a 650-watt variable power microwave oven)

Directions: Place the "bites" on a microwave-safe plate. Microwave, uncovered, at full power for 45 seconds or until the cheese melts, rotating the plate one quarter turn once.

QUICK TIP

A Rose By Any Other Name . . .
Radish roses are a quick and easy way to liven up a salad or buffet. Wash and trim the radish, leaving some of the green leaves on if they are attractive. With a sharp knife, make 5 deep cuts (petals) all around the side of the radish. Place in a bowl of ice water for 15 minutes to make the petals open up.

Savory Stuffed Mushrooms

Serve these tasty morsels either hot or cold.

Makes 18 mushrooms.

*Nutrient Value Per Mushroom:
41 calories, 1 g protein, 4 g fat,
2 g carbohydrate, 47 mg
sodium, 0 mg cholesterol.*

12	ounces white button mushrooms, 1¼ to 1½ inches in diameter (about 18)
3	tablespoons olive oil
⅛	teaspoon plus ¼ teaspoon salt
3	large cloves garlic, sliced crosswise
¼	cup chopped shallots
2	tablespoons brandy
⅓	cup walnuts
1	bunch watercress, for garnish *(optional)*

1. Wipe the dust and dirt off the mushrooms gently with paper toweling. Separate the stems from the caps. Trim the woody or rough parts from the stems. Reserve 1 cup of the stems for the stuffing.
2. Heat 2 tablespoons of the oil in a skillet. Sauté the mushroom caps in the hot oil for 2 to 3 minutes or until the caps are cooked but not too soft. Remove the caps from the skillet with a slotted spoon. Place the mushroom caps, round side up, on a plate. Sprinkle with the ⅛ teaspoon of salt. Set the caps aside.
3. In the same skillet, heat the remaining 1 tablespoon of oil. Add the garlic and sauté for about 1 minute or until it starts to turn golden. Add the reserved mushroom stems and the shallots. Cook the mixture over medium heat for 5 to 8 minutes or until the mushroom stems are soft and well cooked. Be careful not to burn the garlic; the garlic should be a golden color.
4. Add the brandy to the skillet. Cook, stirring constantly, until all the liquid has evaporated.
5. Combine the mushroom stem mixture and the walnuts and chop very fine with a knife or a food processor. Stir in the remaining ¼ teaspoon of salt.
6. Stuff each mushroom cap with about 1 teaspoon of the walnut filling. Serve the mushrooms hot or cold on a bed of watercress. Garnish each stuffed cap with a watercress leaf.

QUICK TIP

Great Garnishes!
Serve stuffed vegetables, fruits, molds, slaws and cheese balls or mixes on a bed of dark, curly greens. Then sprinkle with paprika, grated cheese, nuts or parsley; or use sprigs of greens such as chives, parsley, mint, dill or watercress.

Picadillo Bread

An easy-to-fix picadillo filling goes into packaged frozen bread dough to make this tasty snack. The recipe makes three loaves for eating immediately or freezing for future use.

> *Bake at 350° for 25 to 30 minutes.*
> *Makes 3 loaves (12 slices each).*

> *Nutrient Value Per Slice:*
> *170 calories, 7 g protein, 7 g fat, 20 g carbohydrate, 309 mg sodium, 23 mg cholesterol.*

1½ pounds ground round
1   tablespoon vegetable oil
2   medium-size onions, chopped
1   large clove garlic, finely chopped
1   tablespoon hot chili powder
1   can (15 ounces) tomato sauce
½   teaspoon salt
½   teaspoon leaf oregano, crumbled
3   tablespoons slivered almonds
3   tablespoons sliced black olives
3   tablespoons raisins
⅓   cup grated Monterey Jack cheese
    Cornmeal
1   package (3 pounds) frozen bread dough, thawed
1   egg
1   tablespoon water

1. Sauté the ground beef in the oil in a large skillet over medium-high heat until browned. Stir in the onion and the garlic and cook, stirring often, for 2 minutes. Stir in the chili powder. Add the tomato sauce, salt, oregano, almonds, olives and raisins. Bring the picadillo to boiling. Lower the heat, cover the skillet and simmer for 20 minutes or until the picadillo is thickened. Remove the skillet from the heat. Stir in the Monterey Jack cheese. Cool the picadillo to room temperature.
2. Grease cookie sheets and sprinkle with cornmeal. Set the cookie sheets aside.
3. Roll out 1 loaf (1 pound) of the thawed bread dough on a very lightly floured surface into a rectangle, about 15 x 6 inches. Spoon one third of the picadillo mixture down the center of the dough. Bring together the long sides to enclose the filling. Pinch the dough together along the long seam and the ends to seal well. Place the dough, seam side down, on a prepared cookie sheet. With a pair of scissors, cut 2 rows of 1-inch diagonal slits into the top of the loaf. Repeat the filling and shaping procedure with the remaining dough and filling.

Shrimp in Cilantro Sauce

Cover the loaves and let rise in a warm place, away from drafts, for 15 minutes.

4. Meanwhile, preheat the oven to moderate (350°).

5. Beat together the egg and the water in a small bowl and brush the loaves with the egg-water mixture. Sprinkle the loaves with cornmeal.

6. Bake the loaves in the preheated moderate oven (350°) for 25 to 30 minutes or until the bread is browned on top. Remove the bread to wire racks. Serve the bread warm or at room temperature.

Chill this dish for 5 hours or overnight.

Makes 8 appetizer servings.

Nutrient Value Per Serving: 109 calories, 10 g protein, 7 g fat, 0 g carbohydrate, 266 mg sodium, 65 mg cholesterol.

2   **cups firmly packed coarsely chopped cilantro (coriander)***
1   **pickled jalapeño pepper, seeded**
½   **teaspoon salt**
¼   **cup olive oil**
4   **teaspoons fresh lime juice**
1   **tablespoon salt**
1   **pound large shrimp (about 22) or 1 pound medium-size (about 46), shelled and deveined**

1. Combine the cilantro, jalapeño pepper and the ½ teaspoon of salt in the container of a food processor. Cover and whirl until the pepper is finely chopped. Add the oil and whirl for a few seconds until the mixture is well blended.

2. Pour the sauce into a medium-size bowl. Stir in the lime juice. Cover the bowl and refrigerate.

3. Bring 8 cups of water to boiling in a large saucepan. Add the 1 tablespoon of salt. Add the shrimp and cook for about 2 minutes or until the shrimp are pink and opaque. Drain the shrimp.

4. Toss the warm shrimp in the cilantro sauce. Refrigerate until the shrimp are well chilled, for 5 hours or overnight.

5. Serve the shrimp in a shallow dish with wooden picks.

*Note: Parsley may be substituted if cilantro is not available.

Turkey Ham Logs

The sliced Turkey Ham Logs are delicious served with the Ginger Orange Dip (page 199). Serve as a buffet dish or as part of a light, cold supper.

Everything gets made the day before.

Broil for 15 to 20 minutes.
Makes 32 appetizer servings
(4 slices each).

Nutrient Value Per Serving:
69 calories, 7 g protein, 3 g fat,
2 g carbohydrate, 179 mg
sodium, 38 mg cholesterol.

24   green beans (4 to 6 ounces;
     select straight beans)
2   rolls (1 pound each) frozen
     ground turkey, thawed
2   eggs
⅔   cup unseasoned dry bread
     crumbs
¼   cup chopped chives OR:
     green onions
1   tablespoon Worcestershire
     sauce
¾   teaspoon salt
¼   teaspoon pepper
6   ounces boiled ham, in 1
     piece, cut into eight
     5 x ½ x ½-inch strips
     Ginger Orange Dip
     (recipe, page 199)
     Romaine lettuce leaves

1. Trim the green beans to about 5-inch lengths. Cook the beans in simmering water to cover them in a medium-size saucepan just until crisp-tender. Drain the beans in a colander, rinse under cold running water and pat dry.
2. Combine the turkey, eggs, bread crumbs, chives or green onion, Worcestershire sauce, salt and pepper in a large bowl and mix with a fork. Divide the mixture into 8 equal portions, about 5 ounces each.
3. To shape each log, pat out one portion of turkey mixture on a piece of wax paper to a 6 x 3-inch rectangle. Arrange 3 beans lengthwise, ½ inch apart, in the center of the rectangle. Place a ham strip on top of the center bean. Using the wax paper as an aid, bring the long edges of the meat together to enclose the filling. Seal the edges and ends of the roll, shaping the mixture into a 6-inch log. Place the log on an aluminum foil-lined broiler pan without the rack or in a jelly-roll pan. Make 7 more logs.

Ginger Orange Dip

4. Broil the logs 4 inches from the source of the heat for 15 to 20 minutes, turning the logs every 5 minutes for even browning. Cool the logs to room temperature. Refrigerate the logs, covered, overnight.
5. Prepare and chill the Ginger Orange Dip and the orange shell.
6. To serve, cut the logs crosswise into ¼-inch-thick slices (about 16 slices per log). Line a serving platter with the romaine lettuce leaves. Fill the orange shell with the dip. Place the orange shell on the platter. Surround the dip with the log slices. Refrigerate the remaining slices and dip. Replenish the platter as needed.

Makes about 1 cup.

Nutrient Value Per Teaspoon:
24 calories, 0 g protein, 2 g fat,
1 g carbohydrate, 17 mg
sodium, 2 mg cholesterol.

1	large navel orange
½	cup mayonnaise
½	cup dairy sour cream
2	tablespoons finely chopped crystallized ginger
¼	teaspoon ground ginger
	Pinch salt

Finely grate the rind from the top third of the orange; reserve ½ teaspoon of the grated rind. Cut off and discard the top third of the orange. Squeeze the juice from the orange and reserve 1 tablespoon. Pull out the pulp from the orange and save for another use. Cut the orange rim in a zigzag pattern. Combine the mayonnaise, sour cream, crystallized ginger, reserved orange juice, ground ginger, reserved rind and salt in a small bowl. Wrap the shell, cover the dip and refrigerate until ready to use.

QUICK TIP

From Crouton To Crumbs
If you find yourself out of bread crumbs in the middle of a recipe, just reach for the packaged croutons and your potato masher. It's quick, saves you a trip to the store and there is no blender to wash.

Spreads & Dips

Caviar Dip with Crudités

Tangy Cheese Ball

If using lumpfish caviar, rinse it in a fine sieve under cold running water to wash off the caviar dye. Pat gently with paper toweling.

Makes 8 appetizer servings.

Nutrient Value Per Serving: 178 calories, 8 g protein, 15 g fat, 4 g carbohydrate, 209 mg sodium, 147 mg cholesterol.

1   container (16 ounces) dairy sour cream
1/3 cup sliced green onion, white part only (1 bunch)
2   hard-cooked egg whites, chopped (about 1/2 cup)
2   ounces salmon caviar
2   ounces black caviar, such as beluga, sevruga or lumpfish
1/3 cup sliced green onions, green part only (1/2 bunch)
2   hard-cooked egg yolks, pushed through a fine sieve
     Assortment of vegetables, such as broccoli flowerets, cucumber, carrot and celery sticks, radishes, Belgian endive leaves

1. Combine the sour cream, white part of the green onion, egg whites and 1 tablespoon each of the salmon and black caviars in a bowl. Spoon the dip into a shallow serving dish at least 7 inches in diameter.
2. Spoon the remaining caviars, green onion and egg yolks on top of the sour cream mixture in a decorative design. Cover and refrigerate until serving time. Serve with assorted vegetables.

Caviar Dip, made from red and black caviar smoothed with sour cream, turns vegetables into something special.

Make this cheese ball ahead of time to mellow the flavors and then refrigerate or freeze. If it is not eaten up completely, just press the leftovers together to make a smaller ball and refrigerate for your next unexpected guests.

Makes one 3-cup ball.

Nutrient Value Per Tablespoon: 128 calories, 5 g protein, 11 g fat, 2 g carbohydrate, 171 mg sodium, 27 mg cholesterol.

1   package (10 ounces) sharp Cheddar cheese, cut in pieces
1   package (8 ounces) cream cheese, cut in pieces
4   ounces blue cheese, crumbled
1   teaspoon grated onion
1/2 teaspoon Worcestershire sauce
1/2 teaspoon liquid red-pepper seasoning
1/4 teaspoon dry mustard
1   cup pecan halves

1. Combine the Cheddar cheese, cream cheese and blue cheese in the work bowl of a food processor. Cover and whirl until well mixed. Add the onion, Worcestershire sauce, liquid red-pepper seasoning and mustard and whirl until well mixed. Transfer the cheese mixture to a piece of wax paper. Wrap and refrigerate the cheese mixture until firm.
2. Shape the cheese into a ball. Press the pecan halves into the outside of the ball. Cover the ball and refrigerate until serving time.
3. Place the ball on a serving tray and serve with crisp crackers.

Tuna Spread

Curried Crab Appetizers

8   cloves garlic, peeled
2   cans (6½ ounces each)
     chunk light tuna packed in
     oil, drained
3   tablespoons olive oil
3   flat anchovies
1   tablespoon Dijon-style
     mustard
1   tablespoon lemon juice
⅛   teaspoon ground hot red
     pepper
¼   cup dairy sour cream
4   teaspoons small capers,
     rinsed

1. Blanch the garlic in a small saucepan of boiling water for 4 minutes. Drain the garlic.
2. Combine the blanched garlic, tuna, oil, anchovies, mustard, lemon juice and ground hot red pepper in the work bowl of a food processor or, working in batches, in an electric blender. Cover and whirl until smooth. Transfer the tuna mixture to a small bowl.
3. Stir the sour cream and the capers into the tuna mixture. Refrigerate the spread, covered, until chilled. Serve the spread with bread or crackers.

The crab mixture can be prepared several hours in advance. Remove the mixture from the refrigerator 15 minutes before serving.

1   tablespoon butter
¼   cup finely chopped green
     onion
1   teaspoon curry powder
½   pound lump or backfin
     crabmeat, picked over OR:
     ½ pound imitation
     crabmeat, flaked
½   cup mayonnaise
1   teaspoon lemon juice
     Assorted crackers
     Sliced tops of green onions,
     for garnish *(optional)*

1. Melt the butter in a small saucepan. Add the green onion and the curry powder and sauté for 1 minute over medium heat. Stir in the crabmeat, mayonnaise and lemon juice. Remove the saucepan from the heat.
2. To serve, spread 1 tablespoon of the crab mixture on each cracker. Sprinkle with sliced green onion, if you wish.

Gorgonzola Spread

The tangy taste of Gorgonzola and the crunch of fresh red and green peppers combine beautifully in this molded, make-ahead spread. The spread can be made the day before.

Makes about 5½ cups.

Nutrient Value Per Tablespoon: 28 calories, 1 g protein, 3 g fat, 0 g carbohydrate, 60 mg sodium, 8 mg cholesterol.

1   envelope unflavored gelatin
1   cup chicken broth
½   pound Gorgonzola cheese
2   packages (8 ounces each) cream cheese, softened
¾   cup thinly sliced green onion
¾   cup finely chopped sweet red pepper (1 medium-size)
¾   cup finely chopped sweet green pepper (1 medium-size)
1   round slice sweet red pepper, for garnish *(optional)*
    Thinly sliced green onion (green part only), for garnish *(optional)*
    Party-size rye bread or assorted crackers

1. Lightly grease a 6-cup mold. Sprinkle the gelatin over the chicken broth in a small saucepan. Let the gelatin soften for 5 minutes. Gently warm the gelatin mixture over low heat, stirring, until the gelatin is melted, for about 3 minutes. Cool the gelatin mixture.
2. Combine the Gorgonzola and cream cheese in a large bowl. Beat the cheeses with an electric mixer on medium speed until the cheeses are well blended and smooth. Stir the gelatin mixture into the cheese mixture.
3. Stir the green onion and the red and green peppers into the cheese mixture. Pour the spread into the greased mold. Refrigerate the spread until set, for 4 hours or overnight. To serve, unmold the spread onto a serving plate. Garnish with a round red pepper slice and sliced green onion, if you wish. Serve the spread with party-size rye bread or assorted crackers.

QUICK TIP

The Soft Touch
To quickly soften cream cheese, immerse the unopened package in very warm tap water for 3 to 5 minutes. Check periodically to see if it's soft enough for use by pressing through the wrapping.

203

Mexican Seafood Mousse

This zippy Mexican-inspired spread is made with poached scallops and fish, and it can be made a day ahead.

Makes about 3½ cups.

Nutrient Value Per Tablespoon: 23 calories, 2 g protein, 2 g fat, 0 g carbohydrate, 34 mg sodium, 10 mg cholesterol.

⅓ cup dry white wine
1¼ cups water
½ pound sea scallops
½ pound catfish fillets, thawed if frozen OR: other firm white fish fillets, such as sea bass
1 envelope unflavored gelatin
2 tablespoons fresh lime juice
½ teaspoon salt
1 to 2 tablespoons finely chopped, seeded, canned mild jalapeño peppers
2 to 3 tablespoons chopped fresh cilantro (coriander)
2 to 3 tablespoons finely chopped red onion
  Nonstick vegetable cooking spray
1 cup heavy cream
  Cornmeal Pancakes *(recipe, page 205)*

1. Heat the wine and 1 cup of the water to boiling in a large skillet. Add the scallops, lower the heat and poach the scallops just until firm, for about 1 minute, turning the scallops once. Remove the scallops with a slotted spoon to paper toweling to drain. Add the fish to the skillet and poach until the fish flakes easily, turning the fish once. Drain the fish, reserving ½ cup of the poaching liquid.

2. Sprinkle the gelatin over the remaining ¼ cup of water in a small saucepan. Let the saucepan stand for 5 minutes for the gelatin to soften. Add the reserved poaching liquid. Heat the liquid to dissolve the gelatin. Pour the liquid into the container of a food processor or an electric blender. Remove any tough gristle from the side of each scallop. Remove any bones from the fish, if necessary. Add the seafood, lime juice and salt to the gelatin mixture. Process or blend until the mixture is smooth, for about 1 minute, stopping once and scraping down the side of the bowl.

3. Transfer the seafood mixture to a bowl. Stir in the jalapeño pepper, cilantro and onion until all the ingredients are well mixed. Cover the bowl and refrigerate just until the mixture is slightly thickened.

4. Meanwhile, lightly oil or spray a 1-quart metal mold with nonstick vegetable cooking spray. Beat the cream in a small bowl until stiff. Fold the beaten cream into the seafood mixture and pour the mixture into the oiled mold. Cover the mousse and refrigerate overnight.

5. Just before serving, dip the mold into warm water. Unmold the mousse onto a serving plate. Surround the mousse with the Cornmeal Pancakes.

QUICK TIP

For Whom The Gel Molds

When a gelatin mixture becomes too firm beyond the mounding stage to add any additional ingredients, set the bowl in a larger bowl containing a little warm water. Beat the gelatin mixture with a wire whisk until smooth. Chill the mixture again if necessary to reach the right consistency for adding more ingredients.

Cornmeal Pancakes

Guacamole Smoked Salmon Dip

Makes about 3 to 4 dozen 2-inch pancakes.

Nutrient Value Per Pancake: 30 calories, 1 g protein, 1 g fat, 4 g carbohydrate, 51 mg sodium, 8 mg cholesterol.

A perennial favorite gets extra flavor with the addition of smoked salmon.

Makes about 3 cups.

Nutrient Value Per ¼ Cup: 92 calories, 3 g protein, 8 g fat, 3 g carbohydrate, 597 mg sodium, 6 mg cholesterol.

¾	cup yellow cornmeal
1	tablespoon sugar
½	teaspoon salt
¾	cup boiling water
⅓	cup all-purpose flour
1½	teaspoons baking powder
⅓	cup milk
1½	tablespoons vegetable oil
1	egg
1	to 2 tablespoons vegetable oil for cooking

1. Combine the cornmeal, sugar and salt in a medium-size bowl. Stir in the boiling water. Cover the bowl and let stand for 10 minutes.
2. Sift together the flour and the baking powder. Stir together the milk, the 1½ tablespoons of oil and the egg in a small bowl. Add the milk mixture along with the flour mixture to the cornmeal mixture, stirring just until the dry ingredients are moistened. (The batter will be lumpy.)
3. Heat 1 tablespoon of the remaining oil in a large skillet over medium heat. Drop the batter by heaping measuring teaspoonfuls into the hot skillet. Cook the pancakes until tiny holes form on the top edge of the cakes. Flip the pancakes over and cook for 15 seconds longer. Remove the pancakes to a platter and keep warm while repeating with the remaining batter. Brush additional oil on the skillet, if necessary.

3	small ripe avocados
3	tablespoons lemon juice
⅓	cup dairy sour cream
½	teaspoon pepper
4	ounces thinly sliced smoked salmon
	Crisp crackers

1. Halve the avocados and remove the pit. Scoop out the avocado flesh from the skin into the workbowl of a food processor. Cover and whirl until smooth. (You should have about 2 cups of purée.)
2. Transfer the purée to a medium-size bowl and stir in the lemon juice, sour cream and pepper. Chop the smoked salmon and stir into the avocado mixture. Place a piece of plastic wrap directly on the surface of the dip. Refrigerate the dip until serving time. Serve the dip with crisp crackers.

Note: This dip can be frozen for up to 2 weeks.

205

Wild Mushroom Spread

Wild mushrooms, now available in many markets, add a wonderful, woodsy flavor when added to the white cultivated mushrooms.

Makes about 2 cups.

Nutrient Value Per Tablespoon: 29 calories, 1 g protein, 2 g fat, 2 g carbohydrate, 23 mg sodium, 7 mg cholesterol.

1   **ounce dried wild mushrooms (such as cèpes, porcini or shiitake) OR: ¼ pound fresh wild mushrooms**
12   **ounces fresh white mushrooms**
¼   **cup (½ stick) butter or margarine**
1   **large onion, chopped**
½   **teaspoon leaf thyme, crumbled**
½   **teaspoon salt**
½   **teaspoon white pepper**
2   **tablespoons brandy**
1   **package (3 ounces) cream cheese, cut into chunks**
1   **teaspoon lemon juice Assorted sliced vegetables, such as cucumber, cauliflower, radishes, carrots, zucchini and sweet pepper**

1. If using dried mushrooms, soak them in boiling water to cover in a small bowl for about 30 minutes. Drain the mushrooms, squeeze dry and trim off any tough stems. If using fresh wild mushrooms, rinse and pat dry. Trim and quarter the white mushrooms.
2. Melt the butter or margarine in a 10-inch skillet over medium heat. Add the onion and sauté for 5 minutes or until softened. Add the white mushrooms and the wild mushrooms and sauté for 5 minutes longer. Stir in the thyme, salt, white pepper and brandy. Reduce the heat to low, cover the skillet and cook for 5 minutes. Uncover the skillet and, if there is liquid, cook until all the liquid evaporates.
3. Combine the mushroom mixture, cream cheese and lemon juice in the work bowl of a food processor. Cover and whirl until smooth, scraping down the side of the work bowl as necessary. Transfer the spread to a small serving bowl. Cover the bowl and refrigerate overnight.
4. To serve, place the bowl of mushroom spread on a serving tray. Surround the spread with the sliced vegetables.

QUICK TIP

Much Ado About Mushrooms
When you're buying fresh mushrooms, look for caps that are tightly closed so that the gills on the underside are not visible. Avoid wilted, shriveled, slimy or brown mushrooms. Mushrooms are highly perishable. Store them, unwashed, in an open or ventilated container.
To Prepare:
Mushrooms should be washed quickly in a bowl of cold water. Drain and pat them dry. Wash only the mushrooms you are going to use; never soak them. If the bottom of the stem is dry, trim away a thin slice.

Cucumber Mustard Dip

Zippy Tuna Dip

Hot peppers provide the zip.

Makes about 2 cups.

Nutrient Value Per 2 Tablespoons:
70 calories, 5 g protein, 5 g fat, 0 g carbohydrate, 130 mg sodium, 8 mg cholesterol.

2   cans (6½ ounces each) tuna
¼   cup mayonnaise
¼   cup plain yogurt
2   tablespoons chopped black olives
1   tablespoon finely chopped canned jalapeño peppers
1   tablespoon finely chopped green onion
½   teaspoon dried cilantro (coriander), crumbled
    Tortilla chips

1. Drain the tuna and break it up into flakes. Gently stir together the tuna, mayonnaise, yogurt, olives, jalapeño pepper, green onion and cilantro in a serving bowl. Cover the bowl and refrigerate until serving time.
2. Serve the dip with the tortilla chips.

Delicious as a party dip, and low-calorie, too.

Makes 1½ cups.

Nutrient Value Per Tablespoon:
19 calories, 0 g protein, 2 g fat, 1 g carbohydrate, 48 mg sodium, 2 mg cholesterol.

1   medium-size cucumber, peeled, halved, seeded and coarsely chopped
½   cup nonfat plain yogurt
½   cup reduced-calorie mayonnaise
1   tablespoon grainy coarse mustard
1   tablespoon snipped fresh dill OR: 1 teaspoon dried dillweed
1½ teaspoons lemon juice
⅛   teaspoon black pepper
    An assortment of vegetables

1. Add the cucumber pieces to the container of a food processor. Cover and whirl until the cucumber is finely chopped. Add ¼ cup of the yogurt, cover and whirl until smooth. Turn the mixture into a small bowl.
2. Stir in the remaining ¼ cup of yogurt, the mayonnaise, mustard, dill, lemon juice and black pepper. Serve the dip with the assorted vegetables.

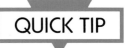
QUICK TIP

Dramatic Presentation
The vivid colors of freshly prepared vegetables are attractive on a buffet table. Mason jars, unusual cut-glass bowls and antique crocks all make interesting containers for fresh crudités or marinated vegetables. Offer fresh raw vegetables in a clay flowerpot or in a basket lined with fresh lettuce leaves. Use raw vegetables for dip containers: hollow out cabbages, tomatoes and peppers, fill them with dip and surround them with fresh vegetables.

Eggplant Hors d'Oeuvre

Make a day before: Eggplant Hors d'Oeuvre tastes even better as flavors blend.

While the eggplant flavor dominates, it is the marinated artichoke hearts that contribute the pizzazz to this delectable dish. Refrigerate for 6 hours or up to 1 day to blend the flavors.

Bake at 350° for 1 hour.
Makes about 3 cups.

Nutrient Value Per Tablespoon: 16 calories, 0 g protein, 1 g fat, 1 g carbohydrate, 49 mg sodium, 0 mg cholesterol.

1 **medium-size eggplant (about 1½ pounds)**
1 **medium-size tomato, peeled, seeded and diced**
2 **ribs celery, chopped**
1 **small onion, chopped**
1 **jar (6 ounces) marinated artichoke hearts, cut up (reserve marinade)**
1 **jar (2½ ounces) sliced mushrooms, drained OR: 6 fresh mushrooms, sliced**
12 **cocktail onions (from a 3-ounce jar), halved**
12 **pimiento-stuffed olives (from a 5-ounce jar), halved**
2 **tablespoons drained capers**
1 **clove garlic, mashed**
¼ **cup red wine vinegar**
2 **tablespoons olive oil**
2 **tablespoons lemon juice**
1 **tablespoon chopped fresh oregano OR: 1 teaspoon leaf oregano, crumbled**
Salt and pepper, to taste
Romaine lettuce leaves
Pitted ripe olive, for garnish (optional)
Party-size bread or assorted crackers

Olive Spread

1. Preheat the oven to moderate (350°).
2. Pierce the eggplant in several places with a fork. Place the eggplant on an aluminum foil-lined cookie sheet.
3. Bake the eggplant in the preheated moderate oven (350°) for 1 hour or until the eggplant is softened. Let the eggplant stand until cool enough to handle.
4. Peel the eggplant, then coarsely chop the pulp. Place the pulp in the container of an electric blender or a food processor. Cover and whirl until the pulp is coarsely chopped. (A little texture is nice, so avoid overprocessing.) Transfer the eggplant to a medium-size bowl.
5. Add the tomato, celery, onion, artichoke hearts and reserved marinade, the mushrooms, cocktail onions, olives, capers and garlic to the eggplant, stirring to blend well.
6. Combine the vinegar, oil, lemon juice, oregano, salt and pepper in a small bowl, stirring to blend well. Add the vinegar mixture to the eggplant mixture, mixing gently but thoroughly. Cover the bowl with plastic wrap and chill for at least 6 hours or up to 1 day to blend the flavors.
7. To serve, mound the eggplant mixture in a serving bowl lined with the romaine lettuce leaves. Garnish the eggplant mixture with a pitted ripe olive, if you wish. Serve with sliced party-size bread or assorted crackers.

Bake garlic at 375° for 45 to 60 minutes.
Makes 1¾ to 2 cups.

Nutrient Value Per Tablespoon: 50 calories, 0 g protein, 5 g fat, 1 g carbohydrate, 107 mg sodium, 0 mg cholesterol.

1	whole head garlic (not 1 clove)
1	can (7 ounces net weight) pitted ripe olives
1	jar (2½ ounces net weight) pitted Spanish olives
¼	to ½ cup olive oil
1	tablespoon grated orange rind
2	tablespoons orange juice
1	tablespoon lemon juice
½	teaspoon fennel seeds
1	tablespoon chopped fresh parsley
	Bread or assorted crackers

1. Preheat the oven to 375°.
2. Peel off the loose papery skin from the garlic head, leaving the cloves intact. Wrap the head in aluminum foil and place in a small baking pan.
3. Bake the garlic in the oven (375°) until it is very soft, for 45 to 60 minutes. With fingers and a pot holder, gently squeeze the foil package; if it gives easily, the garlic is done. When the garlic has cooled, unwrap it. Pinch the cloves to squeeze the garlic paste into a bowl.
4. Working in batches, combine the ripe and Spanish olives, oil, orange rind, orange and lemon juices, fennel seeds and garlic paste in a food processor or an electric blender. Whirl until the mixture is coarsely chopped (chunky, not smooth) and combined. Stir in the parsley. Serve at room temperature with bread or crackers.

QUICK TIP

Eggplant Expertise
To pick the perfect eggplant, find one that is firm and heavy in relation to its size, with a uniformly dark, rich purple color. Use it as quickly as possible after purchasing.

Do-Ahead
Hors d'Oeuvres

Pepper Apricot Chutney

Serve this hot and spicy chutney "as is" on crackers or toast, or mix 2 tablespoons of the chutney into 3 ounces of cream cheese for a delicious variation.

Makes 4 cups.

Nutrient Value Per Tablespoon: 35 calories, 0 g protein, 0 g fat, 9 g carbohydrate, 53 mg sodium, 0 mg cholesterol.

1¼ **pounds sweet red peppers, cored, seeded and cut into ¼-inch dice (3 cups)**
12 **ounces dried apricots, cut into ¼-inch dice**
1 **cup raisins**
1 **large onion, finely chopped (1 cup)**
5 **cloves garlic, thinly slivered**
1 **3-inch piece fresh gingerroot, peeled and thinly slivered (3 tablespoons)**
1½ **teaspoons salt**
1 **to 1½ teaspoons crushed red pepper flakes, or to taste**
1 **teaspoon cumin seeds**
¾ **teaspoon mustard seeds**
1 **cup sugar**
¾ **cup red wine vinegar**

1. Combine the red peppers, apricots, raisins, onion, garlic, gingerroot, salt, red pepper flakes, cumin seeds, mustard seeds and sugar in a large saucepan. Cook the mixture, uncovered, stirring occasionally, over medium heat until the sugar dissolves, for about 5 minutes.
2. Add the vinegar to the saucepan. Cook the chutney, stirring often, until the mixture is shiny and thick, for 30 to 35 minutes. Cool the chutney. Cover and refrigerate.

Menu Idea
Do-Ahead Hors d'Oeuvres for 24 Guests:
Pepper Apricot Chutney*
Egg Roulade* *(recipe, page 212)*
Baked Sweet Pepper Wedges* *(recipe, page 213)*
Mushroom Turnovers* *(recipe, page 214)*
Salmon Pâté *(recipe, page 215)*

QUICK TIPS

Buffet Savvy
● The buffet table should have plenty of space for guests to flow around it freely.
● Arrange the table for easy serving and carrying: first plates, then food, then tableware and napkins.
● Wrap each set of tableware in a napkin.
● Place the proper serving utensils next to each dish.
● Be sure to provide adequate seating and table space.
● If you seat guests at the dining table, set the table with napkins and tableware so guests won't have to pick them up from the buffet.

Do-Ahead Hors d'Oeuvres for 24 Guests (counterclockwise from upper right): Pepper Apricot Chutney, served with cream cheese and crackers; Salmon Pâté (page 215); Mushroom Turnovers (page 214); Sesame Shrimp (page 216); Baked Sweet Pepper Wedges (page 213); and Egg Roulade (page 212).

Egg Roulade

The roulade can be served chilled or at room temperature.

**Bake at 400° for 15 minutes.
Makes 16 servings.**

*Nutrient Value Per Serving:
145 calories, 8 g protein, 10 g fat, 5 g carbohydrate, 217 mg sodium, 22 mg cholesterol.*

Filling:
- 1 medium-size onion, finely chopped (½ cup)
- 2 tablespoons olive oil
- 1 medium-size sweet red pepper, cored, seeded and cut into ½-inch dice
- 1 package (10 ounces) frozen chopped spinach, thawed and squeezed dry
- 1 teaspoon grated lemon rind
- ¼ teaspoon salt
- ⅛ teaspoon sugar
- ⅛ teaspoon pepper
- ¾ cup ricotta cheese, drained

Roulade:
- ¼ cup (½ stick) unsalted butter
- ⅓ cup *un*sifted all-purpose flour
- 1⅓ cups milk, warmed
- ¼ teaspoon pepper
- 6 eggs, separated
- 1¼ cups grated Parmesan cheese

QUICK TIP

Eggs-pert Separation
Eggs separate most easily when cold since the whites hold together better. However, after separating the whites from the yolks, the whites should be brought to room temperature for maximum volume when beating. (Avoid getting any of the yolk mixed with the whites since the fat from the yolk will decrease the volume of the beaten whites.)

1. Prepare the Filling: Sauté the onion in the oil in a large skillet, stirring often, until the onion is soft and golden, for about 8 minutes. Add the red pepper and cook for 4 minutes longer. Add the spinach, lemon rind, salt, sugar and pepper. Transfer the mixture to a medium-size bowl. Stir in the ricotta cheese. Set the bowl aside.
2. Preheat the oven to hot (400°). Grease the bottom of a 15½ x 10½-inch jelly-roll pan. Line the bottom with wax paper; grease and lightly flour the paper, tapping out any excess flour. Set the pan aside.
3. Prepare the Roulade: Melt the butter in a heavy saucepan over low heat. Stir in the flour. Cook, stirring, until the mixture is smooth and lightly colored. Gradually whisk in the warm milk. Cook, stirring, over medium heat until the mixture is quite thick, for 4 to 5 minutes. Stir in the pepper. Remove the saucepan from the heat.
4. Beat the egg yolks, one at a time, into the milk mixture. Stir in ¾ cup of the Parmesan cheese. Transfer the mixture to a large bowl.
5. Beat the egg whites in a large bowl until stiff, but glossy, peaks form. Carefully fold the beaten whites into the milk mixture. Spoon the roulade batter into the prepared pan, smoothing the top with a spatula. Sprinkle the top of the roulade evenly with the remaining ½ cup of Parmesan cheese.

Baked Sweet Pepper Wedges

6. Bake the roulade in the preheated hot oven (400°) for 15 minutes or until golden and a cake tester inserted in the center comes out clean. Carefully invert the roulade onto a kitchen towel or a piece of wax paper. Remove the wax paper from the top of the roulade. Starting with a long side of the roulade, roll up the roulade and the towel together. Place the roll, seam side down, on a wire rack. Cool the roulade at room temperature for 20 minutes.

7. Unroll the roulade and remove the towel. Spread the spinach filling down the length of the roulade, leaving a 2-inch border on one long side and a 1-inch border at each short end. Roll up the roulade, jelly-roll fashion, from the long side without a border. Wrap the roulade tightly with plastic wrap and refrigerate. Unwrap the roulade to serve chilled or at room temperature. Cut the roulade crosswise into slices.

Wedges can be assembled ahead, then baked just before serving.

Bake at 375° for 35 to 40 minutes.
Makes 24 wedges.

Nutrient Value Per Wedge:
49 calories, 1 g protein, 4 g fat,
3 g carbohydrate, 149 mg
sodium, 0 mg cholesterol.

2	medium-size sweet red peppers
2	medium-size sweet yellow peppers
1	medium-size onion, finely chopped
1	can (28 ounces) crushed tomatoes, well drained
¼	cup chopped fresh parsley
¼	cup plus 2 tablespoons olive oil
3	tablespoons pine nuts (pignoli)
4	cloves garlic, finely chopped
1	teaspoon salt
¼	teaspoon pepper, or to taste
¼	cup fresh bread crumbs

1. Preheat the oven to moderate (375°). Lightly oil a 13 x 9-inch baking pan.

2. Trim tops off the peppers. Discard stems; finely chop tops. Cut peppers lengthwise into sixths. Place wedges, cut side up, in the oiled pan; set aside.

3. Combine pepper tops, onion, tomatoes, parsley, ¼ cup oil, pine nuts, garlic, salt and pepper in a bowl; stir well. Spoon into the pepper wedges.

4. Bake wedges in the preheated moderate oven (375°) for 25 to 30 minutes or until just tender. Sprinkle bread crumbs and remaining 2 tablespoons oil over wedges. Bake for 10 minutes longer. Serve warm.

QUICK TIP

Crumbs At Hand
Store your homemade bread crumbs in an empty salt carton — it's easier to pour out the exact amount and cuts down on mess. Feed the crumbs through a funnel into the carton and store in the freezer.

Mushroom Turnovers

The turnovers can be served at room temperature, reheated or baked at the last minute before serving.

Bake nuts at 350° for 10 minutes; bake turnovers at 375° for 12 to 15 minutes.
Makes 32 turnovers.

Nutrient Value Per Turnover: 74 calories, 1 g protein, 5 g fat, 6 g carbohydrate, 72 mg sodium, 11 mg cholesterol.

½   cup pecans (about 2 ounces)
3   medium-size leeks, well washed and finely diced (1½ cups)
3½   tablespoons butter
1   pound mushrooms, trimmed, halved and thinly sliced (about 5 cups)
1½   tablespoons chopped fresh mint OR: 1 teaspoon dried mint
½   teaspoon salt
¼   teaspoon pepper
½   cup dairy sour cream
8   13 x 9-inch sheets phyllo dough (from 8-ounce package)
6   tablespoons melted butter

1. Preheat the oven to moderate (350°).
2. Bake the pecans on a cookie sheet in the preheated moderate oven (350°) until they are toasted, for about 10 minutes. Cool the pecans. Coarsely chop the pecans. Raise the oven temperature to 375°. Place an oven rack in the lowest position.
3. Sauté the leeks in 2½ tablespoons of the butter in a large, heavy skillet over medium heat until the leeks are soft and lightly browned, for about 20 minutes. Add the mushrooms and the remaining 1 tablespoon of butter. Cook the mixture until the mushrooms are soft and the moisture has evaporated, for about 15 minutes longer. Stir in the mint, salt and pepper. Remove the skillet from the heat and stir in the sour cream and the reserved pecans. Cool the mixture slightly.
4. Lightly grease a cookie sheet.
5. Working with one sheet of phyllo at a time, and keeping the others covered with plastic wrap to prevent them from drying out, brush a sheet with the melted butter. Cut the sheet lengthwise into 4 equal pieces. Place a measuring tablespoonful of the filling on the bottom corner of one strip, leaving a 1-inch bottom border. Fold the corner up and over the filling to form a triangle, then fold the triangle up and over. Keep flipping the triangle up and over to the end of the strip. Trim off any excess dough. Repeat making the triangles with the remaining phyllo and filling.
6. Place the turnovers on the prepared cookie sheet. Lightly brush the turnovers with the melted butter.
7. Bake the turnovers in the preheated moderate oven (375°) until crisp and golden, for 12 to 15 minutes.

Salmon Pâté

This mixture keeps for a week in the refrigerator. Serve with toast or cucumber rounds.

Makes 3½ cups.

Nutrient Value Per Tablespoon: 52 calories, 2 g protein, 5 g fat, 0 g carbohydrate, 96 mg sodium, 16 mg cholesterol.

¼	cup heavy cream
¼	cup dairy sour cream
3	cups cold water
1	carrot, peeled and thinly sliced
1	small onion, thinly sliced
1	bay leaf
3	thin lemon slices
1	fresh red chili pepper
1	pound fresh salmon fillets, with skin
4	shallots, finely chopped
1½	tablespoons plus ½ cup (1 stick) unsalted butter, at room temperature
8	ounces smoked salmon, diced
2	tablespoons lemon juice
1½	teaspoons salt
¼	teaspoon white pepper
1	tablespoon finely chopped fresh dill, plus a few sprigs for garnish
	Whole bay leaf and small sweet red pepper strips, for garnish *(optional)*
6	tablespoons butter, clarified*

1. Whisk together the heavy cream and the sour cream in a small bowl. Refrigerate.
2. Combine the cold water, carrot, onion, bay leaf, lemon slices and red chili pepper in a skillet large enough to hold the salmon fillets in one layer. Bring the mixture to boiling; continue to boil for 10 minutes. Lower the heat to a simmer. Add the salmon fillets, skin side up. Simmer very gently over medium-low heat until the salmon is just cooked, for about 10 minutes. (Do not overcook.) Remove the salmon from the poaching liquid. Remove the skin from the salmon and discard. Cool the salmon completely.
3. Sauté the shallots in the 1½ tablespoons of butter in a small skillet over medium heat, stirring, until golden, for about 5 minutes. Transfer the shallots to the bowl of a food processor.
4. Add the salmon fillets, smoked salmon and heavy cream mixture to the bowl of the food processor. Cover and whirl until smooth. With the processor running, add the remaining ½ cup of butter, bit by bit, until the mixture is a smooth purée. Add the lemon juice, salt and white pepper. Fold in the dill.
5. Spoon the pâté mixture into a 4-cup soufflé dish or a decorative serving dish. Smooth the top with a rubber spatula. Garnish the pâté with a few fresh dill sprigs, a whole bay leaf and small sweet red pepper strips, if you wish. Pour the clarified butter over the top of the pâté to cover it completely. Refrigerate the pâté for 4 hours to set it.

*Note: To clarify butter, melt the 6 tablespoons of butter in a saucepan over medium heat. Remove the saucepan from the heat and skim off the foam from the top. With a small ladle, spoon the clear liquid butter into a dish, leaving the milky solids behind. Discard the milky solids. Use the clear or clarified butter.

Sesame Shrimp

The marinade and the dipping sauce can be made ahead.

Makes 38 appetizers.

Nutrient Value Per Serving:
47 calories, 5 g protein, 2 g fat,
1 g carbohydrate, 106 mg
sodium, 7 mg cholesterol.

Marinade:
- 2 tablespoons sesame seeds
- 1 2½-inch piece fresh gingerroot, peeled and coarsely chopped
- 1 tablespoon rice wine vinegar
- 1 tablespoon Oriental sesame oil*
- ¼ cup cold water
- 2 teaspoons honey
- ½ teaspoon salt
- ⅛ teaspoon ground hot red pepper

2½ pounds large shrimp (about 38), shelled and deveined (2 pounds cleaned)

Dipping Sauce:
- 2 tablespoons honey
- 2 tablespoons rice wine vinegar
- 2 tablespoons soy sauce
- 4 teaspoons Oriental sesame oil*
- ½ teaspoon Dijon-style mustard

3 tablespoons peanut oil for cooking shrimp

1. Prepare the Marinade: Combine the sesame seeds and the gingerroot in the container of an electric blender or food processor. Cover and whirl until the mixture is blended. Add the vinegar, sesame oil, cold water, honey, salt and ground hot red pepper. Whirl until the mixture is blended.
2. Transfer the marinade to a large bowl. Add the shrimp and toss to coat the shrimp well. Cover the bowl with plastic wrap and marinate the shrimp in the refrigerator for 45 minutes but no longer than 60 minutes.
3. Prepare the Dipping Sauce: Whisk together the honey, vinegar, soy sauce, Oriental sesame oil and mustard in a small bowl. Reserve.
4. To cook the shrimp, heat the peanut oil in a large skillet over medium-high heat. Working in batches, lift the shrimp from the marinade with a slotted spoon or spatula to the skillet. Sauté the shrimp until they just begin to curl, for 1 to 3 minutes. Serve the shrimp with the Dipping Sauce.

*Note: Oriental sesame oil is richer in flavor and darker in color than regular sesame oil. It can be found in the Oriental food section of many supermarkets or in Oriental specialty food stores.

QUICK TIP

Easy Appetizers
For no-fuss, fancy hors d'oeuvres: Wrap pineapple chunks or water chestnuts in bacon and fasten them with wooden picks. Place them on paper toweling and microwave on high until the bacon is fully cooked.

Planning A Party?

This party planner will help space out your chores so you aren't too exhausted to enjoy your own get-together!

Once you've decided how many people to invite and have planned your menu, it's time to make lists.
List #1: Food: Include everything from snacks — mints and nuts — and "real" food (such as casseroles) to the ingredients needed for all the recipes. Divide the list into two columns: non-perishables and perishables.
List #2: Beverages: Liquor, mixers, juice, soda (have plenty on hand for nondrinkers), coffee, tea.
List #3: Nonfood Items: Cocktail napkins, plastic glasses, dripless candles, ice, flowers or centerpieces.

One Week Before
1. Order the ice, liquor, non-alcoholic drinks, flowers.
2. Shop for the nonperishable foods on List #1.
3. Buy everything for List #3 except the ice and flowers.

Four Days Before
4. Select the serving dishes you'll use; set them aside in your cupboard. Need more? Ask a friend *now.*
5. Check tablecloths, napkins, place mats; wash and press if needed.
6. Make sure you have enough silver, ashtrays, vases, pitchers, etc.

Three Days Before
7. Do the heavy cleaning, such as floors and walls, and tidy up the house. Have the whole family pitch in.
8. Decide where guests' coats will go. If in a closet, have enough hangers on hand.

Two Days Before
9. Buy the perishable foods on List #1. Wash and trim the vegetables and refrigerate.

One Day Before
10. Make extra ice, if needed.
11. Prepare the dishes that can be reheated or served cold.

"The" Day
12. Give the house a once-over in the morning. (If your bedroom is the coat room, neaten it *now.*)
13. Pick up the flowers, ice.
14. Use "kid power" to help clean; set out ashtrays and guest soaps.
15. Arrange the flowers and candles; set up the eating areas and bar.
16. Assemble the ingredients for the dishes that must be cooked that day.
17. Take a deep breath and begin!

Cocktail Party Pluses

When it comes to flexibility — and fun — nothing beats a cocktail party. The menu can be as varied or as simple as you like, depending upon your life style, your guest list and your budget. A nice feature of this kind of entertaining: Because much of the work can be done in advance, you can be a "guest" too, spending time with your friends instead of being tied to the kitchen. For a special look: Spruce up the food with sprigs of rosemary, basil, savory or other herbs; a tiered silver plate stand makes an extra-special serving display; paper and cloth doilies dress up any table. And a garland of ivy around your buffet table can add an inexpensive touch of elegance to charm any guest.

Beverages
for the Party

Berry Punch

Spiced Mocha Mix

Strawberries and cranberry juice flavor this punch.

Makes 32 half-cup servings.

Nutrient Value Per Serving: 71 calories, 0 g protein, 0 g fat, 18 g carbohydrate, 4 mg sodium, 0 mg cholesterol.

Makes 1⅔ cups dry mix (enough for about 8 drinks).

Nutrient Value Per 8-Ounce Drink: 80 calories, 1 g protein, 1 g fat, 20 g carbohydrate, 5 mg sodium, 0 mg cholesterol.

- 1 **package (10 ounces) frozen strawberries in syrup, thawed**
- 1 **can (12 ounces) frozen cranberry-raspberry juice cocktail concentrate**
- 1 **can (12 ounces) frozen lemonade concentrate**
- 1 **bottle (1 liter) ginger ale, chilled**
- 1 **bottle (2 liters) seltzer, chilled**
  Strawberries and cranberries, for garnish *(optional)*

- ½ **cup instant coffee powder or crystals**
- ½ **cup firmly packed dark brown sugar**
- ¼ **cup granulated sugar**
- ¼ **cup unsweetened cocoa powder**
- 1 **teaspoon ground cinnamon**
- ½ **teaspoon ground nutmeg**

1. Place the strawberries with their syrup in the container of an electric blender. Cover and whirl until puréed. (The purée can be prepared ahead and refrigerated.)
2. Just before serving, combine the puréed strawberries, the cranberry-raspberry concentrate, lemonade concentrate and ginger ale in a 6-quart bowl or punch bowl. Stir in the seltzer and serve from a pitcher or punch bowl in glasses, with a garnish of skewered strawberries and cranberries if you wish.

1. Combine the coffee powder or crystals, brown sugar, granulated sugar, cocoa powder, cinnamon and nutmeg in a medium-size bowl until well mixed.
2. Spoon the dry mix into a container with a tight-fitting lid. Cover the container and store the mix at room temperature for up to 2 months.
3. To reconstitute the mix for a hot drink, add 3 level measuring tablespoonfuls of the mix to 8 ounces of boiling water in a heatproof mug. Stir until the mix is completely dissolved.

This nonalcoholic Berry Punch is loaded with fruity flavor and is perfect for any festive occasion.

Very Berry Lemonade

(Counterclockwise from bottom right): Cool down with a glass full of Very Berry Lemonade, a raspberry lemon combo, or a tingly Apple Apricot Spritzer (page 221) made with apricot nectar and sparkling cider. Watermelon Ice (page 263) is a slushy sweet treat.

Makes 6 servings.

Nutrient Value Per Serving:
148 calories, 0 g protein, 0 g fat,
38 g carbohydrate, 1 mg
sodium, 0 mg cholesterol.

5	**cups water**
1	**cup sugar**
3	**sprigs fresh mint *(optional)***
1½	**cups fresh or dry-pack frozen raspberries**
½	**cup fresh lemon juice**
	Ice
	Lemon slices, for garnish *(optional)*

1. Combine the water and the sugar in a large saucepan. Bring the liquid to boiling over high heat, stirring to dissolve the sugar. Remove the saucepan from the heat and add the mint, if you wish. Chill the syrup for 1 hour.

2. Remove the mint, if used. Combine the raspberries and 1 cup of the sugar syrup in the container of an electric blender. Cover and whirl until puréed. Strain the purée into a 1½- to 2-quart pitcher. Add the remaining syrup and the lemon juice. Stir well. Serve the lemonade over ice in 10-ounce tall glasses, garnished with lemon slices, if you wish.

Apple Apricot Spritzer

½   cup apricot nectar, chilled
1½ cups sparkling cider*,
     chilled
2   apple wedges, for garnish
     (optional)
2   mint sprigs, for garnish
     (optional)

Combine the apricot nectar and the
sparkling cider in a 2-cup glass
measure. Pour the drink
immediately into two 10-ounce
wine glasses. Garnish each drink
with an apple wedge and a mint
sprig, if you wish.

*Note: Sparkling cider is available
in most supermarkets and specialty
food stores. If unavailable,
substitute regular cider.*

Peach Blossom Sunrise

5   cups orange juice
⅔   cup peach schnapps
     Ice cubes
1½ to 2 cups champagne OR:
     club soda, chilled
4   to 5 teaspoons grenadine
     Peach slices, for garnish
     (optional)

1. Combine the orange juice and
   the peach schnapps in a pitcher
   or jug. Refrigerate to chill.
2. For each serving, pour ½ cup of
   the chilled juice mixture into
   an 8- to 10-ounce footed glass.
   Add 2 or 3 ice cubes and 3 to 4
   tablespoons of the champagne
   or club soda. Drizzle ½
   teaspoon of the grenadine over
   each drink. Do not mix. Garnish
   each glass with a peach slice
   and serve with a straw.

*Champagne-laced Peach Blossom
Sunrise — the perfect beginning for any
festive occasion.*

Virgin Bellini

Try this refreshing drink as a dessert, served with amaretti cookies.

Makes 4 servings.

*Nutrient Value Per Serving:
72 calories, 1 g protein, 0 g fat,
19 g carbohydrate, 3 mg
sodium, 0 mg cholesterol.*

2   large ripe peaches, peeled,
    pitted and cut into pieces
1   can (5¾ ounces) peach
    nectar
2   tablespoons fresh lime juice
2   to 3 teaspoons sugar
2   cups crushed ice
8   thin slices fresh peach, for
    garnish *(optional)*

1. Combine the peaches, peach nectar, lime juice and sugar in the container of an electric blender. Cover and whirl until puréed, for about 1 minute.
2. Add the ice to the blender and whirl until there are no large chunks of ice, for about 1 minute.
3. Pour the drink into 4 saucer-shaped champagne or daiquiri glasses. Garnish each drink with 2 peach slices, if you wish.

Nectarine Cooler

Cranberry juice adds tanginess to this cool, sweet nectarine drink.

Makes 1 serving.

*Nutrient Value Per Serving:
103 calories, 1 g protein, 1 g fat,
25 g carbohydrate, 1 mg
sodium, 0 mg cholesterol.*

1   medium-size ripe nectarine
¼   cup cranberry juice cocktail
2   to 3 ice cubes

Slice the nectarine from the pit directly into the container of an electric blender. Add the cranberry juice and the ice cubes. Cover and whirl on high speed until the mixture is smooth.

QUICK TIP

Quick Crushed Ice
For perfectly crushed ice every time, keep an empty, clean, half-gallon milk carton filled with fresh water in the freezer. When it's frozen, drop the carton on a cement patio floor or driveway several times, depending on how finely crushed you want the ice.

Mocha Eggnog

Spicy Tomato Cheer

Coffee and chocolate are blended into this creamy drink.

Makes about twenty-eight ½-cup servings.

Nutrient Value Per Serving:
172 calories, 4 g protein, 9 g fat,
11 g carbohydrate, 54 mg
sodium, 139 mg cholesterol.

1	dozen eggs, at room temperature
¾	cup sugar
3	cups milk
2	cups half-and-half
1	cup brandy
1	cup bittersweet chocolate liqueur
1	cup brewed coffee, cold
1	cup heavy cream
	Grated semisweet chocolate, for garnish (optional)

1. Beat the eggs in a large bowl with an electric mixer at high speed until the eggs are frothy, for about 3 minutes. Gradually beat in the sugar until the mixture is pale yellow and fluffy, for about 2 minutes. With the mixer at low speed, beat in the milk, half-and-half, brandy, liqueur and coffee. (The mixture can be made ahead up to this point, then covered and refrigerated.)
2. To serve, pour the mixture into a 4-quart punch bowl. Beat the cream in a small bowl until stiff. Whisk the whipped cream into the eggnog and sprinkle with the grated chocolate, if you wish.

You may wish to add a splash of vodka to this warm, spicy tomato drink.

Makes 12 servings (½ cup each)
or 8 servings (¾ cup each).

Nutrient Value Per ½ Cup:
32 calories, 0 g protein, 0 g fat,
7 g carbohydrate, 389 mg
sodium, 0 mg cholesterol.

1	can (46 ounces) vegetable cocktail juice
2	tablespoons brown sugar
2	tablespoons lemon juice
¼	teaspoon ground allspice
¼	teaspoon ground cinnamon
⅛	teaspoon ground cloves
	Lemon slices and cinnamon sticks, for garnish (optional)

Combine the vegetable juice, brown sugar, lemon juice, allspice, cinnamon and cloves in a medium-size stainless-steel or enamel saucepan. Heat the liquid over medium heat until the mixture just starts to simmer. Reduce the heat to low and simmer for 3 minutes. Serve the drink in heatproof punch cups or mugs, garnished with lemon slices and cinnamon sticks, if you wish.

QUICK TIP

Do The Twist!
To make decorative lemon twists: Finely slice the lemons with a knife. Mark the center of each slice and make a cut to the end. Twist with your fingers. This technique can also be used on limes, oranges and tomatoes. Use the twists to decorate beverages, seafood and poultry platters.

Spiced Tea Mix

Makes 2 cups dry mix (enough for about 10 drinks).

Nutrient Value Per 8-Ounce Drink:
81 calories, 0 g protein, 0 g fat, 20 g carbohydrate, 5 mg sodium, 0 mg cholesterol.

1   cup 100% instant tea powder
1   cup sugar
2   teaspoons ground cloves
2   teaspoons ground ginger
1   teaspoon ground allspice

1. Combine the tea powder, sugar, cloves, ginger and allspice in a bowl until well mixed.
2. Spoon the dry mix into a container with a tight-fitting lid. Cover the container and store the mix at room temperature for up to 2 months.
3. To reconstitute the mix for a hot drink, add 3 level measuring tablespoonfuls of the mix to 8 ounces of boiling water in a heatproof mug. Stir until the mix is completely dissolved.

Rosy Punch

The cinnamon mixture can be prepared ahead, refrigerated and then heated with the cranberry juice mixture just before serving.

Makes about 22 servings.

Nutrient Value Per ½ Cup:
124 calories, 0 g protein, 0 g fat, 21 g carbohydrate, 2 mg sodium, 0 mg cholesterol.

3   cups water
3   cinnamon sticks
8   slices fresh gingerroot, each ⅛ inch thick, unpeeled
10 whole cloves
6   cups cranberry juice cocktail
1½ cups orange juice
3   tablespoons fresh lemon juice
2   cups crème de cassis (black currant liqueur)
½   cup apple schnapps
4   thin orange slices, quartered, for garnish
    Cinnamon sticks and cranberries, for garnish (optional)

1. Combine the water, cinnamon sticks, gingerroot and cloves in a large, nonaluminum saucepan. Bring the mixture to boiling. Reduce the heat and simmer the spice mixture, uncovered, for 30 minutes or until the liquid is reduced to about half (1½ cups).
2. Add the cranberry juice, orange juice, lemon juice, crème de cassis and apple schnapps. Heat the mixture just until heated through. Do not boil.
3. Serve the punch in mugs. Garnish each mug with a quarter of an orange slice, and a cinnamon stick and some cranberries, if you wish.

How To Set Up A Party Bar

One liter each bourbon, gin, scotch*, vodka*, sweet and dry vermouth
*Two liters if you're having 20 or more guests

Two to three six-packs beer

One 750-milliliter brandy

Two 750-milliliter liqueurs (Grand Marnier, Bailey's Irish Cream, etc.)

Two to four quarts seltzer

One quart each cola, diet soda, gingerale, tonic water, orange juice, tomato juice

One bottle Bloody Mary mix

Three limes, One lemon

Green olives, Pearl onions

Cocktail Party Wine Guide

NO. OF GUESTS	BOTTLES WHITE (750 ml)	BOTTLES RED (750 ml)
4	2	1
6	2	2
10	4	2
12	6	2
30	9	4
40	13	6

Note: If you're using wine coolers, plan on 2 to 3 six-packs for 8 to 12 guests, and at least one pound of ice per person.

Don't Get Caught Empty-Handed

Nothing can be more embarrassing than having the bar "run dry." To make sure you won't get caught short, here are some general rules to remember. • A 1-liter bottle of liquor gives you twenty-two 1½-ounce drinks. Assume each guest will have 2 to 3 drinks. • If you are planning to buy in quantity, you might want to consider 1.75-liter bottles. Each one will give you thirty-nine 1½-ounce drinks. • If you prefer wine, a 750-milliliter bottle will provide six 4-ounce drinks of wine. Assume each guest will want 2 to 4 glasses. • Check with the liquor store when you shop to see if they will take back any unopened bottles. • If the party is going to run 3 hours or longer, have coffee on hand. • Assign a friend or family member to tend the bar. Hire a professional bartender if you're having a crowd. • Use all-purpose wine glasses and 8-ounce highball glasses. Figure that at a 2-hour party each guest may use 2 to 3 glasses. • Equipment to have on hand: bottle opener, cocktail shaker, corkscrew, cutting board, juicer, paring knife, shot glass, strainer, tongs and scoops.

QUICK TIPS

As You Like It
Add a little pizzazz to your drinks. Here are some garnishes to consider for both hot and cold beverages at your next party.
- Maraschino cherry
- Lemon/lime slice
- Halved orange slice
- Lemon/lime rind twist
- Orange rind twist
- Lemon/lime wedge
- Fresh mint sprig
- Fresh strawberry
- Peach slice
- Confectioner's 10X sugar
- Shaved chocolate
- Orange wedge
- Fresh stemmed cherry
- Seedless grape
- Fresh raspberry
- Melon chunk
- Banana chunk
- Toasted almond slices
- Cinnamon sugar
- Mandarin orange section
- Pineapple spear
- Coffee bean

225

DESSERTS

Chapter 7 is devoted to dessert. For the busy cook, there are two strategies for dessert time. The first: Keep it simple. Fresh fruits, coffee and cookies, or quick toss-togethers (such as Peaches and Berries with Cassis, *page 229*, or Quick Lemon Mousse, *page 230*) are all time-crunchers. Another time-saver is dessert drinks, served cool and frothy from your blender. Try Melon Slush or Peachy Orange Buttermilk *(pages 268 and 269)*.

If you're organized (unlike most of us!) you'll appreciate the second strategy: When you have the time, prepare make-aheads and stash them in the refrigerator or freezer. Some of our favorites include Strawberry Raspberry Tart *(page 242)*, scrumptious Kiwi Trifle *(page 248)* and fun and festive Striped Fruit Pops *(page 260)*.

One final note on desserts: Most busy cooks are tempted to skip dessert altogether. Our advice: don't. It doesn't have to be high in calories, and doesn't have to take lots of time. Dessert is one wonderful way to complete a meal, and it offers something to linger over. And sometimes, an excuse to linger is just what a busy cook needs.

Delectable, delicious, de-lovely desserts! From top right, clockwise: Raspberry Mousse (page 258), crowned with dollops of fresh whipped cream; Peach Crêpes Melba (page 256) features a heavenly raspberry sauce; Cherry Cheese Tart (page 259) has a glaze of fresh cherries and currant jelly; Peach and Blueberry Compote with Yogurt Sauce (page 251) is lusciously light.

Toss-Togethers

Peaches and Berries with Cassis

A spirited fruit dessert.

Makes 4 servings.

Nutrient Value Per Serving:
135 calories, 1 g protein, 0 g fat,
28 g carbohydrate, 0 mg
sodium, 0 mg cholesterol.

4   firm, ripe peaches
1   pint fresh blackberries,
      raspberries or blueberries
¼   cup cassis (black currant
      liqueur)

1. Peel, halve and pit the peaches.
   Cut into slices.
2. Arrange the peach slices and
   the berries in individual glass
   bowls. Cover and chill.
3. At serving time, pour the cassis
   over the fruit.

An elegant dessert that takes no time at
all — Peaches and Berries with Cassis.

Strawberries Romanoff

A classic combination, and
deliciously quick to make.

Makes 4 servings.

Nutrient Value Per Serving:
245 calories, 1 g protein, 17 g
fat, 19 g carbohydrate, 18 mg
sodium, 61 mg cholesterol.

1   pint fresh strawberries,
      washed, hulled and sliced
1   to 2 tablespoons superfine
      sugar
3   tablespoons plus 1
      teaspoon Cointreau OR:
      other orange-flavored
      liqueur
¾   cup heavy or whipping
      cream
2   tablespoons 10X
      (confectioners' powdered)
      sugar

1. Toss the berries with the
   superfine sugar in a small bowl.
   Let the berries stand for 5
   minutes. Add the 3 tablespoons
   of liqueur.
2. Beat together the cream, 10X
   (confectioners' powdered)
   sugar and the remaining 1
   teaspoon of liqueur in a small
   bowl until soft peaks form.
3. Layer the strawberries and the
   whipped cream in 4 wine
   glasses. Refrigerate for up to 1
   hour.

QUICK TIP

If The Spirit Moves You
Drizzle or sprinkle a
little spirit or liqueur
over fresh fruit, ice
cream or cakes:
orange, anisette,
cherry, mint, berry,
chocolate, amaretto,
coffee, rum, and on
and on.

229

Quick Lemon Mousse

Vary the yogurt flavor in Quick Lemon Mousse to suit your own fancy.

Making this mousse takes, at most, 2 minutes.

Makes 6 servings.

Nutrient Value Per Serving: 159 calories, 2 g protein, 10 g fat, 16 g carbohydrate, 31 mg sodium, 2 mg cholesterol.

1   **container (8 ounces) frozen non-dairy topping, thawed**
1   **container (8 ounces) lemon-flavored yogurt**
    Strawberry Sauce *(recipe follows)*
    Lemon rind, for garnish

1. Spoon the topping into a medium-size bowl. Gently fold in the yogurt. Spoon the mousse into 6 individual bowls. Chill.
2. At serving time, serve the mousse with the Strawberry Sauce and garnish with the lemon rind.

Strawberry Sauce: Rinse and hull 1 pint of strawberries. Slice the strawberries into the container of an electric blender or a food processor. Add ¼ to ⅓ cup of sugar, and 1 tablespoon of kirsch or white rum *(optional)*. Cover and whirl until the berries are puréed. Refrigerate the sauce until serving time. *Makes about 1½ cups. Nutrient Value Per Tablespoon: 13 calories, 0 g protein, 0 g fat, 3 g carbohydrate, 0 mg sodium, 0 mg cholesterol.*

Pineapple Pecan Foster

A tangy alternative to the classic banana dessert, and it takes only minutes to prepare when you're ready to serve it.

Makes 2 servings.

Nutrient Value Per Serving: 439 calories, 2 g protein, 30 g fat, 38 g carbohydrate, 129 mg sodium, 51 mg cholesterol.

⅓ cup pecan halves
2 tablespoons butter
4 fresh ripe pineapple rings
   OR: 4 canned pineapple rings packed in natural syrup, drained
2 tablespoons firmly packed light brown sugar
2 tablespoons dark rum
2 tablespoons heavy cream
   Light whipped cream OR: vanilla ice cream OR: butter pecan ice cream

1. Sauté the pecans in the butter in a medium-size skillet over medium heat until toasted. (Watch carefully to avoid burning the pecans or the butter.) Remove the pecans from the skillet with a slotted spoon to drain on paper toweling.
2. Sauté the pineapple rings on both sides in the remaining butter in the skillet. Push the rings to the side of the skillet. Lower the heat.
3. Add the brown sugar to the skillet and stir rapidly to dissolve the sugar. Add the rum and the heavy cream. Continue heating, stirring constantly, until the mixture forms a thin caramel sauce. Coat the pineapple rings with the sauce.
4. Divide the pineapple rings and the caramel sauce between 2 plates. Sprinkle the pineapple with the sautéed pecans. Serve with dollops of softly whipped cream or a scoop of vanilla ice cream or butter pecan ice cream.

QUICK TIP

Billowy Whipped Cream
For the lightest whipped cream, chill the beaters and bowl in the refrigerator for about an hour first. Begin beating at low speed, then increase the speed as the cream gains in volume. Beat until stiff peaks form. Remember, ultra-pasteurized heavy cream doesn't whip up as well as plain pasteurized.

231

Make-Ahead Cakes,
Cookies and Such

Sponge Cake with Chocolate Glaze

The more gently you fold the egg whites in Step 3, the higher and lighter the cake will be. Prepare and refrigerate the cake on a weekend for weekday eating. And don't tell anyone the cake is low-calorie.

Bake at 350° for 40 to 45 minutes.
Makes 16 servings.

Nutrient Value Per Serving:
115 calories, 3 g protein, 5 g fat, 16 g carbohydrate, 46 mg sodium, 57 mg cholesterol.

7	egg whites
⅛	teaspoon cream of tartar
¾	cup sugar
3	egg yolks
1	teaspoon vanilla
1	cup sifted cake flour
3	tablespoons butter, melted and cooled to lukewarm

Chocolate Glaze:

1½	ounces semisweet chocolate
2	tablespoons vegetable shortening

1. Preheat the oven to moderate (350°).
2. Beat the egg whites with the cream of tartar in a large bowl until the whites are foamy. Beat in the sugar, 1 tablespoon at a time, until the meringue forms stiff, but not dry, peaks.
3. Stir together the egg yolks and the vanilla in another large bowl. Fold in one third of the beaten egg whites. Fold in the remaining whites until no streaks of white remain. Sprinkle the flour over the top of the mixture, then gently fold in the flour. Very gently fold in the melted butter; do not overfold. Turn the batter into a 9-inch tube pan, spreading the batter evenly.
4. Bake the cake in the preheated moderate oven (350°) for 40 to 45 minutes or until a wooden pick inserted near the center comes out clean.
5. Invert the tube pan onto a large funnel or bottle and let the cake hang until it is completely cooled, for at least 1½ hours.
6. Run a knife around the inner and outer edges of the tube pan. Turn the cake out onto a wire rack and cool completely, with the crusty portion up. The cake can be stored in the refrigerator after it's cooled.
7. At serving time, melt together the chocolate and the vegetable shortening in the top of a double boiler over hot, not boiling, water, stirring occasionally, until the mixture is smooth. Cool the mixture slightly. Spoon the melted chocolate evenly over the top of the cake, letting the excess run down the sides.

Velvety-smooth Sponge Cake with Chocolate Glaze is easy to make.

QUICK TIP

The Yoke's On You
Leftover egg yolks? Refrigerate them in a jar with a screw-top lid, adding water to cover, for up to 4 days. Add to scrambled eggs.

Chocolate Roll with Orange Ginger Meringue

The cake can be prepared a day ahead. Or, for a less "wet" cake, the roll can be prepared ahead and then filled just before serving. And who would guess one serving has fewer than 100 calories!

Bake at 375° for 10 to 12 minutes.
Makes 12 servings.

Nutrient Value Per Serving:
98 calories, 3 g protein, 2 g fat, 18 g carbohydrate, 85 mg sodium, 69 mg cholesterol.

	Nonstick vegetable cooking spray
½	cup sifted cake flour
3	tablespoons unsweetened cocoa powder
¾	teaspoon baking powder
3	eggs, separated
¼	cup plus 3 tablespoons sugar
2	tablespoons water
1	egg white
⅛	teaspoon salt
	Orange Ginger Meringue Filling *(recipe follows)*
1	tablespoon 10X (confectioners' powdered) sugar
	Orange twists, for garnish *(optional)*

1. Spray a 15 x 10 x 1-inch jelly-roll pan with nonstick vegetable cooking spray. Line the bottom of the pan with a piece of wax paper and spray the paper.
2. Preheat the oven to moderate (375°).
3. Sift together the flour, cocoa powder and baking powder onto wax paper.
4. Beat the egg yolks in a large bowl with an electric mixer at high speed until the yolks are foamy. Gradually beat in the ¼ cup of sugar, 1 tablespoon at a time, until the yolks are very thick, for about 3 minutes. Add the water and beat well. Stir in the flour mixture until smooth.
5. Beat the 4 egg whites with the salt in a large bowl with clean beaters until the whites are foamy. Gradually beat in the

Chocolate Roll with Orange Ginger Meringue is a dieter's dream come true.

remaining 3 tablespoons of sugar until soft peaks form. Fold one third of the whites into the batter to lighten it. Fold in the remaining whites until no streaks of white remain. Spread the batter evenly in the pan.

6. Bake the cake in the preheated moderate oven (375°) for 10 to 12 minutes or until the center springs back when pressed with a fingertip.

7. Spray a second, clean piece of wax paper with nonstick vegetable cooking spray. Loosen the cake around the edges of the pan with a knife and invert the cake onto the wax paper. Peel off the first piece of wax paper from the cake. Starting at a short end, roll up the cake and the second piece of wax paper together. Place the roll, seam side down, on a wire rack and cool completely.

8. Unroll the cake and remove and discard the paper. Spread with the Orange Ginger Meringue Filling. Reroll the cake, sprinkle with the 10X (confectioners' powdered) sugar, and garnish with orange twists if you wish. Serve immediately.

Orange Ginger Meringue Filling: Beat together 3 egg whites and ¾ teaspoon of cream of tartar in a large bowl until the whites are foamy. Gradually beat in 3 tablespoons of sugar, a tablespoon at a time, until firm peaks form. Gently fold in 2 tablespoons of orange marmalade and 1 tablespoon of chopped perserved candied ginger (½ ounce). Use at once, or refrigerate the filling until ready to use.

QUICK TIPS

Make Marvelous Meringue

● Choose a cool, dry day—humid air tends to soften meringues. Be sure your tools—non-plastic bowl and beater—are clean and dry. The tiniest speck of fat will spoil meringues.

● Egg whites will beat higher if allowed to stand at room temperature to warm slightly.

● Depend on your electric mixer, since long beating is a must to dissolve sugar completely and prevent meringue from "weeping." To test if sugar is completely dissolved: Rub a bit of meringue between your fingers. The meringue should feel smooth.

235

QUICK TIPS

The Cookie "Store"
- Store soft cookies in an airtight container, with a slice of apple on a piece of wax paper to keep the cookies soft and moist.
- Store crisp cookies in a container with a loose fitting lid. If the cookies soften, place them in a slow oven (300°) for a few minutes to make them crisp again.

Buttery Almond Cookies

(Basic Dough; third row from top in photo, page 236)

Bake at 375° for 8 to 10 minutes. Makes about 8 dozen cookies.

Nutrient Value Per Undecorated Cookie: 51 calories, 1 g protein, 2 g fat, 7 g carbohydrate, 43 mg sodium, 11 mg cholesterol.

3   **cups sifted all-purpose flour**
4   **teaspoons baking powder**
1   **teaspoon salt**
1   **cup (2 sticks) unsalted butter, at room temperature, cut into tablespoons**
2   **cups sugar**
2   **eggs, slightly beaten**
½   **cup finely ground blanched almonds**
1   **teaspoon almond extract**

1. Sift together the flour, baking powder and salt onto a piece of wax paper.
2. Beat the butter in a large bowl until light. Gradually add the sugar, beating until the mixture is fluffy. Stir in the eggs, almonds and almond extract. Stir in the dry ingredients.
3. Divide the dough in half. If too sticky, wrap each half in plastic wrap. Refrigerate the dough for 30 minutes to 1 hour, or chill in the freezer for 5 to 15 minutes to firm the dough.
4. Roll each half into a 12-inch-long log. Wrap the rolls in wax paper and twist the ends closed. Freeze the rolls for 1 to 1½ hours or until frozen solid, or overwrap the wrapped rolls in plastic bags and freeze for up to 1 month.
5. When ready to bake the cookies, preheat the oven to moderate (375°).
6. Cut each log into ¼-inch-thick slices. Arrange the slices, 2 inches apart, on ungreased cookie sheets.
7. Bake the cookies in the preheated moderate oven (375°) for 8 to 10 minutes or until the edges are lightly browned.
8. Loosen the cookies from the cookie sheets with a spatula. Transfer the cookies to a wire rack. Cool completely to crisp.

Decorations (left to right in photo, page 236):
Variations A and B: Drizzle half of each cookie with the Shiny Chocolate Glaze *(page 240)*, using a spoon, and allow to set. For A, pipe the Fluffy Decorator Frosting *(page 238)* along the chocolate edge with a pastry bag fitted with a small plain round tip (#7); press in the cinnamon red-hot candies.
Variation C: Drizzle the Shiny Chocolate Glaze *(page 240)* from a spoon in a crisscross pattern over the cookie and let the chocolate set. Pipe or spread a small round of Fluffy Decorator Frosting *(page 238)* in the center of each cookie. Press in the candy-coated chocolate candy.

From top down: Tangy Lemon Sunshine Cookies (page 239); three-alarm Cinnamon Hotshots (page 238); chocolate-covered Buttery Almond Cookies; Chewy Spearmint Drops (page 239); sweet Chocolate Snowflakes (page 240); Ginger Orange Ornaments (page 240), are covered with fruity candy orange slices.

Cinnamon Hotshots

(second row from top in photo, page 236)

Nutrient Value Per Undecorated Cookie: 51 calories, 1 g protein, 2 g fat, 7 g carbohydrate, 43 mg sodium, 11 mg cholesterol.

Cookie Changes: Prepare 1 recipe of the Buttery Almond Cookies *(page 237)* with the following changes. Eliminate the almond extract. Grind 2 tablespoons of cinnamon red hot candies in a food processor. Add to the egg-and-almond mixture with 2 drops of red coloring just before adding the dry ingredients in Step 2.

Decorations *(left to right in photo, page 236):*
Variations A, B and C: Spread Fluffy Decorator Frosting *(below)* in a candy cane shape (A), circle (B) or flower petal shape (C). Garnish each cookie with crushed cinnamon red-hot candies.

Fluffy Decorator Frosting

Beat together 1 egg white and ½ teaspoon cream of tartar in a small bowl until foamy. Slowly beat in 1½ cups sifted 10X (confectioners' powdered) sugar, part at a time, beating well after each addition. Add ½ teaspoon almond extract. Continue to beat until the whites are stiff and creamy, for about 3 minutes. Work with small amounts of the frosting; cover any remaining frosting in the bowl with damp toweling to prevent it from drying out. *Makes ¾ cup (enough to decorate 2 dozen cookies). Nutrient Value Per 1½ Teaspoons: 25 calories, 0 g protein, 0 g fat, 6 g carbohydrate, 2 mg sodium, 0 mg cholesterol.*

Butterscotch Crisps

(not shown in photo)

Nutrient Value Per Undecorated Cookie: 55 calories, 1 g protein, 3 g fat, 8 g carbohydrate, 43 mg sodium, 11 mg cholesterol.

Cookie Changes: Prepare 1 recipe of the Buttery Almond Cookies *(page 237)* with the following changes. Eliminate the almond extract. Melt 3 ounces (about ½ cup) of butterscotch chips in a small bowl over hot water. Cool slightly. Add the melted butterscotch to the egg-and-almond mixture just before adding the dry ingredients in Step 2.

Decorations:
Variation A: Decorate each cookie with Fluffy Decorator Frosting *(below left).* Press a candied cherry half and silver dragées into the frosting.
Variation B: Pipe Fluffy Decorator Frosting around each cookie edge. Press in butterscotch chips and candied red cherry pieces.
Variation C: Spread Fluffy Decorator Frosting in the center of each cookie. Press walnut pieces, candied red cherry halves, butterscotch chips and chocolate sprinkles into the frosting.

Chewy Spearmint Drops

Lemon Sunshine Cookies

(fourth row from top in photo, page 236)

(top row in photo, page 236)

Nutrient Value Per Undecorated Cookie: 53 calories, 1 g protein, 2 g fat, 8 g carbohydrate, 43 mg sodium, 11 mg cholesterol.

Nutrient Value Per Undecorated Cookie: 51 calories, 1 g protein, 2 g fat, 7 g carbohydrate, 43 mg sodium, 11 mg cholesterol.

Cookie Changes: Prepare 1 recipe of the Buttery Almond Cookies (page 237) with the following changes. Eliminate the almond extract. Chop very finely 1½ ounces (6) green spearmint leaf candies with 2 tablespoons of granulated sugar, separating the pieces of candy as you chop and coating them with the sugar. Add the chopped candies to the egg-and-almond mixture just before adding the dry ingredients in Step 2.

Decorations *(left to right in photo, page 236):*
Variation A: Slice spearmint leaf candies in half horizontally. Press a silver dragée into each candy half. Spread Fluffy Decorator Frosting *(page 238)* in the center of each cookie. Press a spearmint leaf into the frosting.
Variations B and C: Spread Fluffy Decorator Frosting *(page 238)* in the center of each cookie. Press small pieces of spearmint leaf candies and a cinnamon red-hot candy into the frosting.

Cookie Changes: Prepare 1 recipe of the Buttery Almond Cookies *(page 237)* with the following changes. Eliminate the almond extract. Add 1 tablespoon of lemon juice, 1 tablespoon of grated lemon rind and 8 to 10 drops of yellow food coloring to the egg-and-almond mixture just before adding the dry ingredients in Step 2.

Decorations *(left to right in photo, page 236):*
Variation A: Spread Fluffy Decorator Frosting *(page 238)* in the center of each cookie. Sprinkle with yellow crystal sugar and garnish with thin strips of lime zest.
Variation B: Spoon a band of Shiny Chocolate Glaze *(page 240)* across the top of each cookie. Sprinkle with chopped pistachios.
Variation C: Same as variation A, but garnish each cookie with a pecan half instead of lime zest.

QUICK TIP

Foiled Again
When you have a lot of cookies to bake and are short of space and time, try a foil assembly line. Cut aluminum foil and slip the foil over your cookie sheets. You can prepare all the cookies ahead of time and just slip the foil sheet liners on as soon as the sheets come out of the oven.

239

Ginger Orange Ornaments

(sixth row from top in photo, page 236)

Nutrient Value Per Undecorated Cookie: 51 calories, 1 g protein, 2 g fat, 7 g carbohydrate, 43 mg sodium, 11 mg cholesterol.

Cookie Changes: Prepare 1 recipe of the Buttery Almond Cookies *(page 237)* with the following changes. Eliminate the almond extract. Add 1 teaspoon of grated orange rind, ⅛ to ¼ teaspoon of orange food coloring and 1 tablespoon of finely chopped crystallized ginger pieces, to the egg-and-almond mixture just before adding dry ingredients in Step 2.

Decorations *(left to right in photo, page 236):* Spread or pipe Fluffy Decorator Frosting *(page 238)* in the center of each cookie.
Variation A: Press candied orange slices in frosting; decorate with pecans and silver dragées.
Variation B: Press a piece of candied orange slice and 2 almond slices into the frosting.
Variation C: Press pieces of candied orange slice and candy-coated chocolate candy into the frosting.

Shiny Chocolate Glaze

Melt together 4 squares (1 ounce each) semisweet chocolate and two tablespoons vegetable shortening in a small saucepan. Cool the glaze slightly before using. *Makes scant ½ cup (enough to decorate 3½ dozen cookies). Nutrient Value Per ½ Teaspoon: 17 calories, 0 g protein, 1 g fat, 1 g carbohydrate, 0 mg sodium, 0 mg cholesterol.*

Chocolate Snowflakes

(fifth row from top in photo, page 236)

Nutrient Value Per Undecorated Cookie: 57 calories, 1 g protein, 3 g fat, 7 g carbohydrate, 43 mg sodium, 11 mg cholesterol.

Cookie Changes: Prepare 1 recipe of the Buttery Almond Cookies *(page 237)* with the following changes. Eliminate the almond extract. Melt 4 squares (1 ounce each) of unsweetened chocolate in a small bowl over hot water. Cool slightly. Add the chocolate to the egg-and-almond mixture just before adding the dry ingredients in Step 2.

Decorations *(left to right in photo, page 236):*
Variation A: Drizzle each cookie with Shiny Chocolate Glaze *(below left).* Let the chocolate set. Drizzle with Sugar Glaze *(below).*
Variation B: Spread Fluffy Decorator Frosting *(page 238)* in the center of each cookie. Arrange sliced walnuts around a candied red cherry half.
Variation C: Spread each cookie with Fluffy Decorator Frosting *(page 238).* Sprinkle with toasted and untoasted shredded coconut and silver dragées.

Sugar Glaze

Whisk together 1 cup sifted 10X (confectioners' powdered) sugar and 1 tablespoon of milk in a small bowl until blended. Whisk in enough of a second tablespoon of milk to reach a good drizzling consistency. *Makes ½ cup (enough to decorate 4 dozen cookies). Nutrient Value Per ½ Teaspoon: 8 calories, 0 g protein, 0 g fat, 2 g carbohydrate, 0 mg sodium, 0 mg cholesterol.*

Lemon Sponge Cake with Strawberry Sauce

A delicious make-ahead—and it's low-calorie.

Bake at 400° for 12 to 14 minutes.
Makes 12 servings.

Nutrient Value Per Serving:
87 calories, 3 g protein, 2 g fat, 14 g carbohydrate, 47 mg sodium, 91 mg cholesterol.

Nonstick vegetable cooking spray

Basic Sponge Cake:
- 4   **eggs, separated**
- ⅛   **teaspoon salt**
- ¼   **cup sugar**
- ½   **teaspoon grated lemon rind**
- 1   **teaspoon lemon juice**
- ⅔   **cup sifted all-purpose flour**

Strawberry Sauce:
- 3   **cups fresh strawberries, washed, hulled and sliced**
- ¼   **cup 10X (confectioners' powdered) sugar**
- 1   **teaspoon raspberry brandy (optional)**
- 12 **strawberries, for garnish (optional)**

1. Preheat the oven to hot (400°). Spray the bottom of a 9 x 9 x 2-inch square baking pan with nonstick vegetable cooking spray. Line the bottom with aluminum foil and spray the foil.
2. Prepare the Basic Sponge Cake: Beat the egg whites with the salt in a large bowl until the whites are fluffy. Gradually beat in the sugar until the whites form firm, but not dry, peaks.
3. Beat together the egg yolks, lemon rind and juice in a second large bowl until well combined. Fold ½ cup of the beaten whites into the yolk mixture. Fold in the remaining whites. Then fold in the flour, 1 tablespoon at a time. Spread the batter evenly into the pan.
4. Bake the cake in the preheated hot oven (400°) for 12 to 14 minutes or until the top springs back when touched with a fingertip.
5. Loosen the cake around the edges of the pan with a knife and invert it onto a wire rack. Remove the pan and foil. Invert the cake again so the golden side is on top. Cool the cake completely on the wire rack.
6. Prepare the Strawberry Sauce: Combine the strawberries, 10X (confectioners' powdered) sugar, and the raspberry brandy if you wish, in the container of a blender. Cover and whirl until the mixture is smooth. (The sauce can be made the day ahead, covered and refrigerated.)
7. To serve, cut the cake into 12 equal pieces and set on individual dessert plates. Spoon a generous 2 tablespoons of the sauce over each piece, and garnish each serving with a strawberry, if you wish.

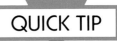
QUICK TIP

Sweet And Saucy
A spoonful of syrup or sweet sauce can make all the difference between "ho-hum" and "wow!" desserts. On cakes or ice cream, try chocolate syrup, or sauces such as fudge, butterscotch, caramel, or fruit and berry.

Strawberry Raspberry Tart

Prepare this tart a day ahead in a spare moment. For a slightly sweeter taste, add a little sugar to the cooled filling.

Bake crust at 400° for 10 to 12 minutes.
Makes 10 servings.

Nutrient Value Per Serving:
126 calories, 1 g protein, 7 g fat, 15 g carbohydrate, 119 mg sodium, 3 mg cholesterol.

½   **of 11-ounce package piecrust mix**
2   **pint baskets strawberries, hulled**
5   **tablespoons low-sugar raspberry preserves or jam**

QUICK TIPS

Caution: Soggy When Wet!
Rinse strawberries just before using and before hulling to prevent the berries from becoming soggy.

The Incredible Shrinking Pie Shell
If you are baking a pie shell ahead and the shell shrinks, it means you've probably rolled out the dough unevenly or you stretched the dough while fitting it into the pie plate. To remedy, disguise the shell as an open-face fresh fruit tart with a whipped cream border.

1. Preheat the oven to hot (400°). Prepare the piecrust mix following the package directions for a single 9-inch crust. Line a 9-inch tart pan with a removable bottom with the piecrust dough. Prick the bottom all over with a fork. Refrigerate the tart shell for 10 minutes to set.
2. Bake the tart shell in the preheated hot oven (400°) for 10 to 12 minutes or until the shell is pale golden. Transfer the pan to a rack to cool.
3. Reserve 1 pint of the strawberries for the garnish. Halve the remaining berries.
4. Combine the halved strawberries with the raspberry preserves or jam in a medium-size saucepan. Bring the mixture to boiling. Lower the heat and simmer the strawberries, stirring occasionally, until the berries have softened, for about 7 minutes.
5. Strain the berries over a bowl. Transfer the berries to a small bowl. Pour the fruit syrup back into the saucepan. Cook the syrup over low heat, stirring constantly, until thickened to a jamlike consistency, for about 5 minutes. Add the thickened syrup to the cooked berries in the small bowl. Cool the mixture to room temperature.
6. Spread the cooked strawberry mixture into the tart shell. Refrigerate the tart, lightly covered, until ready to serve. (The tart may be kept overnight.)
7. Just before serving, remove the outer ring from the tart pan. Cut the reserved pint of whole berries into ½-inch-thick slices and arrange on the tart.

Teatime Pastries

Make these pastries on a weekend, and use during the week for coffee or tea breaks, brown paper bag lunches or for a dinner dessert.

Bake at 400° for 10 to 15 minutes.
Makes 3 dozen.

Nutrient Value Per Pastry:
103 calories, 3 g protein, 2 g fat, 19 g carbohydrate, 57 mg sodium, 0 mg cholesterol.

1   **cup milk**
¼   **cup (½ stick) butter**
½   **cup granulated sugar**
½   **teaspoon salt**
2   **packages active dry yeast**
¼   **cup warm water**
2   **eggs, slightly beaten**
4   **to 5 cups *un*sifted all-purpose flour**
     Nonstick vegetable cooking spray
1   **cup low-sugar jam or preserves**
2   **egg whites**
2   **tablespoons water**
½   **cup 10X (confectioners' powdered) sugar**
2   **to 3 teaspoons water**

1. Heat together the milk, butter, sugar and salt in a medium-size saucepan until the butter is melted and the sugar is dissolved. Cool the liquid to lukewarm.
2. Sprinkle the yeast over the warm water in a large bowl and stir to dissolve the yeast. Add the butter mixture, eggs and 3 cups of the flour to the yeast mixture and beat until blended. Stir in 1 cup of the flour and as much of the remaining flour as necessary to make a soft dough.
3. Turn the dough out onto a lightly floured surface. Knead the dough until smooth, for about 8 minutes. Spray a medium-size bowl with nonstick vegetable cooking spray. Press the dough into the bowl and bring the oiled side up. Cover the bowl with plastic wrap. Let the dough rise in a warm place, away from drafts, for 45 minutes to 1 hour or until doubled in bulk.
4. Punch the dough down. Divide into thirds. Roll each third into a 12 x 9-inch rectangle. Cut each rectangle into 3-inch squares. Spoon about 1 teaspoon of the jam or preserves into the center of each square.
5. Fold two opposite corners of each square toward the center until the points touch; pinch the points together to seal. Set the pastries on a cookie sheet. Cover the pastries lightly with plastic wrap and let rise in a warm place, away from drafts, for 20 minutes or until doubled in bulk.
6. Preheat the oven to hot (400°).
7. Stir together the egg whites and the 2 tablespoons of water in a small cup. Brush the tops of the pastries with the egg wash.
8. Bake the pastries in the preheated hot oven (400°) for 10 to 15 minutes or until golden. Transfer the pastries to a wire rack to cool.
9. Place the 10X (confectioners' powdered) sugar in a small bowl. Stir in enough of the 2 to 3 teaspoons of water to make an icing with a good drizzling consistency. Drizzle the icing over the pastries.

Chilled Delights

Lemon Swirl Cheesecake

Bake crust at 350° for 5 minutes, bake cake at 350° for 40 minutes.
Makes 12 servings (one 10-inch cake).

Nutrient Value Per Serving: 342 calories, 7 g protein, 25 g fat, 25 g carbohydrate, 173 mg sodium, 127 mg cholesterol.

4   ounces toasted blanched almonds
5   Italian amaretti
2   to 3 tablespoons melted butter
3   packages (8 ounces each) cream cheese, at room temperature
1   cup plus 2 tablespoons sugar
     Grated rind of 2½ lemons
     Juice of 2½ lemons
4   eggs
1   cup dairy sour cream
2   tablespoons sugar
2   tablespoons prepared lemon curd (available at food specialty stores)
     Raspberry Purée *(recipe follows)*
     Fresh blueberries
     Mint sprigs, for garnish

1. Preheat the oven to moderate (350°). Combine the almonds and the amaretti in a food processor. Cover and whirl until the crumbs are medium coarse. Transfer the crumbs to a small bowl. Add the butter and toss to coat. (The mixture should hold together; if it does not, add an additional tablespoon of melted butter.)
2. Press the crumbs on the bottom and up the side of a 10-inch springform pan.

Lemon Swirl Cheesecake is served with fresh blueberries and raspberry purée.

3. Bake the crust in the preheated moderate oven (350°) for 5 minutes. Let the pan stand on a wire rack while preparing the filling. Leave the oven temperature at 350°.
4. Beat together the cream cheese and the 1 cup and 2 tablespoons of sugar in a medium-size bowl with an electric mixer at high speed until smooth. Add the lemon rind and lemon juice and beat until smooth. Add the eggs, one at a time, scraping down the side of the bowl as needed. Pour the filling into the crust.
5. Bake the cheesecake in the preheated moderate oven (350°) for 40 minutes or until the filling is set but still slightly soft in the center. Let it stand for 5 minutes.
6. Mix together the sour cream and the 2 tablespoons of sugar in a small bowl. Place the lemon curd in a pastry bag fitted with a ¼-inch plain tube.
7. After the cake has stood for 5 minutes, top with the sour cream mixture. With the lemon curd, make dots evenly around the top of the cake. Make a decorative swirl through each dot with the tip of a knife.
8. Cool the cheesecake completely, then refrigerate.
9. At serving time, remove the side of the pan and cut the cheesecake into wedges. Spoon some Raspberry Purée on one side of each slice and the blueberries on the other side. Garnish with mint sprigs.

Raspberry Purée: Thaw 1 package (10 ounces) frozen raspberries in heavy syrup. Place in the container of a food processor. Cover and whirl until puréed. Strain through a very fine sieve. Add sugar to taste.

Ginger Melon

A refreshing combination of melons with a zesty taste of fresh ginger. For best flavor, make the day before serving.

Makes 4 servings.

Nutrient Value Per Serving: 239 calories, 3 g protein, 1 g fat, 62 g carbohydrate, 35 mg sodium, 0 mg cholesterol.

½ cup water
½ cup sugar
2 tablespoons finely chopped, peeled fresh gingerroot
1 lemon
2 small cantaloupes (2 pounds each)
½ medium-size honeydew melon (2¼-pound melon half)
1 piece watermelon (¾ pound)
    Fresh mint sprigs, for garnish *(optional)*

1. Combine the water and the sugar in a small saucepan. Bring the mixture to boiling over high heat, stirring to dissolve the sugar. Reduce the heat to medium and stir in the gingerroot. Boil the syrup gently for 5 minutes, watching carefully to prevent any boiling over the side of the pan. Remove the saucepan from the heat. Strain the syrup into a medium-size, heatproof bowl. Discard the gingerroot.

2. Use a citrus zester to remove the lemon zest (the outermost part of the yellow rind with no white pith) in narrow 2- to 3-inch-long strips. Or use a swivel-bladed vegetable peeler to remove wide strips of the zest, and cut each wide strip into narrow strips. Add the zest to the hot syrup.

3. Cut the cantaloupes in half. Remove and discard the seeds from the cantaloupes and the honeydew half. Scoop out the pulp from the cantaloupes and the honeydew with a melon ball cutter. Reserve the cantaloupe shells. Add the melon balls to the syrup.

4. Cut the watermelon into ¾-inch cubes (about 1⅔ cups), removing and discarding the seeds and the rind. Add the watermelon to the syrup. Cover the bowl with plastic wrap and refrigerate overnight.

5. Hollow out the cantaloupe shells with a spoon to even out the pulp inside the shells. Place the shells in a plastic bag and refrigerate them until serving time.

6. To serve, spoon the melon balls into the cantaloupe shells. Arrange the lemon zest on top. Garnish with fresh mint sprigs, if you wish.

QUICK TIP

Ripe For The Pickin'
A ripe cantaloupe will have a distinct aroma and be somewhat springy when pressed lightly between your hands. Look for heavily netted skin and a smooth sunken scar at the stem end. Cantaloupe is in season from May to November, but can be found in some cities year-round. Plan to store the melon for 2 to 3 days at room temperature so the flesh will soften and be juicier. Refrigerate when ripe.

Lime Cheesecake

Make this smooth, tart cheesecake a day ahead, if you wish.

Bake crust at 350° for 2 minutes, bake cake at 350° for 40 to 50 minutes.
Makes 12 servings.

Nutrient Value Per Serving:
141 calories, 9 g protein, 3 g fat, 19 g carbohydrate, 323 mg sodium, 49 mg cholesterol.

	Nonstick vegetable cooking spray
½	**cup finely crushed zwieback biscuits**
2	**tablespoons reduced-calorie margarine**
3	**cups 1% lowfat cottage cheese**
¾	**cup sugar**
3	**tablespoons all-purpose flour**
2	**eggs, slightly beaten**
¾	**cup skim milk**
1	**to 2 tablespoons lime juice**
½	**teaspoon grated lime rind**
¼	**teaspoon salt**
	Limes, for garnish (optional)

1. Preheat the oven to moderate (350°). Spray only the tight-fitting removable bottom of a 9 x 3-inch springform pan with nonstick vegetable cooking spray.
2. Combine the zwieback crumbs and the margarine with your fingers in a bowl until well blended. Scatter the crumb mixture over the bottom of the prepared pan. Press the crumbs down slightly.
3. Bake the crust in the preheated moderate oven (350°) until crisp, for about 2 minutes. Cool the crust on a wire rack while preparing the cheese filling. Leave the oven on.
4. Place the cottage cheese in the work bowl of a food processor. Whirl until the cottage cheese is smooth (*no* lumps), scraping down the side of the bowl occasionally, for 3 to 5 minutes. Add the sugar and the flour and whirl until blended. Add the eggs, one at a time, whirling after each addition. Add the milk, lime juice, lime rind and salt and whirl just until the mixture is well blended.
5. Place the prepared springform pan on a cookie sheet. Ladle the cheesecake mixture into the crust; do not pour, or else air bubbles will form on the top.
6. Bake the cheesecake in the preheated moderate oven (350°) for 40 to 50 minutes or until a wooden pick inserted near the center comes out clean. Do not overbake the cake.
7. Cool the cake in the pan on a wire rack. Refrigerate, covered, for several hours until chilled. Run a sharp knife around the edge of the cake; loosen and remove the side of the pan. Garnish the cheesecake with lime slices cut into quarters and strips of lime rind, if you wish.

QUICK TIPS

Baker's Secrets
- Always remember to preheat the oven to the proper temperature 10 minutes before baking.
- Don't open the oven door to check the cake until the minimum baking time is up. The cake will fall if the baking process is interrupted too early.

247

Kiwi Trifle

Kiwi Trifle — a new version of an old favorite.

Kiwi makes a delicious and colorful addition to this version of trifle.

Makes 10 servings.

*Nutrient Value Per Serving:
167 calories, 4 g protein, 8 g fat,
20 g carbohydrate, 44 mg
sodium, 114 mg cholesterol.*

Custard:
- 2   tablespoons cornstarch
- ¼   cup sugar
- 3½ cups milk
- 4   egg yolks
- 2   tablespoons cream sherry

Sherry Syrup:
- ⅓   cup water
- 3   tablespoons sugar
- 2   tablespoons cream sherry

- 2   frozen poundcakes (10¾ ounces each), thawed
- 5   kiwis, peeled and cut crosswise in ¼-inch-thick slices
- 2   tablespoons seedless raspberry jam
- ½   cup heavy cream whipped with 1 tablespoon 10X (confectioners' powdered) sugar, for garnish
- 2   tablespoons seedless raspberry jam, for garnish *(optional)*

1. Prepare the Custard: Combine the cornstarch and the ¼ cup of sugar in a medium-size saucepan. Stir in 3 cups of the milk. Cook the mixture over medium heat, stirring gently with a wooden spoon, until the mixture comes to a boil and is slightly thickened. Remove the saucepan from the heat.

2. Combine the egg yolks and the remaining ½ cup of milk in a small bowl. Slowly stir 1 cup of the hot milk mixture into the egg yolks in a small bowl; then stir the egg yolk mixture into the hot milk mixture. Return the saucepan to the heat and cook, stirring, for 1 minute longer or until the mixture thickens. Do not boil the mixture. Remove the saucepan from the heat. Stir in the 2 tablespoons of sherry. Strain the custard into a medium-size bowl. Cover the surface with plastic wrap and refrigerate until chilled, for about 2 hours.

3. Prepare the Sherry Syrup: Combine the water and the 3 tablespoons of sugar in a small saucepan. Cook over high heat, stirring until the sugar dissolves and the mixture boils. Reduce the heat to medium and boil gently for 2 minutes longer. Remove the saucepan from the heat. Stir in the 2 tablespoons of sherry. Cool to room temperature, for about 1 hour.

4. To assemble the trifle, remove 1 pound cake from the foil package. Cut the cake in half horizontally, placing the halves next to each other on a cutting board. Measure the diameter of a straight-sided 2¾- to 3-quart bowl. The bowl should be about 7 inches in diameter and about 4 inches tall. Make a round pattern on a piece of wax paper using the top of the bowl. Place the pattern on the 2 cake halves. Cut around the pattern with a knife to make a round cake layer, filling in any spaces with the cake trimmings. Repeat the tracing and cutting with the second cake.

5. Cut 4 kiwi slices in half. Place the halves, round side up, around the base of the bowl, spacing them evenly and pressing the kiwi firmly against the side of the bowl. Carefully spoon one third of the custard (about 1⅓ cups) into the bottom of the bowl. Fit the pieces forming 1 cake round on the custard in the bowl. Brush half the Sherry Syrup over the layer. Stir the 2 tablespoons of raspberry jam to break up, then brush 1 tablespoon of the jam over the cake.

6. Reserve 6 to 8 kiwi slices for the garnish. Layer the remaining kiwi slices in an overlapping spiral over the cake. Carefully spoon another third of the custard over the kiwi. Place the second cake layer on the custard, fitting the pieces as necessary. Brush the cake with the remaining syrup, then brush with the remaining tablespoon of raspberry jam. Spoon on the remaining custard. Refrigerate the trifle, covered, for 4 hours or overnight.

7. Garnish the top of the trifle with the whipped cream and the reserved kiwi slices. Spoon 2 tablespoons of raspberry jam around the outside edge of the trifle, if you wish.

Refreshing Cantaloupe Whip

Make ahead, cool and delicious.

Makes 16 servings (½ cup each).

Nutrient Value Per Serving:
78 calories, 3 g protein, 0 g fat,
17 g carbohydrate, 13 mg
sodium, 0 mg cholesterol.

4   **pounds cantaloupe melon**
      (about 2 melons)
¼   **cup fresh lemon juice**
      (about 2 lemons)
¼   **cup fresh lime juice (about**
      4 to 5 limes)
2½   **cups water**
¾   **cup plus 2 tablespoons**
      sugar
5   **envelopes unflavored**
      gelatin
2   **tablespoons Grand Marnier**
      OR: other orange-flavored
      liqueur
2   **egg whites**
      Nonstick vegetable cooking
      spray
      Melon balls, for garnish
      (optional)

1. Working in batches, purée the
   melon with the lemon and lime
   juices in an electric blender.
   Pour the purée into a large
   metal bowl. You should have
   about 5½ to 6 cups of purée.
2. Combine 1 cup of the water, the
   ¾ cup of sugar and the gelatin
   in a 4-cup glass measure and
   stir. Let the mixture stand for 3
   minutes for the gelatin to
   soften. Microwave the mixture
   at full power, uncovered, for 3
   to 4 minutes or just to boiling.
   Stir to dissolve the sugar. Or

place the mixture in a small
saucepan and heat over
medium heat until boiling,
stirring to dissolve the sugar.
Pour the gelatin mixture into
the bowl with the melon purée.
Add the remaining 1½ cups of
water and the Grand Marnier or
other orange-flavored liqueur
to the melon mixture. Place the
bowl in a pan of ice and water
and quick-chill the mixture just
until it begins to mound when
spooned.
3. Beat the egg whites with the
   remaining 2 tablespoons of
   sugar in a small bowl until soft
   peaks form. Fold the whites
   into the gelatin mixture.
4. Spray an 8-cup decorative ring
   mold with nonstick vegetable
   cooking spray. Pour the melon
   mixture into the prepared
   mold. Refrigerate until set, for
   about 4 to 6 hours.
5. To serve, loosen the edges of
   the mold with a small metal
   spatula. Invert a serving dish
   over the mold and turn the
   mold and the plate right side
   up. Gently tap the mold to
   loosen the whip and carefully
   remove the mold. Just before
   serving, arrange melon balls in
   the center of the cantaloupe
   whip, if you wish.

QUICK TIP

It Just Doesn't Gel
If a mixture with
added gelatin doesn't
gel, there's probably
not enough gelatin for
the amount of liquid,
or the gelatin was not
completely dissolved.
To remedy,
completely dissolve
more gelatin in a little
additional liquid and
add to the original
mixture. Chill.

250

Peach and Blueberry Compote with Yogurt Sauce

Poached peaches and fresh blueberries served with a tangy yogurt sauce make this the perfect finale for a summer meal.

Makes 8 servings.

*Nutrient Value Per Serving:
106 calories, 2 g protein, 1 g fat,
25 g carbohydrate, 23 mg
sodium, 2 mg cholesterol.*

½   cup water
2½ tablespoons honey
1   tablespoon lemon juice
4   large peaches (1¾ pounds)
½   cup orange juice
1½ cups blueberries
1   container (8 ounces) plain
    yogurt
2   tablespoons orange
    marmalade

1. Combine the water, honey and lemon juice in a medium-size saucepan.
2. Peel and quarter the peaches, discarding the peels and pits. Add the peaches to the honey mixture in the saucepan; turn the peaches to coat with the honey mixture. Bring the mixture to boiling over high heat. Reduce the heat to medium-low. Simmer, covered, for 8 minutes or until the peaches are tender. Stir the peach mixture gently with a wooden spoon several times. Remove the saucepan from the heat.
3. Stir the orange juice and the blueberries into the peach mixture. Spoon into a 2-quart serving bowl. Refrigerate the fruit mixture, covered, until well chilled, for 4 hours or overnight.
4. Combine the yogurt and the marmalade in a small bowl. Refrigerate the yogurt, covered, until ready to serve.
5. Serve the compote with the yogurt sauce.

Microwave Instructions
(for a 650-watt variable power microwave oven)

Directions: Combine the water, honey and lemon juice in a microwave-safe 1½-quart casserole. Peel, pit and quarter the peaches as directed in the above recipe and add to the casserole. Stir the peaches to coat with the honey mixture. Cover the casserole with the lid. Microwave at full power for 4 to 5 minutes or until the peaches are tender, stirring once. Continue with Step 3 in the above recipe.

QUICK TIP

Peachy Keen!
Peaches are at their peak from May to September—so make the most of them during the summer. Peaches will not mature or get sweeter once they've been picked (they only get soft and wither), so choose firm—but not hard—fruit with a good color for the best flavor. Refrigerate and use within five days.

251

Italian Spumoni Bombe

An ice cream bombe can be made with any ice cream and/or sherbet combination desired. Select those with contrasting colors for the best effect.

Makes 10 servings.

Nutrient Value Per Serving:
245 calories, 4 g protein, 11 g
fat, 31 g carbohydrate, 102 mg
sodium, 48 mg cholesterol.

¼ cup finely chopped **maraschino cherries**
2 tablespoons candied lemon peel OR: candied orange peel
2 tablespoons candied citron OR: angelica
2 tablespoons light rum OR: brandy
1 quart pistachio OR: mint ice cream
1 pint vanilla ice cream
1 pint strawberry ice cream **Whipped cream, for garnish (optional)**

1. Combine the maraschino cherries, candied lemon or orange peel, candied citron or angelica and rum or brandy in a small bowl and let stand for 30 minutes.
2. Meanwhile, place an 8-cup ice cream mold or metal bowl in the freezer. Soften the pistachio or mint ice cream in the refrigerator for about 30 minutes.
3. Pack the softened ice cream into the chilled mold to make a 1- to 1½-inch-thick layer. Smooth the surface with a large spoon. Place the mold in the freezer for 2 hours or until the ice cream is firm.
4. Soften the vanilla ice cream in the refrigerator for about 30 minutes. Transfer the ice cream to a small bowl. Fold in the candied fruit mixture. Spread the vanilla ice cream over the pistachio layer in the mold, smoothing the surface with a large spoon. Freeze until firm, for about 2 hours.
5. Soften the strawberry ice cream in the refrigerator for about 30 minutes. Pack the strawberry ice cream into the mold, pressing firmly. Cover the surface of the mold with plastic wrap. Freeze for 2 hours or until firm.
6. To unmold the bombe, immerse the mold in a large bowl of hot water for 5 to 10 seconds. Quickly invert the bombe onto a chilled serving plate. If not ready to serve, place the plate with the bombe in the freezer.
7. At serving time, garnish the bombe with rosettes of whipped cream, if you wish. Cut the bombe into wedges with a long, sharp knife dipped in warm water.

QUICK TIP

Overwhipped Cream
If the cream is only slightly overwhipped, you can revive it by whipping in 1 to 2 tablespoons of half-and-half or evaporated milk.

Mocha Amaretti Loaf

An elegant, easy-to-slice loaf to make ahead for a delectable dessert.

Makes 8 servings.

Nutrient Value Per Serving: 224 calories, 4 g protein, 11 g fat, 27 g carbohydrate, 93 mg sodium, 46 mg cholesterol.

2 **pints chocolate ice cream**
1 **pint coffee ice cream**
12 **amaretti cookies, crumbled**
2 **tablespoons coffee liqueur**
  Chocolate curls, for garnish

1. Soften 1 pint of the chocolate ice cream in the refrigerator for 30 minutes. Line a 9 x 5-inch metal loaf pan with plastic wrap and place in the freezer.
2. With a large wooden spoon, pack the softened chocolate ice cream into the bottom of the lined pan. Smooth the top and freeze for 30 minutes.
3. Meanwhile, soften the coffee ice cream in the refrigerator. Combine half the amaretti cookie crumbs with the liqueur in a small bowl and let stand for 15 minutes.
4. Add the coffee ice cream to the crumb mixture and mix until blended. Then spread the coffee ice cream mixture over the chocolate layer in the pan. Freeze for 30 minutes.
5. Meanwhile, soften the second pint of chocolate ice cream in the refrigerator. Spread the chocolate ice cream over the coffee layer in the pan, smoothing the top. Cover the loaf with plastic wrap and freeze for 4 hours or until firm.
6. Invert the loaf onto an aluminum foil-lined cookie sheet. Peel off the plastic wrap. Press the remaining amaretti crumbs onto the outside of the loaf. Return the loaf to the freezer until serving time.
7. To serve, transfer the loaf to a chilled serving plate. Garnish with the chocolate curls.

QUICK TIPS

Crazy About Chocolate
Cakes, pies, cookies, candies, puddings and ice cream desserts take on a professional look with a garnish of grated chocolate or chocolate curls.
● *Chocolate Curls:* Warm a square of chocolate slightly at room temperature. For little curls, shave thin strips with a vegetable parer from the narrow side; for large ones, from the bottom. Pick up the curls with a wooden pick (otherwise they shatter) and chill until firm before arranging them on food.
● *Grated Chocolate:* Start with cold chocolate, a dry, cold grater and cold hands. Rub the square up and down over the grating surface, working quickly and handling the chocolate as little as possible.

253

Chocolate Confetti Spumoni

This showy dessert can be made several days in advance, then unmolded and garnished just before serving.

Makes 16 servings.

Nutrient Value Per Serving: 282 calories, 3 g protein, 19 g fat, 25 g carbohydrate, 85 mg sodium, 63 mg cholesterol.

3   **pints chocolate ice cream**
½   **cup chopped mixed glacé fruits**
2   **tablespoons Grand Marnier OR: other orange-flavored liqueur**
1½   **cups heavy cream**
¼   **cup 10X (confectioners' powdered) sugar**
½   **cup chopped pistachio nuts**
½   **cup finely crushed chocolate chocolate-chip cookies**
¾   **cup heavy cream beaten with 1½ tablespoons 10X (confectioners' powdered) sugar until stiff**
1   **teaspoon coarsely chopped pistachio nuts, for garnish (optional)**

1. Line a 2-quart bowl with aluminum foil, smoothing the foil next to the bowl. Place the bowl in the freezer to chill for 15 minutes.
2. Remove the ice cream from the freezer to soften slightly, for about 15 minutes. Remove 1 cup of the ice cream to a small bowl, cover the bowl and reserve in the freezer. Gently spread the remaining ice cream over the inside of the 2-quart bowl to form a shell. Place the bowl in the freezer until the ice cream is firm, for about 2 hours.
3. Meanwhile, combine the glacé fruits and the Grand Marnier or other orange-flavored liqueur in a small bowl. Reserve.
4. When the ice cream is firm, beat the 1½ cups of heavy cream with the ¼ cup of 10X (confectioners' powdered) sugar in a small bowl until stiff. Fold in the glacé fruit mixture and ¼ cup of the chopped pistachio nuts.
5. Remove the chocolate ice cream shell from the refrigerator. Sprinkle ¼ cup of the crushed cookies over the chocolate ice cream shell. Gently press the cookies into the ice cream with the back of a spoon. Spoon the whipped cream mixture into the mold, shaping a 1¼-cup cavity in the center. Freeze until the cream mixture is firm, for about 2 hours. Sprinkle the remaining ¼ cup of crushed cookies into the cavity and press the cookies into the frozen whipped cream mixture.
6. Soften the reserved 1 cup of ice cream in the refrigerator for 15 minutes. Stir the remaining ¼ cup of chopped pistachio nuts into the reserved ice cream. Spoon the ice cream mixture into the cavity. Smooth the top of the ice cream. Cover the bowl with plastic wrap and freeze until serving time, for at least 4 hours or overnight.
7. To serve, remove the bowl from the freezer. Unmold the ice cream onto a serving platter and carefully peel off the aluminum foil. Smooth the surface of the ice cream with a spatula. Garnish the dessert with the sweetened whipped cream, and sprinkle with a teaspoon of coarsely chopped pistachio nuts, if you wish.

QUICK TIP

Going Nuts
Toasted, untoasted, whole, chopped or slivered—nuts are a wonderful dessert garnish. Try almonds, pecans, pistachios, hazelnuts and walnuts. Sprinkle them on ice cream, cake and the like, or add them to sauce on top of a dessert.

Peach Crown

A frozen charlotte-like dessert with a peach-flavored ricotta cheese filling that adds elegance to any occasion.

Makes 8 servings.

Nutrient Value Per Serving:
282 calories, 8 g protein, 8 g fat,
46 g carbohydrate, 87 mg
sodium, 67 mg cholesterol.

Ladyfingers pair nicely with the rich filling in Peach Crown.

10   plain ladyfingers*, split
1   bag (20 ounces) frozen peach slices, thawed OR: 3 cups fresh peach slices
4   tablespoons sugar
¾   cup peach preserves
⅛   teaspoon ground cinnamon
1   container (15 ounces) part-skim ricotta cheese
½   cup dairy sour cream
2   teaspoons lemon juice
     Whipped cream, for garnish

1. Line the bottom of a 5½-cup brioche mold or 1½-quart bowl with aluminum foil. Arrange 3 or 4 ladyfinger halves on the bottom, cutting the ladyfingers so they fit exactly in a single layer. Line the sides of the mold with ladyfinger halves, slightly overlapping them. (The brioche mold needs 17 halves; the bowl may require more.)

2. Combine 1 cup of the peach slices, 2 tablespoons of the sugar, the preserves and cinnamon in the container of an electric blender or a food processor. Cover and whirl until the mixture is smooth. Transfer the purée to a clean bowl. Stir in the ricotta cheese and the sour cream. Pour into the prepared mold. Cover the mold with plastic wrap. Freeze for at least 8 hours or overnight.

3. Prepare the peach sauce up to 1 hour before serving: Set aside 6 or 7 peach slices for the garnish. Combine the remaining peaches, the remaining 2 tablespoons of sugar and the lemon juice in the container of the blender or food processor. Cover and whirl until puréed. Set the purée aside in the refrigerator.

4. To serve, turn the mold out onto a serving platter. Let stand at room temperature for 15 to 20 minutes before serving. Garnish the top with the reserved peach slices and the whipped cream. Serve with the peach sauce on the side.

*Note: Make sure the ladyfingers are very fresh, or they will "float."

Peach Crêpes Melba

Try the peaches and melba sauce on waffles or French toast.

Makes 8 servings.

Nutrient Value Per Serving:
142 calories, 3 g protein, 3 g fat,
27 g carbohydrate, 68 mg
sodium, 41 mg cholesterol.

1½ **cups raspberries**
1   **tablespoon raspberry brandy (optional)**
2   **teaspoons cornstarch**
3   **tablespoons sugar**
¾   **cup orange juice**
3⅓ **cups peeled, sliced peaches (1½ pounds)**
8   **crêpes (5 to 6 inches each) (recipe follows)**

1. Reserve ½ cup of the raspberries for the garnish. Purée the remaining berries in the container of a food processor or an electric blender, with the raspberry brandy if you wish. Strain the purée into a small bowl. Refrigerate the purée, covered.
2. Combine the cornstarch and the sugar in a small saucepan. Stir in the orange juice. Cook the mixture over medium-high heat until boiling. Boil gently, stirring, for 1 minute.
3. Place the peaches in a large bowl. Pour the orange sauce over the peaches and stir to combine well. Refrigerate the peach mixture, covered, for 2 hours or until serving time.
4. To serve, use a slotted spoon to lift out 16 peach slices. Set the slices aside for the garnish. Using the slotted spoon, divide the remaining peach slices among the 8 crêpes, about ¼ cup of slices per crêpe. Roll up each crêpe and place on a dessert plate. Brush each crêpe with the orange sauce remaining in the bowl. Spoon a little of the raspberry purée sauce over each crêpe, dividing evenly. Garnish each serving with the reserved whole raspberries and peach slices.

Crêpes: Combine 1 egg, ⅔ cup of milk, ½ cup of *un*sifted all-purpose flour, ⅛ teaspoon of salt and 1 tablespoon of melted butter or margarine in the container of an electric blender. Cover and whirl at medium speed for 1 minute or until the batter is smooth. Refrigerate the batter for ½ hour. Heat a small skillet (5 to 6 inches across bottom) over medium-high heat. Butter the skillet lightly, pour in the batter, 2 to 3 tablespoons at a time, and quickly rotate the skillet to spread the batter evenly over the bottom of the skillet. Cook the crêpe over medium heat to brown lightly, for about 1 minute on each side. Slide the crêpe onto a plate. Repeat with the remaining batter. When the crêpes are cool, stack them with 2 sheets of wax paper between each. Wrap the crêpes with plastic wrap and refrigerate for up to 2 days or freeze for up to 2 weeks.

Microwave Instructions
(for a 650-watt variable power microwave oven)

Directions: Combine the cornstarch and the sugar in a microwave-safe 4-cup measure and stir to mix well. Stir in the orange juice. Microwave, uncovered, at full power for 2 minutes. Whisk the mixture well. Microwave, uncovered, at full power for 30 seconds to a full rolling boil. Stir the peaches into the sauce. Continue with Step 3 in the above recipe.

Red Raspberry Ice Cream

Spectacular make-ahead desserts to wow your guests! From top, Red Raspberry Ice Cream, Italian Spumoni Bombe (page 252) and Mocha Amaretti Loaf (page 253).

Crushed strawberries or blackberries may be substituted for the raspberries. Or use a combination.

Makes about 3 quarts.

Nutrient Value Per ½ Cup: 268 calories, 5 g protein, 16 g fat, 28 g carbohydrate, 81 mg sodium, 55 mg cholesterol.

1½   **quarts light cream**
2   **cans (14 ounces each) sweetened condensed milk**
2   **cups mashed red raspberries**
¼   **cup freshly squeezed lemon juice**
  Few drops red food coloring (optional)

1. Combine the cream, condensed milk, raspberries and lemon juice in a large bowl. Stir with a wire whisk until well blended. Tint the mixture a delicate pink with a few drops of food coloring, if you wish.
2. Transfer the mixture to an ice-cream maker. Freeze, following the manufacturer's directions.

QUICK TIP

Side Show
Small cookies or little pastries can look very elegant placed on top or served alongside of puddings, creams, trifles, sherbets and ice creams.

257

Raspberry Mousse

Whip up this cool treat a day ahead and refrigerate until serving. Or serve frozen.

Makes 6 servings.

Nutrient Value Per Serving:
153 calories, 2 g protein, 11 g fat, 12 g carbohydrate, 24 mg sodium, 41 mg cholesterol.

2   egg whites
⅛   teaspoon cream of tartar
¼   cup sugar
1   cup heavy cream
1½   cups Raspberry Purée
         (recipe follows)
¼   cup heavy cream whipped
         with 1 teaspoon 10X
         (confectioners' powdered)
         sugar, for garnish
         (optional)
8   raspberries, for garnish
         (optional)
         Chocolate curls, for garnish
         (optional)

1. Beat the egg whites with the cream of tartar in a large bowl with an electric mixer at high speed until soft peaks form. Beat in the sugar, 1 tablespoon at a time, until the sugar is dissolved and the whites form almost stiff peaks.
2. Beat the 1 cup of cream in a small bowl until stiff.
3. Fold the Raspberry Purée into the egg whites. Fold the whipped cream into the raspberry mixture. Pour the mousse mixture into a 6-cup soufflé dish or bowl. Refrigerate the mousse, covered, until ready to serve.
4. To serve, garnish the mousse with ¼ cup of whipped cream, raspberries and chocolate curls, if you wish.

Raspberry Purée: Purée 3 cups of raspberries, a few at a time, in the container of a food processor or an electric blender. You should have 1½ cups of purée.

Note: For a frozen dessert, cover the mousse, ungarnished, with plastic wrap. Freeze the mousse for 4 hours or overnight. To serve, remove the mousse from the freezer, and garnish as above if you wish.

QUICK TIP

Measure For Measure
As a general rule, 1 pint of fresh berries will equal 1¾ cups; 1 cup of heavy cream will make 2 cups of whipped cream.

Cherry Cheese Tart

If you like cheesecake, you'll love this easy almond crumb crust tart with creamy cheese filling and fresh cherry topping. You can make the crust several days in advance and freeze, and you can fill the pie 3 or 4 hours before dinner.

Makes 8 servings.

Nutrient Value Per Serving:
450 calories, 7 g protein, 36 g
fat, 27 g carbohydrate, 188 mg
sodium, 92 mg cholesterol.

Almond Crumb Crust:
1	**cup vanilla wafer crumbs (about 28 cookies)**
1	**can (4 ounces) blanched slivered almonds, ground (about 1 cup)**
¼	**cup melted butter**
¼	**teaspoon almond flavoring**

Cream Cheese Filling:
1	**envelope gelatin**
2	**tablespoons water**
1	**cup (½ pint) heavy cream**
1	**package (8 ounces) cream cheese, softened**
⅓	**cup sugar**
1	**teaspoon grated lemon zest**
1	**tablespoon fresh lemon juice**
14	**fresh sweet cherries (4 ounces), halved and pitted**
3	**tablespoons currant jelly, melted**

1. Prepare the Almond Crumb Crust: Combine the vanilla wafer crumbs, ground almonds, melted butter and almond flavoring in a medium-size bowl. Stir the mixture with a fork to blend thoroughly.
2. Pour the crumb mixture into a 9-inch tart pan with a removable bottom. Press the crumbs firmly with your fingertips to form a crust over the bottom and up the sides of the pan. Cover the pan with plastic wrap and place in the freezer to set the crust, for about 30 minutes. Or make the crust several days in advance and freeze, wrapped, until 30 minutes before you are ready to fill the crust.
3. Prepare the Cream Cheese Filling: Sprinkle the gelatin over the water in a 1-cup glass measure or custard cup; let the mixture stand for 5 minutes for the gelatin to soften. Place the measuring cup in a small saucepan with 1 inch of hot water. Heat the water over medium heat and stir the gelatin until it is dissolved, for about 1 minute. Remove the measuring cup from the water and set aside to cool slightly.
4. Beat the cream in a medium-size bowl until stiff. Set the whipped cream aside.
5. Combine the cream cheese, sugar, lemon zest and lemon juice in a large bowl. Beat with an electric mixer until smooth, for about 2 minutes. Stir the gelatin into the cream cheese mixture. Gently fold in the whipped cream. Pour the filling into the crust. Refrigerate for 3 hours or until serving time.
6. To serve, arrange the cherry halves on the cheese tart and brush with the melted jelly.

QUICK TIP

Getting Even
To insure a more even bottom and side crust when making a crumb crust, press the sides and bottom of a standard measuring cup along the sides and bottom of the pie plate.

Striped Fruit Pops

Colorful layers of frozen cranberry juice, plus lemonade and limeade mixed with yogurt make these Striped Fruit Pops so irresistible kids won't realize they're good for them.

Keep these citrusy pops on hand in the freezer for hot afternoon coolers.

Makes 25 pops.

Nutrient Value Per Pop:
56 calories, 0 g protein, 0 g fat, 14 g carbohydrate, 5 mg sodium, 0 mg cholesterol.

²⁄₃ cup vanilla yogurt
1   can (6 ounces) frozen limeade concentrate, thawed
1   can (6 ounces) frozen lemonade concentrate, thawed
1   can (6 ounces) frozen cranberry juice concentrate, thawed
25 three-ounce paper cups
25 wooden sticks

1. Place ⅓ cup of the yogurt in a small bowl and stir in the limeade concentrate until the mixture is smooth. Stir in 3 concentrate cansful of water. Repeat with the remaining ⅓ cup of yogurt, the lemonade concentrate and water in a second bowl. Combine the cranberry juice concentrate and 2 cups of water in a third bowl. Keep the mixtures cold.

2. Divide the lime-yogurt mixture into the paper cups. Freeze until almost firm. Insert a wooden stick into each cup and then freeze until firm. Pour in a layer of the cranberry juice and freeze until firm. Top the pops with the lemon-yogurt mixture and freeze until the pops are firm. Peel off the paper cups to serve.

Nectarine Sorbet

Makes 12 servings (½ cup each).

Nutrient Value Per ½ Cup:
72 calories, 1 g protein, 0 g fat,
18 g carbohydrate, 4 mg
sodium, 0 mg cholesterol.

1   **cup water**
½   **cup sugar**
2   **pounds ripe nectarines**
2   **tablespoons fresh lemon**
      juice
½   **cup fresh orange juice**
1   **egg white, slightly beaten**
      with a fork
      Nectarine slices, for garnish
      (optional)

1. Combine the water and the sugar in a medium-size saucepan over medium-high heat. Bring the mixture to boiling, stirring. Cook until all the sugar is dissolved. Remove the saucepan from the heat.
2. Peel the nectarines and cut them in half. Remove and discard the pits. Add the nectarine halves to the hot sugar syrup along with the lemon juice.
3. Return the saucepan to the heat and cook, covered, over low heat until the nectarines are soft, for about 10 minutes. Let the mixture cool for 15 minutes.
4. Working in small batches, place the nectarines and the syrup in the container of an electric blender. Cover and whirl until the mixture is puréed. Pour the purée into a large mixing bowl (you should have 4 cups of purée). Add the orange juice and the egg white to the purée, stirring to combine. Refrigerate the mixture until chilled, for about 2 hours.
5. Process the nectarine mixture in an ice-cream maker following the manufacturer's instructions. OR: Still-freeze the mixture following the Quick Tip directions on page 262. For the best flavor and texture, serve the sorbet immediately. Garnish the sorbet with nectarine slices, if you wish.

Note: If the sorbet becomes too firm to scoop, soften it slightly in the refrigerator.

Elegant Nectarine Sorbet; delicious Blueberry Sorbet (page 262); tangy Raspberry Granita (page 263) and refreshing Virgin Bellini (Chapter 6, page 222.)

Blueberry Sorbet

Place the make-ahead blueberry mixture in the ice cream maker just as you sit down to dinner.

1   cup water
¾   cup sugar
1   lemon
2   cups fresh or frozen
        blueberries
1   egg white, slightly beaten
        with a fork
      Pinch ground cinnamon
      Blueberries, for garnish
      (optional)

QUICK TIP

Simple Sorbet
Pour the fruit mixture into a 13 x 9 x 2-inch metal pan. Cover the pan with plastic wrap and freeze the mixture until firm 1½ inches from the edge of the pan, for about 1½ hours. Scrape the mixture into a large bowl. Beat the mixture with an electric mixer at low speed until slushy, for about 1 minute. Pour the mixture back into the pan. Freeze, covered, until almost firm, for about 30 minutes. Repeat the beating process and return the mixture to the pan. Freeze until the mixture is just firm, for about 2 hours.

1. Combine ⅓ cup of the water and the sugar in a medium-size saucepan over medium-high heat. Bring the mixture to boiling, stirring to dissolve the sugar. Reduce the heat to low.
2. Using a swivel-bladed vegetable peeler, peel the zest (the outermost yellow rind with no white pith) from the lemon in 2½ x ½-inch strips. Add the zest strips to the syrup and simmer for 5 minutes. Remove the saucepan from the heat. With a slotted spoon, remove the zest from the syrup to use as a garnish. Cool the syrup for 15 minutes.
3. Meanwhile, combine the blueberries with the remaining ⅔ cup of water in the container of an electric blender. Cover and whirl until puréed. Pour the purée into a large bowl. Add the egg white, cinnamon and the sugar syrup and stir to combine the mixture. Refrigerate the mixture until chilled, for about 2 hours.
4. Process the blueberry mixture in an ice-cream maker following the manufacturer's instructions. OR: Still-freeze the mixture following the Quick Tip directions at left. Serve the sorbet immediately for the best flavor and texture, garnished with the candied lemon zest, and with additional blueberries, if you wish.

Note: If the mixture becomes too firm to scoop, soften it slightly in the refrigerator.

Raspberry Granita

Watermelon Ice

If the granita is made the day before or earlier in the day, place it in the refrigerator to soften slightly before serving.

Makes 6 servings (½ cup each).

*Nutrient Value Per ½ Cup:
159 calories, 1 g protein, 0 g fat,
40 g carbohydrate, 0 mg
sodium, 0 mg cholesterol.*

1 cup water
1 cup sugar
3 cups fresh or dry-pack
    frozen raspberries
1 teaspoon fresh lemon juice
    Additional raspberries, for
    garnish *(optional)*

1. Combine the water and the sugar in a medium-size saucepan over medium-high heat. Bring the mixture to boiling, stirring. Cook until all the sugar is dissolved. Let the mixture cool for 30 minutes.
2. Combine the raspberries, sugar syrup and lemon juice in the container of an electric blender. Cover and whirl until puréed.
3. Strain the purée through a coarse sieve into a bowl. Discard the seeds. Chill the purée for 2 hours.
4. Pour the purée into a 9 x 9 x 2-inch square metal pan. Cover the pan with plastic wrap and freeze until the mixture is firm around the edges, for about 45 minutes. Use a fork to gently stir the mixture. Freeze until fairly firm, for about 1 hour. Gently stir the mixture and serve. For the best flavor and texture, serve immediately. Garnish the granita with additional raspberries, if you wish.

Makes 8 servings (½ cup each).

*Nutrient Value Per ½ Cup:
86 calories, 1 g protein, 1 g fat,
21 g carbohydrate, 3 mg
sodium, 0 mg cholesterol.*

½ cup water
½ cup sugar
4 pounds watermelon (about
    ¼ large watermelon)

1. Combine the water and the sugar in a small saucepan. Bring the mixture to boiling over medium-high heat, stirring until the sugar is dissolved. Let the syrup cool for 30 minutes.
2. Remove the rind from the watermelon and discard. Cut the pulp into 1-inch pieces and remove the seeds. Purée the pulp in an electric blender, working in batches if necessary (you should have 4 cups.) Pour the purée into a large bowl. Stir the sugar syrup into the purée.
3. Pour the mixture into a 9 x 9 x 2-inch square metal pan. Cover the pan with plastic wrap. Freeze the mixture for 45 minutes or until frozen around the edges to about 1 inch. Break up the mixture with a fork to mix evenly. Freeze until the mixture is almost firm, for 45 minutes to 1 hour. Serve immediately. OR: One hour before serving, remove the pan to the refrigerator so the ice softens slightly. Chip the ice with a fork and spoon into bowls.

QUICK TIPS

The Big Chill
● To make sure your sorbets have a rich, smooth texture, stir them frequently during the freezing process.
● Granitas and ices should have a much coarser texture, so just stir them gently once or twice while they're in the freezer.
● Sorbets, ices and granitas all taste best served freshly made. If you store them in the freezer, remove to the refrigerator to soften, covered, for 15 to 45 minutes before serving.

Plum Ice

1   **pound ripe red plums**
      (6 to 8)
½   **cup water**
¾   **cup sugar**
1   **can (5½ ounces) apple juice**

1. Cut the plums in half and remove and discard the pits.
2. Add the plums to a medium-size saucepan with the water. Cook the plums, covered, over medium heat until they are soft, for 10 to 15 minutes, depending on the ripeness of the fruit. Add the sugar and stir until the sugar is dissolved. Remove the saucepan from the heat. Let the mixture cool for 30 minutes.
3. Place the plums with their liquid in the container of an electric blender. Cover and whirl until you have a smooth purée. Add the apple juice and blend to combine.
4. Pour the purée into an 8 x 8 x 2-inch square metal pan. Cover the pan with plastic wrap and place in the freezer until the mixture is frozen around the edges, for about 45 minutes. Stir the mixture with a fork to break it up and redistribute the mixture. Stir the mixture again after 45 minutes. Freeze the mixture just until firm, but easy to scoop, for about 20 minutes longer. For the best flavor and texture, serve the ice immediately.

Note: If the mixture becomes too firm to scoop, soften it slightly in the refrigerator.

Microwave Instructions
(for a 650-watt variable power microwave oven)

Directions: Combine the plums, water and sugar in a microwave-safe 1½-quart casserole. Cover the casserole. Microwave at full power for 8 minutes. Uncover and let the mixture cool for 30 minutes. Continue with Step 3 in the recipe above.

QUICK TIP

Plum Wonderful
Plums are at their peak from June to October, so make the most of them during this time. Look for plums that are soft but not mushy, shriveled or brown. Refrigerate them loosely covered or in a plastic produce bag with air holes. Use within five days of purchase.

Frozen Blueberry Yogurt

Makes about 3 cups.

Nutrient Value Per ½ Cup:
98 calories, 4 g protein, 1 g fat,
19 g carbohydrate, 54 mg
sodium, 5 mg cholesterol.

1   container (16 ounces) plain
      yogurt
½   cup fresh or frozen
      blueberry purée*
1   tablespoon sugar
3   tablespoons honey
½   teaspoon grated orange rind
      Almond Crêpe Cups
      (optional; recipe, page
      266)

Combine the yogurt, blueberry purée, sugar, honey and orange rind in a small bowl. Freeze the mixture in an electric ice-cream maker following the manufacturer's directions. Store the yogurt in the freezer. To serve, scoop the yogurt into Almond Crêpe Cups or dessert dishes.

Note: *One cup of fresh or thawed frozen blueberries yields ⅔ cup of purée.*

Refreshing Frozen Blueberry Yogurt, served by itself or in a crusty Almond Crêpe Cup (page 266), is a cooling snack or dessert.

Almond Crêpe Cups

Bake in toaster oven for 4 to 6 minutes.
Makes 12 crêpes.

Nutrient Value Per Crêpe:
94 calories, 3 g protein, 6 g fat, 7 g carbohydrate, 38 mg sodium, 53 mg cholesterol.

⅔ cup milk
2 eggs
1 tablespoon honey
1 tablespoon vegetable oil
¼ teaspoon almond extract
½ cup *un*sifted all-purpose flour
⅓ cup coarsely chopped blanched almonds
2 tablespoons butter, melted

1. Combine the milk, eggs, honey, oil, almond extract, flour and chopped almonds in the container of an electric blender. Cover and whirl until the mixture is smooth. Transfer to a small bowl. Cover the bowl and refrigerate for 1 hour.
2. Heat a 6-inch crêpe pan or a nonstick skillet. Brush the pan with a little of the melted butter. Pour in about 3 tablespoons of the batter and tilt and turn the pan to cover the bottom of the pan with the batter. Cook until the crêpe is lightly browned on the underside. Turn the crêpe over and lightly brown the other side. Stack the crêpes with a piece of wax paper between each. Fit the crêpes into 5-ounce custard cups and place an aluminum foil ball in the center of each.
3. Bake 4 cups at a time in a toaster oven set at 350° for 4 to 6 minutes (or in a conventional oven at 400°). Remove the foil balls. Cool the crêpes to room temperature. To serve, fill each crêpe with a scoop of Frozen Blueberry Yogurt *(recipe, page 265)*.

Note: *Flat crêpes can be made ahead and frozen. Thaw before fitting into cups.*

QUICK TIP

La Crêpe — C'est Bonne!
Crêpes are one of the easiest—and most elegant—desserts imaginable. Make the crêpes ahead of time. Use the recipe in our Almond Crêpe Cups, substituting vanilla extract for the almond extract. Refrigerate or freeze. When you want to use the crêpes, thaw them, fill, roll and garnish as you like. Try cherry pie filling with sour cream, finely chopped canned pears with chocolate sauce— the variations are limitless.

Frozen Yogurt in Vacherins

Such an elegant dessert—and it's all make-ahead. Prepare the vacherins in advance and store them in an airtight container.

Bake meringue at 225° for 1 hour.
Makes 6 servings.

Nutrient Value Per Serving:
142 calories, 3 g protein, 0 g fat, 32 g carbohydrate, 17 mg sodium, 0 mg cholesterol.

2   egg whites
⅛   teaspoon cream of tartar
½   cup sugar
1½   cups lowfat frozen yogurt (60 to 115 calories per ¼ cup)
¼   cup low-sugar raspberry or strawberry jam or preserves, stirred well

1. Preheat the oven to very slow (225°). Cover a large cookie sheet with heavy brown paper. Draw six 2-inch diamond shapes, about 3 inches apart from each other, on the paper.

2. Beat the egg whites with the cream of tartar in a small bowl until foamy. With an electric mixer at high speed, beat in the sugar, a tablespoon at a time, until the meringue forms stiff, glossy peaks.

3. Spread or pipe the meringue with a pastry bag fitted with a decorative #5 (plain or star) tip, following the diamond outlines. Repeat the spreading or piping to make a second meringue layer on top of the first, building up a rim.

4. Bake the meringues in the preheated very slow oven (225°) for 1 hour. Turn off the oven and leave the meringues in the oven with the door closed until cool. The vacherins can be stored for a day or two in an airtight container.

5. Place the vacherins on dessert plates. Scoop ¼ cup of the frozen yogurt into each vacherin and spoon about 2 teaspoons of the jam or preserves over each. Serve the vacherins immediately.

QUICK TIP

Egg Whites: Turn Up The Volume

If egg whites are refrigerator-cold, they should be warmed slightly, just to get the chill off. Place them in a bowl; place the bowl over another bowl of warm water; stir briefly, just until they are no longer ice-cold.

Add a pinch of salt to help egg whites liquefy to a point where they will begin absorbing air. Then start beating the egg whites slowly. If using a machine, set it on medium speed. Continue whipping on medium speed until the egg whites are very white and opaque. *Then,* increase the speed to high and beat until whites are the desired consistency, soft peaks or firm. If sugar is added, it should be added in a very slow, thin stream when the speed is increased.

267

Gingered Melon Drink

Peachy Orange Buttermilk

Any seasonal melon will do for this gingery drink. Blend the melon with the ginger ale and yogurt, add a touch of spice and enjoy.

Makes 2 servings.

Nutrient Value Per Serving: 197 calories, 6 g protein, 2 g fat, 42 g carbohydrate, 100 mg sodium, 6 mg cholesterol.

2 cups cubed, peeled melon*
   (honeydew, Persian,
   cantaloupe or cassava)
1 cup cold ginger ale
1 cup vanilla yogurt

Combine the melon, ginger ale and yogurt in the container of an electric blender. Cover and whirl until the mixture is smooth and frothy.

Note: Watermelon is not recommended for this drink.

Recharge with this tangy combination of fresh peaches (or nectarines), orange juice and buttermilk. Buttermilk is low in calories, but has a pleasant tartness and slight thickness that adds a smooth texture to blended drinks.

Makes 2 servings.

Nutrient Value Per Serving: 142 calories, 5 g protein, 1 g fat, 29 g carbohydrate, 130 mg sodium, 5 mg cholesterol.

1 cup cold buttermilk
1 cup peeled and sliced
   peaches*
¼ cup frozen orange juice
   concentrate

Combine the buttermilk, peaches and orange juice concentrate in the container of an electric blender. Cover and whirl until the mixture is smooth and frothy.

Note: Peeled and sliced nectarines or mangos may be substituted for the peaches in this recipe.

QUICK TIP

Eat, Drink And Be Healthy
Have more than just a cooling drink when you're on the run— a low-fat yogurt- or buttermilk-based blender drink is low in calories and can contribute nutrients such as protein and calcium to a skimpy meal.

268

Raspberry Frosted

When raspberries are plentiful, this is a superb way to feature them.

Makes 2 servings.

Nutrient Value Per Serving:
151 calories, 6 g protein, 5 g fat,
22 g carbohydrate, 60 mg
sodium, 17 mg cholesterol.

⅔ cup fresh raspberries,
     rinsed
1   cup cold milk
1   scoop frozen vanilla yogurt

Combine the raspberries, milk and frozen yogurt in the container of an electric blender. Cover and whirl until the mixture is smooth and frothy.

Strawberry Yogurt Drink

Vanilla yogurt is a good base to use for fruit drinks. Vary the fruit, using one or a mixture of whatever berries are in season. If your breakfast or lunch is really a quickie, this liquid dessert will add protein to your meal.

Makes 2 servings.

Nutrient Value Per Serving:
214 calories, 13 g protein, 3 g
fat, 35 g carbohydrate, 171 mg
sodium, 12 mg cholesterol.

8   large strawberries
1   pint vanilla yogurt
⅓ cup skim milk, chilled

Rinse and hull the strawberries. Slice into the container of an electric blender. Add the yogurt and the milk. Cover and whirl until the mixture is smooth and frothy.

Melon Slush

Makes 2 servings.

Nutrient Value Per Serving:
80 calories, 1 g protein, 0 g fat,
21 g carbohydrate, 13 mg
sodium, 0 mg cholesterol.

¼ honeydew melon, seeded,
     peeled and cut into cubes
     (1½ cups)
¼ cup grapefruit juice
1   tablespoon sugar
     Cracked ice

Combine the melon, grapefruit juice, sugar and ½ cup of cracked ice in the container of an electric blender. Cover and whirl until puréed. Pour the slush over ⅓ cup of cracked ice in each of two 10-ounce glasses.

Strawberry Yogurt Drink is a mellow blend of vanilla yogurt and fresh strawberries.

STEP BY STEP MENUS IN MINUTES

Chapter 8 eliminates all the guess work from meal planning. Here we offer step-by-step menus, and each includes a shopping list, a list of items to have on hand in your pantry, the work plan, and of course, delicious recipes. What could be easier? It's almost as good as having a private cook!

The quickest menu, Hot Deli Platter *(page 272)* clocks in at a mere 14 minutes — start to finish! The longest takes only 50 minutes, the South-of-the-Border Fiesta *(shown here; menu, page 298).*

As for what's in between, there's a lot to choose from: our Special Seafood Dinner *(page 274)* takes only 17 minutes to fix; in half an hour, you can serve Apple Chicken Cutlets with Cream Sauce *(page 282)* or Beef Teriyaki *(page 290.)* And that's just to name a few.

These step-by-step menus are offered as guidelines, for days when you just don't want to *think* about what to prepare. This chapter is designed to offer options, not chain you to a set pattern. By all means, substitute your favorite side dishes and desserts, or mix and match the recipes to please your family. What's important here is that it works for *you*, and makes being a busy cook a little easier.

The Turkey in Chili Mole Sauce (page 299) can be made 1 or 2 days ahead. A few hours before meal time, assemble the different parts of the Fruit and Cream Brûlée (page 301), mix the Sangria (page 301) and assemble the salad without the avocado. Then just reheat the turkey and finish the Mixed Vegetable Salad (page 300) to serve. Olé!

14-Minute Hot Deli Platter

14-Minute Hot Deli Platter

Hot Turkey
  Sandwich with
  Chutney
  Mayonnaise*

Deli Coleslaw

Low-Salt Potato Chips

Vanilla Ice Cream
  with Butterscotch
  Sauce and Chopped
  Walnuts

GROCERY LIST

1   pound sliced cooked turkey
      breast
1   head leaf lettuce
1   medium-size red onion
1   medium-size sweet red pepper
    Vanilla ice cream
4   club rolls
    Deli coleslaw
    Chutney
    Low-salt potato chips
    Butterscotch sauce
    Chopped walnuts

To Have on Hand:

• Butter or margarine • Mayonnaise
• Ground cumin • Ground hot red
pepper

WORK PLAN

1. Prepare the Hot Turkey
    Sandwich through Step 1.
2. Prepare the Chutney
    Mayonnaise.
3. Complete the turkey sandwich.
4. Place the slaw and the chips in
    serving bowls.
5. Scoop the ice cream and top
    with the sauce and the walnuts
    when ready to serve dessert.

Hot Turkey Sandwich with Chutney Mayonnaise

*Makes 4 open-face sandwiches
(2 halves per serving).*

*Nutrient Value Per Sandwich:
537 calories, 40 g protein, 22 g
fat, 44 g carbohydrate, 564 mg
sodium, 103 mg cholesterol.*

2   tablespoons butter or
      margarine
1   pound thinly sliced cooked
      turkey breast
4   club (rectangular) rolls,
      split and toasted
    Leaf lettuce
    Chutney Mayonnaise *(recipe
      follows)*
1   medium-size red onion,
      cut into rings
1   medium-size sweet red
      pepper, cut into rings

1. Melt the butter or margarine in
    a large skillet over medium-
    high heat. Add the sliced turkey
    and heat, turning the slices
    often, for about 3 minutes.
2. Place the rolls, cut side up, on
    the work surface. Cover both
    halves of each roll with leaf
    lettuce. Arrange the hot turkey
    over the lettuce and spread
    with the Chutney Mayonnaise.
    Top the sandwiches with the
    onion and the red pepper.

Chutney Mayonnaise: Combine ¼
cup of mayonnaise, ¼ cup of
chutney, ½ teaspoon of ground
cumin and a pinch of ground hot
red pepper in the container of an
electric blender or a food
processor. Cover and whirl until
fairly smooth.

15-Minute Pasta Presto!

Tortellini with Cream Sauce

GROCERY LIST

1   pound frozen cheese tortellini
1   bunch broccoli, or ½ pound flowerets from salad bar
½   cup heavy cream
½   cup grated Parmesan cheese
1   can (10½ ounces) chick peas
1   jar (6 ounces) marinated artichoke hearts
1   pint cherry tomatoes
1   loaf Italian bread
1   pint raspberry sherbet
    Shredded coconut

To Have on Hand:
• Butter • Pepper

WORK PLAN

1. In the morning, refrigerate the jar of marinated artichoke hearts and the can of chick-peas.
2. When ready to prepare dinner, heat the water for the tortellini.
3. Trim the broccoli and save the stems for another use.
4. Prepare the Marinated Artichoke Salad.
5. Slice the bread and place it in a bread basket or serving plate.
6. Prepare the Tortellini with Cream Sauce.
7. Scoop the sherbet and sprinkle with the coconut when ready to serve dessert.

Makes 4 servings.

Nutrient Value Per Serving: 410 calories, 21 g protein, 22 g fat, 33 g carbohydrate, 752 mg sodium, 90 mg cholesterol.

1   **pound frozen cheese tortellini**
2   **cups broccoli flowerets**
½   **cup heavy cream**
½   **cup grated Parmesan cheese Pepper, to taste**

1. Cook the tortellini in 3 quarts of boiling water in a large pot for 5 minutes. Add the broccoli and continue cooking for 1 to 2 minutes or until the tortellini are tender. Drain the tortellini and broccoli; set aside.
2. In the same pot, heat the cream to boiling; cook for 1 minute.
3. Add the tortellini and the broccoli to the cream. Sprinkle the tortellini with the Parmesan. Gently toss to coat. Add pepper. Serve immediately.

Marinated Artichoke Salad

Makes 4 servings.

Nutrient Value Per Serving: 150 calories, 5 g protein, 8 g fat, 16 g carbohydrate, 129 mg sodium, 0 mg cholesterol.

Combine 1 jar (6 ounces) marinated artichoke hearts, halved and undrained, with 1 can (10½ ounces) chick peas, drained, and 1 pint cherry tomatoes in a serving bowl. Add pepper to taste. Let the salad stand to blend the flavors.

15-Minute Pasta Presto!

Tortellini with Cream Sauce*

Marinated Artichoke Salad*

Italian Bread

Raspberry Sherbet with Shredded Coconut

273

17-Minute
Special Seafood
Dinner

17-Minute Special Seafood Dinner

Fillet of Flounder
with Vegetables
and Lobster*

Mixed Green Salad

Croissant

Fresh Pears with
Roquefort Cheese

White Wine or Soda

Just fill and fold! Foil packets make Fillet of Flounder with Vegetables and Lobster deliciously easy.

GROCERY LIST

4	flounder fillets (1¼ to 1½ pounds)
1	medium-size leek
1	stalk fennel or celery
1	medium-size carrot
	Greens for salad
4	ripe pears
1	package (6½ ounces) frozen lobster newburg in boilable bag
4	croissants or French rolls
4	ounces Roquefort cheese
	Bottled creamy garlic dressing
	Dry white wine or soda

To Have on Hand:
● Vegetable oil ● Salt and pepper ● Leaf tarragon

WORK PLAN

1. Place the Roquefort cheese on a serving plate and let it stand at room temperature until ready to serve dessert. Place a large cookie sheet in the oven to heat. Preheat the oven to very hot (500°). Cut out the aluminum foil squares.
2. Rinse and dry the fish. Rinse the pears and place them in a serving bowl. Cut the vegetables.
3. Assemble the foil packages.
4. Prepare the salad.
5. Arrange the fish packages on the cookie sheet in the oven. Bake the fish packages.
6. Heat the croissants.
7. Place the fish packages on dinner plates and open.

Fillet of Flounder with Vegetables and Lobster

Bake at 500° for 10 minutes.
Makes 4 servings.

Nutrient Value Per Serving:
270 calories, 34 g protein, 12 g
fat, 6 g carbohydrate, 628 mg
sodium, 75 mg cholesterol.

4   **flounder fillets (1¼ to 1½**
     pounds)
1   **medium-size carrot, peeled**
1   **medium-size leek**
1   **stalk fennel OR: celery**
     Vegetable oil
½   **teaspoon salt**
⅛   **teaspoon pepper**
¼   **teaspoon leaf tarragon,**
     crumbled
1   **package (6½ ounces) frozen**
     lobster newburg in
     boilable bag, partially
     thawed

1. Place a cookie sheet in the oven. Preheat the oven to very hot (500°).
2. Cut out four 12-inch squares of aluminum foil.
3. Rinse the flounder fillets and blot dry on paper toweling.
4. Cut the carrot, leek and fennel or celery into julienne strips, 2½ x ¼ inch.
5. Brush the lower half of each foil square with a little oil. Place a flounder fillet on each, folding the fillet to fit. Spread the vegetables equally over each fillet. Sprinkle the fillets with the salt, pepper and tarragon. Divide the lobster newburg into 4 equal portions and spread over each fillet.
6. Fold the top half of the foil over the filling to meet the lower edge. Fold the edges all around twice to make a double pleat to seal. Place the packages on the hot cookie sheet in the oven, one inch apart.
7. Bake the fish packages in the preheated very hot oven (500°) for 10 minutes. Remove the packages to dinner plates. Cut an X in the top of each package and carefully open up the foil. Serve in the foil.

QUICK TIP

"Brain Food" Facts
Fresh fish should be used immediately whenever possible; however, you can refrigerate it for 1 or 2 days or even freeze it for up to 9 months. Before refrigerating, rinse fish thoroughly in cold water. Pat dry with paper toweling and cover loosely with wax paper. Store in the coldest part of your refrigerator. To freeze fillets, wrap them well in moisture/vapor-proof wrapping. *Don't forget to label and date your fish!*

17-Minute Mexi-Burger Supper

Mexi-Burgers with Cheddar Cheese

17-Minute Mexi-Burger Supper

Mexi-Burgers with Cheddar Cheese*

Spicy Lettuce Relish*

Sunshine Sundae*

GROCERY LIST

1   pound lean ground beef
1   sweet green pepper
1   head iceberg lettuce
1   ripe tomato
1   egg
1   package (6 ounces) sliced Cheddar cheese
4   sesame seed buns
    Plain bread crumbs
1   small jar mild taco sauce
2   containers plain yogurt
    Granola
    Fresh fruit

To Have on Hand:
● Vegetable oil ● Liquid red pepper seasoning ● Leaf oregano ● Chili powder ● Ground cumin ● Salt and pepper ● Orange marmalade

WORK PLAN

1. Prepare the Mexi-Burgers with Cheddar Cheese.
2. While the burgers are cooking, prepare the Spicy Lettuce Relish and the Sunshine Sundaes, but do not garnish the sundaes.
3. When ready to serve dessert, garnish the Sunshine Sundaes with the fresh fruit of your choice.

Makes 4 burgers.

Nutrient Value Per Burger:
535 calories, 31 g protein, 31 g fat, 32 g carbohydrate, 783 mg sodium, 170 mg cholesterol.

1   pound lean ground beef
¼   cup mild taco sauce
1   egg
2   tablespoons plain bread crumbs
1   teaspoon leaf oregano, crumbled
½   teaspoon chili powder
½   teaspoon ground cumin
½   teaspoon salt
⅛   teaspoon pepper
6   drops liquid red pepper seasoning
1   tablespoon vegetable oil
4   sesame seed buns
4   square slices Cheddar cheese (part of 6-ounce package)
4   large slices ripe tomato
8   thin sweet green pepper rings

1. Mix together the beef, taco sauce, egg, crumbs, oregano, chili powder, cumin, salt, pepper and liquid red pepper seasoning in a medium-size bowl until combined. Shape the meat into four 4-inch burgers.
2. Cook the hamburgers in the oil in a large skillet for 3 minutes on each side or until the burgers are the desired doneness.
3. Split the buns in half. Place a burger on the bottom of each bun. Top the burgers with the Cheddar cheese, tomato, green pepper and the top of the bun.

276

Spicy Lettuce Relish

Sunshine Sundae

By varying the flavor of the yogurt and the preserves, you have almost unlimited possibilities for future desserts.

Makes about 4 servings (2 cups).

Nutrient Value Per Serving: 74 calories, 1 g protein, 4 g fat, 10 g carbohydrate, 249 mg sodium, 0 mg cholesterol.

1   tablespoon vegetable oil
6   cups shredded iceberg
      lettuce
⅓   cup mild taco sauce
¼   teaspoon salt
      Pinch pepper
      Liquid red pepper
      seasoning

Heat the oil in a large skillet over high heat. Add the lettuce and stir-fry for 1 minute or until wilted. Transfer the lettuce to a serving dish. Lightly toss the lettuce with the taco sauce, salt, pepper and liquid red pepper seasoning.

Makes 4 servings.

Nutrient Value Per Serving: 150 calories, 7 g protein, 4 g fat, 21 g carbohydrate, 90 mg sodium, 7 mg cholesterol.

2   containers (8 ounces each)
      plain yogurt
2   tablespoons orange
      marmalade
2   tablespoons granola
      Fresh fruit

1. Combine the yogurt and the marmalade in a small mixing bowl. Place 1 tablespoon of the granola in each of four sundae glasses. Spoon one quarter of the yogurt mixture into each dish. Sprinkle the remaining 4 tablespoons of granola over the yogurt, dividing evenly.
2. Garnish with the fresh fruit.

QUICK TIP

Make A Note Of That!
As soon as you run out of a stock item, jot it down on a list you keep handy in the kitchen. Your brain power should be used for more important things than trying to remember whether you are supposed to buy flour or canned chicken broth.

20-Minute Pork And Apple Dinner

Brandied Pork Cutlets

20-Minute Pork And Apple Dinner

Brandied Pork Cutlets*

Winter Applesauce*

Whipped Potatoes with Bacon and Chives*

Banana Chocolate Chip Mousse*

GROCERY LIST

4   boneless pork loin cutlets (1 pound)
1   envelope (3½ ounces) instant mashed potatoes
2   medium-size ripe bananas
2   apples
2   small parsnips
1   can (8 ounces) jellied cranberry sauce
    Frozen chopped chives
    Real bacon bits
1   small bag mini-chocolate pieces
    Brandy or apple juice
½   pint heavy cream

To Have on Hand:
● Milk ● Butter or margarine
● Vegetable oil ● Garlic
● Leaf thyme ● Salt and pepper ● Sugar ● Vanilla ● Lemon juice ● Cinnamon

WORK PLAN

1. Prepare the Banana Chocolate Chip Mousse. Prepare the Winter Applesauce through Step 2.
2. Prepare the Brandied Pork Cutlets through Step 2.
3. Prepare the Whipped Potatoes with Bacon and Chives, following the package directions, but using 2 cups of milk, ¾ cup of water and 4 tablespoons of butter. After whipping the potatoes, beat in 1 tablespoon of real bacon bits, 2 tablespoons of frozen chopped chives and salt and pepper to taste.
4. Complete the Winter Applesauce.
5. Complete the pork cutlets.

Makes 4 servings.

Nutrient Value Per Serving: 299 calories, 25 g protein, 17 g fat, 0 g carbohydrate, 407 mg sodium, 87 mg cholesterol.

4   boneless pork loin cutlets (about 1 pound), trimmed of excess fat
½   teaspoon salt
¼   teaspoon leaf thyme, crumbled
⅛   teaspoon pepper
2   tablespoons butter or margarine
1   tablespoon vegetable oil
1   clove garlic, finely chopped
¼   cup brandy or apple juice

1. Pound the cutlets to a ¼-inch thickness between 2 pieces of wax paper. Season the cutlets with the salt, thyme and pepper.
2. Meanwhile, heat a large, heavy skillet over medium-high heat. Add 1 tablespoon of the butter or margarine and the oil to the skillet. Sauté the cutlets for 3 minutes on each side or until cooked through. Remove the cutlets to a platter and cover to keep warm. Discard the fat from the skillet.
3. Lower the heat to medium. Add the remaining 1 tablespoon of butter or margarine and the garlic to the skillet. Sauté for 30 seconds. Add the brandy or apple juice and cook for 30 seconds or until the liquid is syrupy. Add any accumulated meat juices from the platter to the skillet and stir. Pour the sauce over the cutlets and serve.

Winter Applesauce

Makes 4 servings.

*Nutrient Value Per Serving:
195 calories, 1 g protein, 0 g fat,
50 g carbohydrate, 21 mg
sodium, 0 mg cholesterol.*

½ cup cold water
¼ cup sugar
2 tablespoons lemon juice
2 all-purpose apples (about ¾ pound), pared, cored and cut into chunks
2 small parsnips (about ¼ pound), pared and cut into chunks
1 can (8 ounces) jellied cranberry sauce
⅛ teaspoon ground cinnamon

1. Combine the water, sugar and lemon juice in a saucepan. Bring to boiling, stirring, until the sugar is dissolved.
2. Working in batches, place the apples and parsnips in a blender or food processor. Pulse on and off to chop fine. Stir into the boiling sugar syrup. Cover and cook over medium heat, until the apples and parsnips are soft, for about 5 minutes.
3. Combine the apple mixture, cranberry sauce and cinnamon in the container of an electric blender or processor. Cover; whirl until puréed. Serve warm.

Banana Chocolate Chip Mousse

Makes 4 servings.

*Nutrient Value Per Serving:
249 calories, 2 g protein, 19 g
fat, 21 g carbohydrate, 18 mg
sodium, 61 mg cholesterol.*

¾ cup heavy cream
1 tablespoon sugar
1 teaspoon vanilla
2 medium-size ripe bananas, peeled and broken into chunks
2 tablespoons mini-chocolate pieces

1. Beat together the cream, sugar and vanilla in a small bowl until stiff.
2. Place the bananas in the container of an electric blender or a food processor. Cover and whirl until puréed. Fold the banana purée into the whipped cream along with the chocolate pieces. Spoon the mousse into 4 dessert dishes and refrigerate for up to 1 hour.

QUICK TIP

A Master Plan
Plan your menus for the week, and you'll be less frazzled when you're running late and the gang is wondering where dinner is. You may also discover that you're spending a little less on groceries every week—less impulse buying.

28-Minute
Pizza Parlor

Overstuffed Italian Bread Pizza

28-Minute Pizza Parlor

Overstuffed Italian Bread Pizza*

Green Salad

Creamy Italian Dressing*

Raspberry Almond Dream*

GROCERY LIST

1   package (3½ ounces) sliced pepperoni
1   package (8 ounces) shredded mozzarella cheese
     Grated Parmesan cheese
1   small container dairy sour cream
     Greens for salad
1   bunch curly parsley
1   lemon
8   oil-cured black olives
1   small jar (7 ounces) roasted red peppers
1   small jar marinara spaghetti sauce
1   large loaf Italian bread (½ pound)
1   package (12 ounces) individually frozen raspberries
1   container (8 ounces) frozen nondairy whipped topping

To Have on Hand:
● Garlic ● Leaf oregano
● Pepper ● Olive oil
● Mayonnaise ● Dijon-style mustard ● 10X (confectioners' powdered) sugar ● Almond extract

WORK PLAN

1. Prepare the Raspberry Almond Dream, spoon it into dessert dishes and freeze.
2. Clean and assemble the ingredients for the green salad and refrigerate. Prepare the Creamy Italian Dressing and refrigerate.
3. Prepare the Overstuffed Italian Bread Pizza.

Makes 4 pizzas.

*Nutrient Value Per Pizza:
509 calories, 23 g protein, 29 g fat, 40 g carbohydrate, 1,351 mg sodium, 64 mg cholesterol.*

1   large loaf Italian bread (about ½ pound), cut in half horizontally and crosswise
½   cup prepared marinara spaghetti sauce
1   package (8 ounces) shredded mozzarella cheese
16   slices pepperoni (part of 3½-ounce package)
¼   cup drained roasted red peppers (part of 7-ounce jar), cut into strips
8   oil-cured black olives, halved and pitted
2   tablespoons grated Parmesan cheese
1   teaspoon olive oil
½   teaspoon leaf oregano, crumbled

1. Place the bread on a broiler rack. Broil the bread 4 inches from the source of the heat for 2 minutes on each side or until the bread is crisp.
2. Spread the cut sides of the bread with the marinara sauce. Sprinkle the bread with the mozzarella cheese and top with the pepperoni, red peppers, olives, Parmesan cheese, oil and oregano, dividing the ingredients equally among the bread slices.
3. Broil the pizzas for 2 minutes or until the cheese is melted and bubbly.

Creamy Italian Dressing

Makes about 1 cup.

Nutrient Value Per 2 Tablespoons:
132 calories, 1 g protein, 14 g fat, 1 g carbohydrate, 115 mg sodium, 14 mg cholesterol.

½   cup dairy sour cream
½   cup mayonnaise
¼   cup chopped parsley
1½ teaspoons lemon juice
1½ teaspoons Dijon-style mustard
1   or 2 cloves garlic, finely chopped
¼   teaspoon leaf oregano, crumbled
⅛   teaspoon pepper

Combine the sour cream, mayonnaise, parsley, lemon juice, mustard, garlic, oregano and pepper in a small bowl and mix until well combined. Store the dressing in an airtight container in the refrigerator for up to 1 week.

Raspberry Almond Dream

Makes 8 servings.

Nutrient Value Per Serving:
131 calories, 1 g protein, 7 g fat, 16 g carbohydrate, 7 mg sodium, 0 mg cholesterol.

1   package (12 ounces) individually frozen raspberries
1   container (8 ounces) frozen nondairy whipped topping, thawed
⅓   cup 10X (confectioners' powdered) sugar
½   teaspoon almond extract
    Additional frozen nondairy whipped topping, for garnish *(optional)*

Place the raspberries in the container of an electric blender or a food processor. Cover and whirl until the raspberries are puréed. Place the whipped topping in a large bowl. Gradually fold in the raspberry purée, 10X (confectioners' powdered) sugar and almond extract. Spoon the mixture into 8 dessert dishes and refrigerate or freeze until ready to serve. Garnish each dessert with a dollop of whipped topping, if you wish.

QUICK TIP

Location Logic
Organize your grocery list in categories according to their location in the supermarket. For example, if you enter the store through the produce department, begin your list with fruits and vegetables.

281

30-Minute Autumn Weekend Dinner

30-Minute Autumn Weekend Dinner

Apple Chicken Cutlets with Cream Sauce*

Broccoli and Wild Rice*

Chocolate Cake with Cherry Sauce*

Coffee Supreme*

GROCERY LIST

1   bunch broccoli (1¼ pounds)
1   bunch green onions
1   large apple (Rome Beauty or Granny Smith)
4   boneless, skinned chicken breast halves (about 1¼ pounds)
½   cup (1 stick) butter
1   container (½ pint) heavy cream
1   package (6 ounces) original-style long grain and wild rice mix
1   can (5½ ounces) apple juice
1   can (1 pound, 5 ounces) cherry pie filling
1   frozen frosted chocolate cake with sliced almond topping (11½ ounces)

To Have on Hand:
● Coffee ● Cloves ● Anise seeds
● Vanilla bean ● Cinnamon sticks
● Natural or light brown sugar
● Milk or whipping cream

WORK PLAN

1. Prepare the Chocolate Cake with Cherry Sauce, allowing enough advance time for the cake to thaw.
2. Wash and trim the broccoli.
3. Start the rice cooking.
4. Prepare the Apple Chicken Cutlets with Cream Sauce, and cook the broccoli. Brew the coffee for Coffee Supreme.
5. Before serving dinner, pour the coffee into a carafe with the spice bag for the Coffee Supreme. Serve with the Chocolate Cake with Cherry Sauce.

Apple Chicken Cutlets with Cream Sauce

Use part of the seasoning mix from the packaged rice in the Broccoli and Wild Rice for extra spice in this apple-flavored chicken dish.

Makes 4 servings.

Nutrient Value Per Serving: 464 calories, 35 g protein, 30 g fat, 15 g carbohydrate, 176 mg sodium, 179 mg cholesterol.

4   boneless, skinned chicken breast halves (about 1¼ pounds)
1   container (½ pint) heavy cream
2   tablespoons butter
1   large apple (Rome Beauty or Granny Smith)
1   bunch green onions, white parts and some of green tops, sliced
1   can (5½ ounces) apple juice
½   of packet herb and seasoning mix (reserved from Broccoli and Wild Rice; *recipe, page 284)*

1. Lightly pound the chicken breasts between 2 pieces of wax paper, using a meat mallet, a rolling pin or the bottom of a heavy skillet, to flatten the breasts slightly to ½-inch thickness.

2. Bring the cream to boiling in a medium-size saucepan over medium heat. Gently boil the cream until it is reduced by about half, for about 5 minutes.

3. Meanwhile, sauté the flattened chicken in the butter in a 10-inch skillet over medium-high heat until lightly browned, turning once, for about 4 minutes. Remove the chicken to a plate.

4. Core the apple and slice it crosswise into ⅓-inch-thick rings. Add the apple rings to the skillet and sauté over high heat until the rings are lightly browned, turning once, for about 2 minutes. Remove the rings to the plate.

5. Add the green onion to the skillet and sauté for several seconds. Add the apple juice, reduced cream and the herb and seasoning mix, stirring with a wooden spoon to scrape up any browned bits from the bottom of the skillet. Boil the mixture for 1 minute to reduce slightly. Return the chicken to the skillet. Lower the heat to medium and simmer, covered, until the chicken is cooked through, for about 5 minutes. (The chicken should offer slight resistance when pressed with a finger.)

6. Add the apple rings to the skillet and cook to heat the rings through, for about 1 minute. Arrange the chicken and the apple rings on a warmed serving platter. Spoon the sauce over the chicken.

QUICK TIP

Divide And Conquer!
For today's busy two-career couple, division of labor is a must. Once a week, sit down and write out complete menus for the week ahead. Make a list of things to buy, what can be done in advance and what should be started by whomever arrives home first. By having a thorough "plan of attack," you'll save time and energy in the kitchen — and by sharing the burden of meal preparation, you'll have more leisure time to spend together.

283

Broccoli and Wild Rice

Makes 4 servings.

*Nutrient Value Per Serving:
221 calories, 8 g protein, 6 g fat,
35 g carbohydrate, 398 mg
sodium, 16 mg cholesterol.*

1	**bunch broccoli (1¼ pounds)**
1	**package (6 ounces) original-style long grain and wild rice mix**
2	**tablespoons butter**
½	**cup water**

1. Wash the broccoli and trim the leaves. Separate the broccoli into flowerets. If the stalks are large, split the broccoli lengthwise through the stem and flower. Set the broccoli aside.
2. Pour the contents of the herb and seasoning packet into a custard cup and stir to mix.
3. Prepare the rice following the package directions, using half the herb and seasoning mix, 1 tablespoon of the butter and the amount of water specified in the package directions. Reserve the remaining herb and seasoning mix for the Apple Chicken Cutlets with Cream Sauce *(recipe, page 282)*.
4. Bring the ½ cup of water to boiling in a large saucepan. Add the broccoli and cook, covered, over medium heat for 8 minutes or until the stalks are just tender when pierced with a fork.
5. Drain the water from the broccoli in the saucepan. Add the remaining tablespoon of butter to the broccoli in the saucepan and toss to coat the broccoli with the butter.
6. Spoon the rice into the center of a warmed serving dish. Arrange the broccoli around the rice.

Microwave Instructions
(for a 650-watt variable power microwave oven)

Ingredient Changes: Reduce the butter to 1 tablespoon.
Directions: Combine 2⅓ cups of water, 1 tablespoon of butter and half the herb and seasoning mix in a microwave-safe, 3-quart casserole. Cover the casserole with the lid. Microwave the mixture at full power for 6 to 8 minutes until boiling. Stir in the rice. Cover the casserole. Microwave at half power for 18 minutes. Stir the rice and place the broccoli on top of the rice with the floweret ends toward the center of the casserole. Cover the casserole. Microwave at full power for 4 to 5 minutes until the broccoli is crisp-tender. Let the broccoli and rice stand, covered, for 5 minutes.

Chocolate Cake with Cherry Sauce

Coffee Supreme

Makes 6 servings.

Nutrient Value Per Serving:
346 calories, 2 g protein, 12 g
fat, 62 g carbohydrate, 198 mg
sodium, 0 mg cholesterol.

1   frozen frosted chocolate
    cake with sliced almond
    topping (11½ ounces)
1   can (1 pound, 5 ounces)
    cherry pie filling

1. Thaw the cake following the
   package directions.
2. Place the cake on a small
   serving platter.
3. Pour the cherry pie filling into a
   coarse sieve over a medium-
   size bowl. Tap the sieve to
   drain the sauce from the
   cherries.
4. Using a fork, arrange some of
   the cherries on the cake top in
   diagonal lines. Arrange more of
   the cherries around the cake
   base.
5. Gently stir the remaining
   cherries back into the sauce.
   Pour the sauce into a serving
   dish and serve the sauce with
   the cake, spooning some over
   each serving.

Makes 8 to 10 servings.

Nutrient Value Per Serving:
7 calories, 0 g protein, 0 g fat,
1 g carbohydrate, 3 mg sodium,
0 mg cholesterol.

6   cups hot, freshly brewed,
    strong coffee
12 whole cloves
1¼ teaspoons anise seeds,
    crushed
1   2-inch vanilla bean, split
    lengthwise
2   cinnamon sticks
    Natural or light brown
    sugar, for garnish
    Hot milk OR: softly whipped
    cream, for garnish

1. Prepare the coffee, using your
   favorite method. Tie the cloves,
   anise seeds and vanilla bean in
   a small cheesecloth bag. Add
   the bag and the cinnamon
   sticks to the coffee carafe.
   Leave the carafe on a warmer
   to steep for 15 minutes. Or pour
   the freshly made coffee into a
   thermos, add the spice bag and
   the cinnamon sticks and allow
   the coffee to steep for at least
   15 minutes.
2. Serve the coffee in small mugs
   or cups garnished with the
   sugar and hot milk or whipped
   cream to taste.

30-Minute Meat and Potatoes

Marinated Flank Steak

30-Minute Meat And Potatoes

Marinated Flank Steak*

Hash Browns Piquante*

Asparagus Vinaigrette*

Strawberries and White Chocolate*

GROCERY LIST

1 pound fresh asparagus
1 lemon
1 pint fresh strawberries
1 medium-size red onion
1 flank steak (1¼ pounds)
1 container (½ pint) heavy cream
1 bottle (12 ounces) malt or balsamic vinegar
1 bar (3 ounces) white chocolate candy
1 bag (2 pounds) frozen hash brown potatoes

To Have on Hand:
● Olive oil ● Pepper

WORK PLAN

1. Prepare the marinade for the flank steak and marinate the steak for at least 1 hour.
2. Trim and clean the asparagus. Wash and hull the strawberries.
3. Prepare the Hash Browns Piquante.
4. Prepare the Asparagus Vinaigrette.
5. Broil the flank steak.
6. Prepare the Strawberries and White Chocolate.

By marinating the flank steak earlier in the day (or overnight), once you begin cooking, this meal is ready in less than 30 minutes.

Broil for 10 to 11 minutes for rare.
Makes 4 servings.

Nutrient Value Per Serving:
348 calories, 27 g protein, 25 g fat, 2 g carbohydrate, 90 mg sodium, 75 mg cholesterol.

½ cup malt vinegar OR: balsamic vinegar
¼ cup olive oil
½ cup chopped red onion (about ¾ of medium-size onion, saving remaining onion for Asparagus Vinaigrette; *recipe, page 287*)
¼ teaspoon pepper
1 flank steak (1¼ pounds)

1. Combine the malt or balsamic vinegar, the oil, onion and pepper in a heavy plastic food-storage bag.
2. Score the steak in a diamond pattern on both sides. Add the steak to the marinade in the plastic bag. Expel the excess air from the bag, seal the bag and place in a pan. Let the steak stand for 30 minutes. Turn the bag over and marinate the steak for another 30 minutes.
3. Remove the steak from the marinade and save the marinade for the Hash Browns Piquante *(recipe, page 287)*.
4. Adjust the broiler pan 4 to 5 inches from the source of the heat. Preheat the broiler.
5. Broil the steak for 5 minutes. Turn the steak over and broil for another 5 to 6 minutes for rare.

Asparagus Vinaigrette

Serve hot, or make ahead and serve chilled, if you wish.

Makes 4 servings.

Nutrient Value Per Serving:
49 calories, 2 g protein, 4 g fat,
5 g carbohydrate, 2 mg sodium,
0 mg cholesterol.

1   pound fresh asparagus
1   lemon
1   tablespoon olive oil
1   tablespoon chopped red
       onion

1. Break off the woody ends of the asparagus and discard. Wash the stalks thoroughly. If the asparagus are large, peel the bottom half of the stalks with a swivel-bladed vegetable peeler.
2. Bring 2 cups of water to boiling in a 10-inch skillet. Add the asparagus and cook, covered, over medium-high heat for 8 to 10 minutes or until the stalks are just fork-tender. Drain the asparagus on paper toweling. Arrange the asparagus on a platter.
3. Cut the lemon in half crosswise. Cut one half into slices for the garnish. Squeeze the juice from the other half and combine with the oil in a small cup. Drizzle the vinaigrette over the asparagus. Sprinkle the asparagus with the chopped onion. Garnish the platter with the lemon slices.

Hash Browns Piquante

Makes 4 servings.

Nutrient Value Per Serving:
172 calories, 2 g protein, 9 g fat,
20 g carbohydrate, 26 mg
sodium, 0 mg cholesterol.

2   tablespoons olive oil
½   of 2-pound bag frozen hash
       brown potatoes
3   tablespoons reserved
       marinade from Marinated
       Flank Steak *(recipe, page*
       286)

1. Cook the hash browns in the oil, following the package directions for the skillet method, for 10 minutes.
2. Add the reserved marinade and cook for another 10 minutes or until the potatoes are crisp.

Strawberries and White Chocolate

Makes 4 servings.

Nutrient Value Per Serving:
242 calories, 2 g protein, 18 g
fat, 20 g carbohydrate, 29 mg
sodium, 44 mg cholesterol.

½   cup heavy cream
1   bar (3 ounces) white
       chocolate candy
1   pint fresh strawberries,
       hulled, halved if large

Heat the cream to boiling in a small saucepan; remove from the heat. Break the chocolate into the hot cream. Stir the mixture gently until the chocolate is melted. Spoon the sauce into dessert dishes. Place the strawberries on top of the sauce.

30-Minute Winter's Evening Dinner

Beef Paprika with Noodles

30-Minute Winter's Evening Dinner

Beef Paprika
  with Noodles*
Cucumber Salad
Red Wine or Soda
Cherry Cheesecake

GROCERY LIST

1¼ pounds ground round
¼   pound small mushrooms
1   small green cabbage
    Fresh dill
1   small cucumber
1   small red onion
1   head Boston lettuce
½   cup dairy sour cream
1   envelope onion soup mix
8   ounces wide egg noodles
    Bottled vinaigrette dressing
1   can cherry pie filling
1   cheesecake, fresh or frozen
    Red wine or soda

To Have on Hand:
● Butter or margarine ● Paprika
● Poppy or caraway seeds

WORK PLAN

1. Heat the water for the noodles and the cabbage.
2. Cook the beef patties.
3. Add the noodles and the cabbage to the boiling water.
4. Prepare the salad.
5. Sauté the mushrooms and prepare the sauce.
6. Drain the noodles and season. Arrange the noodles on a platter with the patties.
7. Finish the sauce. Spoon some of the sauce over the patties.
8. Garnish the cheesecake with some of the cherry pie filling when ready to serve dessert.

Makes 4 servings.

*Nutrient Value Per Serving:
770 calories, 37 g protein, 45 g fat, 52 g carbohydrate, 1,113 mg sodium, 195 mg cholesterol.*

1¼ pounds ground round
2   tablespoons butter or margarine
8   ounces wide egg noodles
3   cups shredded green cabbage (1 small)
¼   pound small mushrooms, halved or sliced
1   tablespoon paprika
1   envelope onion soup mix
1½ cups water
2   tablespoons butter
½   teaspoon poppy or caraway seeds
½   cup dairy sour cream
    Dill sprigs, for garnish

1. Bring 3 quarts of lightly salted water to boiling in a saucepan.
2. Shape the beef into 4 patties.
3. Heat 2 tablespoons butter in a skillet. Add patties; cook over medium heat for 4 to 6 minutes each side.
4. Boil noodles and cabbage for 6 minutes or until tender.
5. Remove patties; keep warm. Sauté mushrooms in same skillet for 3 minutes. Stir in paprika, onion soup mix and water. Bring to boiling, stirring often. Reduce heat; cover and simmer 5 minutes.
6. Drain noodles and cabbage; return to saucepan. Stir in 2 tablespoons butter and poppy or caraway seeds. Arrange noodles, cabbage and meat patties on a platter.
7. Stir sour cream into paprika sauce. Heat, stirring, but do not boil. Spoon sauce over meat and noodles. Garnish with dill.

30-Minute Frittata Fiesta

Tomato Onion Frittata

GROCERY LIST

1   dozen eggs
2   ounces grated Parmesan cheese
4   ounces mozzarella cheese OR: Provolone
2   large onions
1   sweet green pepper or 1 package frozen diced sweet green pepper
1   pound fresh spinach
¼   pound mushrooms
3   to 4 ripe tomatoes
1   can (16 ounces) peach halves
     Bottled salad dressing
1   loaf Italian bread
     Packaged cookies
     Marsala wine

To Have on Hand:
● Olive oil ● Salt and pepper
● Fresh bread crumbs ● Leaf oregano ● Garlic ● Coffee

WORK PLAN

1. Preheat the oven to moderate (350°). Start heating the oil in the skillet.
2. Cook the onion and the pepper. Prepare the frittata through Step 4.
3. Prepare the frittata crumb topping. Slice the tomatoes, the mozzarella cheese or Provolone and the bread. Place the bread in a bread basket or serving plate.
4. Prepare the salad.
5. Arrange the peaches in dessert bowls and sprinkle with the Marsala wine. Place the cookies on a serving plate.
6. Remove the skillet from the oven and add the toppings. Broil the frittata. Cut the frittata into wedges and serve from the skillet.

Bake at 350° for 10 minutes, broil for 2 to 4 minutes. Makes 6 servings.

Nutrient Value Per Serving: 317 calories, 17 g protein, 23 g fat, 11 g carbohydrate, 660 mg sodium, 475 mg cholesterol.

2   large onions, sliced
3   tablespoons plus 1 teaspoon olive oil
½   cup diced sweet green pepper
10 eggs, at room temperature
⅓   cup grated Parmesan cheese
1   teaspoon salt
¼   teaspoon pepper
½   cup fresh bread crumbs
½   teaspoon leaf oregano
1   clove garlic, finely chopped
3   to 4 ripe tomatoes, sliced
4   ounces mozzarella, sliced

1. Preheat the oven to 350°.
2. Sauté onion in 3 tablespoons oil in a skillet with an oven-safe handle until tender. Sauté the pepper for 1 minute.
3. Beat the eggs, ¼ cup of the Parmesan cheese, salt and pepper in a large bowl; add to skillet. Cook over medium-low heat, lifting bottom of frittata with a spatula as eggs set, for about 3 minutes.
4. Bake in the oven (350°), uncovered, for 10 minutes or until top is almost set.
5. Combine remaining Parmesan cheese, crumbs, oregano, garlic and 1 teaspoon of oil.
6. Remove skillet from oven. Turn oven to broil. Overlap tomato slices with mozzarella on the frittata. Sprinkle with crumbs.
7. Broil frittata 4 inches from source of heat until cheese melts and crumbs are golden brown, for 2 to 4 minutes.

30-Minute Frittata Fiesta

Tomato Onion Frittata*
Spinach Salad
Italian Bread
Peaches in Marsala
Cookies
Coffee

QUICK TIP

How Low Can You Go?
You can lower the cholesterol in any frittata or omlette dish by using an egg substitute. And try one of the many varieties of low-fat cheeses, such as skim-milk mozzarella cheese.

289

30-Minute Beef Teriyaki For The Gang

Beef Teriyaki and Stir-Fried Vegetables

30-Minute Beef Teriyaki For The Gang

Chicken Broth with Tofu and Spinach

Beef Teriyaki and Stir-Fried Vegetables*

Cellophane Noodles or Rice

Vanilla Ice Cream

Tea

GROCERY LIST

1   flank steak (about 1½ pounds)
     Chicken broth
¼   pound fresh spinach
1   medium-size sweet potato
12   small mushrooms (about ¼ pound)
1   sweet green pepper
1   cup fresh bean sprouts
4   green onions
1   square tofu
     Cellophane noodles or long-grain rice
     Dry sherry
     Vanilla ice cream

To Have on Hand:
● Soy sauce ● Garlic ● Sugar
● Vegetable oil ● Tea

WORK PLAN

1. Prepare the teriyaki sauce. Marinate the steak.
2. Preheat the broiler. Start the water for the noodles or rice.
3. Prepare the vegetables (Step 2).
4. Heat the chicken broth to boiling. Add the cubed tofu and the spinach.
5. Broil the meat. Cook the noodles or rice.
6. Stir-fry the vegetables (Step 4).
7. Slice the meat and arrange with the vegetables on a platter. Place the noodles or rice in a bowl.
8. Scoop the ice cream when ready to serve dessert.

Makes 6 servings.

*Nutrient Value Per Serving:
286 calories, 24 g protein, 16 g
fat, 11 g carbohydrate, 790 mg
sodium, 60 mg cholesterol.*

1   flank steak (1½ pounds)
⅓   cup dry sherry
⅓   cup chicken broth
½   cup soy sauce
1   clove garlic, finely chopped
1   teaspoon sugar
1   medium-size sweet potato
12   small mushrooms (about ¼ pound)
1   sweet green pepper, cored and seeded
4   green onions
1   tablespoon vegetable oil
1   cup fresh bean sprouts

1. Place steak in a shallow glass dish. Prepare teriyaki sauce: mix together the sherry, broth, soy sauce, garlic and sugar. Pour about two-thirds over the steak. Turn steak to coat; marinate for 15 minutes. Reserve remaining teriyaki sauce. Preheat the broiler.
2. Peel sweet potato and slice very thin. Cut mushrooms in half. Cut green pepper into 1-inch squares. Cut green onion into 1-inch lengths. Set aside.
3. Drain the steak, pat dry. Broil 4 inches from source of heat, 2 to 3 minutes on each side for rare. Keep the steak warm.
4. Heat oil in a wok. Add the sweet potato slices and stir-fry for 1 minute. Add mushrooms, green pepper and green onion. Stir-fry for 2 to 3 minutes or until vegetables are crisp-tender. Add bean sprouts; stir-fry for 1 minute to heat through.
5. Thinly slice steak crosswise on the diagonal. Serve with sauce.

35-Minute Curry Chicken Dinner

Curried Chicken in Yogurt Sauce

GROCERY LIST

2 whole chicken breasts
   (12 ounces each)
1 cup plain yogurt
1 can (6 ounces) tomato paste
1 package (11 ounces) frozen
   French-style rice
1 medium-size onion OR: 1
   package frozen diced onion
1 small cauliflower
2 small zucchini
1 small ripe avocado
1 lime
1 bunch watercress
   Chutney, peanuts, kumquats
   and raisins
   Bananas
   Flaked coconut

To Have on Hand:
● Butter or margarine ● Garlic
● Curry powder ● Ground cardamom
● Ground ginger ● Honey

WORK PLAN

1. Sauté the chicken breasts.
2. Steam the cauliflower for 12 to 15 minutes and steam the zucchini for 8 to 10 minutes.
3. Prepare the rice following the package directions.
4. Sauté the onion and the garlic. Finish the yogurt sauce (Steps 2 and 3).
5. Prepare the condiments and place them in serving bowls.
6. Complete the chicken.
7. At dessert time, slice the bananas into 4 dessert bowls. Drizzle the bananas with the honey and sprinkle with the coconut.

Makes 4 servings.

Nutrient Value Per Serving: 434 calories, 39 g protein, 16 g fat, 33 g carbohydrate, 739 mg sodium, 98 mg cholesterol.

2 tablespoons butter or margarine
2 whole chicken breasts, split (about 12 ounces each)
¾ cup fresh or frozen diced onion
1 clove garlic, finely chopped
1 teaspoon curry powder
¼ teaspoon ground cardamom
¼ teaspoon ground ginger
2 tablespoons tomato paste
1 cup plain yogurt
1 package (11 ounces) frozen French-style rice, cooked according to package directions
1 avocado, halved, pitted, peeled and sliced
1 lime, thinly sliced
   Watercress, for garnish (optional)

1. Heat the butter in a large skillet. Add the chicken breasts, skin side down, and sauté until the chicken is golden, for 8 to 10 minutes per side. Push chicken to the side of skillet.
2. Stir the onion and the garlic into the skillet and sauté for 5 minutes. Stir in the curry powder, cardamom and ginger and cook, stirring, for 1 minute.
3. Mix together the tomato paste and the yogurt in a small bowl and stir into the skillet. Heat the mixture to *almost* boiling. Spoon sauce over chicken and heat gently for 5 minutes.
4. Arrange chicken breasts with sauce and rice on a platter. Garnish with the avocado and lime slices, and watercress.

35-Minute Curry Chicken Dinner

Curried Chicken in Yogurt Sauce*

Chutney

Peanuts

Raisins

Kumquats

Steamed Cauliflower and Zucchini

Banana with Coconut and Honey

35-Minute French Country Dinner

Garlic Chicken Ragoût

35-Minute French Country Dinner

Garlic Chicken Ragoût*

Toasted French Bread Slices

Steamed Green Beans

White Wine or Soda

Chocolate Cake

Coffee

GROCERY LIST

1   barbecued or roasted chicken (1½ to 2 pounds), from the deli department
     Chicken broth
2   bottles dry white wine or soda
4   carrots (½ pound)
1   pound green beans
9   small red new potatoes (½ pound)
1   bunch parsley
1   large or 2 small bulbs garlic
1   loaf French bread
     Chocolate cake

To Have on Hand:
● Olive or vegetable oil ● Leaf thyme ● Leaf rosemary ● Bay leaf ● Coffee

WORK PLAN

1. Start cooking the oil, garlic and herbs in a skillet.
2. Prepare the carrots and the potatoes and add to the skillet.
3. Steam the green beans. Toast the French bread slices.
4. Cut the chicken into quarters. Add the chicken to the skillet.
5. Arrange the chicken and the vegetables in a serving dish.
6. Press the purée from the garlic skin with a fork and spread on the French bread toast.
7. Place the chocolate cake on a serving plate.

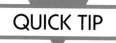

QUICK TIP

Put Thyme On Your Side
Give herbs time to season foods. If the cooking time is short, let the herbs soak in part of the cooking liquid while preparing the other ingredients.

Makes 4 servings.

Nutrient Value Per Serving: 522 calories, 40 g protein, 26 g fat, 33 g carbohydrate, 767 mg sodium, 117 mg cholesterol.

2   tablespoons olive or vegetable oil
20   cloves unpeeled garlic (1 large or 2 small bulbs)
½   teaspoon leaf thyme, crumbled
½   teaspoon leaf rosemary, crumbled
1   bay leaf
½   cup dry white wine
½   cup chicken broth or water
4   carrots (about ½ pound)
9   small red new potatoes (about ½ pound)
1   barbecued or roasted chicken (about 1½ to 2 pounds)
1   tablespoon chopped fresh parsley, for garnish

1. Heat the oil in a large, deep skillet or Dutch oven. Add the garlic, thyme and rosemary and sauté for 1 minute. Add the bay leaf, wine and broth or water. Cover; simmer while preparing the vegetables.
2. Peel the carrots and cut on a diagonal into 1-inch lengths. Add to the skillet. Scrub the potatoes and cut in half; add to the skillet. Cook, covered, until the carrots and potatoes are tender, for about 25 minutes.
3. Cut the chicken into quarters and add to the skillet for the last 5 minutes of cooking time. Cook until the chicken is heated through. Remove the garlic; reserve for the toast.
4. Arrange the chicken and the vegetables in a serving platter and garnish with the parsley.

292

35-Minute Norwegian Fireside Dinner

Norwegian Fish Chowder

GROCERY LIST

1½ to 2 pounds fresh or frozen cod or haddock fillets
2 leeks
2 carrots
1 small cucumber
Fresh dill
1 package (24 ounces) frozen O'Brien potatoes
1 can (10¾ ounces) condensed cream of celery soup
1 quart milk
Cheese and fruit
Whole-grain and flat bread
Bundt cake from bakery

To Have on Hand:
● Butter or margarine ● Salt
● Coffee

WORK PLAN

1. Prepare the Norwegian Fish Chowder.
2. Arrange the breads in a bread basket, the fruit and cheese on a platter and the cake on a serving plate. Brew the coffee.

Makes 6 servings.

Nutrient Value Per Serving: 375 calories, 31 g protein, 13 g fat, 33 g carbohydrate, 989 mg sodium, 95 mg cholesterol.

2 leeks, sliced
2 carrots, sliced
3 tablespoons butter or margarine
1½ to 2 pounds fresh or frozen cod or haddock fillets
2 cups water
1 teaspoon salt
1 can (10¾ ounces) condensed cream of celery soup
3 cups frozen O'Brien potatoes
1 small cucumber, peeled and halved lengthwise
3 cups hot milk
1 tablespoon chopped fresh dill

1. Sauté leeks and carrots in 2 tablespoons of butter in a kettle for 4 to 5 minutes or until tender but not browned. Cut fish into serving-size pieces and place in kettle. Add the water and salt; bring to boiling. Lower heat, cover and simmer for 15 minutes or until fish flakes easily when tested with fork. Remove fish from kettle with a slotted spoon, set aside.
2. Add celery soup and potatoes to kettle. Bring mixture to boiling. Cover, lower heat. Simmer for 5 minutes.
3. Remove seeds from cucumber, slice crosswise into ⅛-inch-thick slices. Sauté cucumber in remaining tablespoon of butter for 3 to 4 minutes; add to kettle with milk, reserved fish and dill. Bring just to boiling; serve hot.

35-Minute Norwegian Fireside Dinner

Norwegian Fish Chowder*

Whole-Grain Bread and Flat Bread

Fruit and Cheese Platter

Bundt Cake

Coffee

293

35-Minute After-The-Game Spaghetti Squash Dinner

35-Minute After-The-Game Spaghetti Squash Dinner

Spaghetti Squash Picadillo*

Lettuce with Tomato Slices

Hot Buttered Tortillas

Beer or Soda

Orange Sherbet with Kiwi

GROCERY LIST

1	pound ground chuck
1	spaghetti squash (2½ pounds)
1	large onion
1	sweet green pepper
1	head lettuce
3	to 4 ripe tomatoes
1	kiwi
1	jar homestyle tomato cooking sauce
1	bottle red wine vinegar
1	box raisins
1	package tortillas
1½	to 2 ounces slivered almonds
1	jar (2¼ ounces) pitted green olives
	Orange sherbet
	Beer or soda

To Have on Hand:
● Garlic ● Ground cinnamon ● Ground cumin ● Ground hot red pepper ● Salt

WORK PLAN

1. Heat the water for the squash. Cut the squash into quarters and steam.
2. Prepare the picadillo (Steps 2 and 3).
3. Wash the lettuce. Slice the tomatoes. Heat the tortillas following the package directions.
4. Scoop the sherbet into 4 dessert dishes and place in the freezer. Slice the kiwi.
5. Finish the squash and the picadillo (Step 4). Serve.

Spaghetti Squash Picadillo

Makes 4 servings.

Nutrient Value Per Serving: 564 calories, 27 g protein, 38 g fat, 32 g carbohydrate, 863 mg sodium, 85 mg cholesterol.

1	spaghetti squash (2½ pounds)
1	pound ground chuck
1	cup chopped onion (1 large)
1	sweet green pepper, cored, seeded and diced
1	large clove garlic, minced
1	cup bottled homestyle tomato cooking sauce
1	tablespoon red wine vinegar
½	teaspoon ground cinnamon
¼	teaspoon ground cumin
⅛	teaspoon ground hot red pepper
¼	cup raisins
1	jar (2¼ ounces) pitted green olives
½	cup plus 2 tablespoons slivered almonds
	Salt, to taste

1. Heat about 1½ inches of water in a large saucepan. Cut squash in quarters; discard seeds. Place squash in saucepan, rind side down. Cover pan; steam for 25 minutes or until tender.
2. Meanwhile, brown beef over high heat until all pink disappears, about 5 minutes. Add onion, green pepper, garlic. Cook 5 minutes, stirring often.
3. Stir in tomato sauce, vinegar, cinnamon, cumin, red pepper, raisins and olives. Cover skillet; cook for 10 minutes. Add ½ cup of almonds. (Add water if mixture is too thick.) Add salt.
4. Remove squash from saucepan; scrape pulp into "spaghetti" and pile back into shell. Spoon picadillo mixture over squash; sprinkle with almonds.

35-Minute Oriental Lemon Chicken Dinner

Lemon Chicken

GROCERY LIST

4	boneless, skinless chicken breast halves (1 to 1¼ pounds)
5	lemons
4	navel oranges
1	fresh pineapple
2	green onions
1	small sweet red pepper
½	pound snow peas
1	head iceberg or romaine lettuce
1	jar (2.6 ounces) sesame seeds Long-grain rice
1	box seasoned bread crumbs White wine or soda

To Have on Hand:
- Egg • Soy sauce • Sugar
- Cornstarch • Vegetable oil
- Butter

WORK PLAN

1. Cut pieces of pineapple and section the oranges.
2. Start the rice, following the package directions.
3. Coat the chicken.
4. Start the lemon sauce (Step 2).
5. Cook the vegetables. Cook the chicken. Shred and arrange the lettuce on a serving platter.
6. Stir-fry the snow peas.
7. Finish the lemon sauce (Step 4).
8. Press the cooked rice into a mold, then unmold.
9. Cut the chicken and arrange on the lettuce. Spoon the lemon sauce over the chicken. Garnish the platter.

Makes 4 servings.

Nutrient Value Per Serving: 486 calories, 39 g protein, 24 g fat, 29 g carbohydrate, 917 mg sodium, 167 mg cholesterol.

¼	cup sesame seeds
½	cup seasoned dry bread crumbs
1	egg
4	boneless, skinless chicken breast halves, slightly flattened (1 to 1¼ pounds)
⅓	cup fresh lemon juice
4	teaspoons soy sauce
2	to 3 tablespoons sugar
1	tablespoon cornstarch
1	cup water
3	tablespoons vegetable oil
2	green onions, chopped
1	small sweet red pepper, cut into julienne strips
2	tablespoons butter
4	cups shredded crisp lettuce
½	lemon, sliced, for garnish

1. Combine sesame seeds and crumbs on wax paper. Beat the egg in a saucer. Dip chicken pieces in the egg, then the crumb mixture. Pat chicken to help coating stick. Set aside, uncovered, for 10 minutes.
2. Mix together the lemon juice, soy sauce, sugar, cornstarch and water; set aside. Heat 1 tablespoon of oil. Add the green onion and red pepper; sauté for 1 minute. Remove from heat.
3. Heat 2 tablespoons oil and the butter over medium-high heat. Add chicken; sauté until golden brown, 4 to 5 minutes each side. Cut chicken into ½-inch strips; arrange on lettuce.
4. Add lemon mixture to saucepan. Bring to boiling; stir until thickened. Spoon over chicken; garnish with lemon.

35-Minute Oriental Lemon Chicken Dinner

Lemon Chicken*

Rice

Stir-Fried Snow Peas

Fresh Pineapple and Oranges

White Wine or Soda

295

45-Minute Far-Eastern Feast

Teriyaki Meatball Skewers with Yellow Rice

45-Minute Far-Eastern Feast

Teriyaki Meatball Skewers with Yellow Rice*

Spinach and Orange Salad Oriental*

Peaches and Cream

GROCERY LIST

1   large sweet green pepper
1   pint cherry tomatoes
1   navel orange
½   pound fresh spinach
1   large sweet onion (8 ounces)
1   pound lean ground beef
1   package (10 ounces) yellow rice mix
1   bottle (5 ounces) teriyaki sauce
1   package (10 ounces) quick-thaw peach slices
1   pint vanilla ice cream

To Have on Hand:
● Pepper

WORK PLAN

1. Prepare the marinade and the meatballs and marinate the meatballs. Thaw the peach slices.
2. Prepare the yellow rice following the package directions.
3. Prepare the Spinach and Orange Salad Oriental.
4. Complete the meatballs and yellow rice.
5. At dessert time, divide the ice cream among 4 dessert dishes. Spoon the peach slices over each serving, dividing evenly.

Broiled or barbecued, these marinated meatballs are tasty either way.

Broil for 12 to 14 minutes. Makes 4 servings.

Nutrient Value Per Serving: 502 calories, 27 g protein, 16 g fat, 61 g carbohydrate, 1,569 mg sodium, 70 mg cholesterol.

Marinade:
3   tablespoons teriyaki sauce
1   tablespoon grated sweet onion

Meatballs:
1   pound lean ground beef
2   teaspoons teriyaki sauce
1   tablespoon grated sweet onion
    Pinch pepper

1   package (10 ounces) yellow rice mix
¾   of large sweet green pepper (reserve remainder for Spinach and Orange Salad Oriental; *recipe, page 297*)
1   pint cherry tomatoes, washed

1. Prepare the Marinade: Combine the teriyaki sauce and the onion in a pie plate.
2. Prepare the Meatballs: Gently break apart the ground beef, using 2 forks, in a medium-size bowl. Sprinkle the teriyaki sauce, onion and pepper over the meat and gently toss to combine.
3. Shape the mixture into twelve 1¼-inch meatballs. Place the meatballs in the marinade, turning the meatballs to coat evenly. Let the meatballs stand for 10 minutes. Turn the meatballs and let stand for 10 minutes longer.

Spinach and Orange Salad Oriental

4. Cook the yellow rice, using water, following the package directions.
5. Cut the green pepper into 1-inch pieces. Thread the cherry tomatoes alternately with the green pepper and the meatballs onto 4 large skewers. Be careful not to break the meatballs. Brush the marinade over the green peppers and the tomatoes.
6. Broil the skewers 4 to 5 inches from the source of the heat for 6 to 8 minutes or until the meatballs are browned on one side. Turn the skewers carefully. Brush the skewers with the marinade. Broil the skewers for 6 minutes longer or until the meatballs are browned and cooked through. Serve the skewers on the rice.

A teriyaki dressing gives a new taste to this old favorite.

Makes 4 servings.

*Nutrient Value Per Serving:
39 calories, 2 g protein, 0 g fat, 8 g carbohydrate, 183 mg sodium, 0 mg cholesterol.*

1	navel orange
1	tablespoon teriyaki sauce
2	tablespoons water
1	tablespoon grated onion
½	pound fresh spinach, well washed and stems removed
½	of large sweet onion, thinly sliced into rings
¼	of large sweet green pepper, cut lengthwise into very thin slices

1. Cut the peel from the orange, holding the orange over a pie plate to catch the juices. Section the orange, again catching the juices; set the sections aside in a small bowl. Squeeze about 2 tablespoons of the juice remaining from the sections into the pie plate.
2. Combine the juice from the orange, the teriyaki sauce, water and grated onion in a small bowl.
3. Toss together the orange sections, spinach, onion rings and green pepper in a salad bowl. Briskly whisk the dressing. Pour the dressing over the salad and toss lightly to combine.

QUICK TIP

Veggie-Matic
To cut down on preparation time, wash vegetables as soon as you get home from the market. Keep bags of pre-cut carrots, celery, radishes, cucumber, pepper and the like in the refrigerator. Then you can literally throw together salads or stir-fries as you need them.

297

55-Minute South-of-the-Border Fiesta

55-Minute South-Of-The-Border Fiesta

Turkey in Chili Mole Sauce*

Mixed Vegetable Salad*

Sangria*, Beer or Soda

Fruit and Cream Brûlée*

GROCERY LIST

1   fresh or frozen turkey (about 10 pounds)
1   head lettuce
3   medium-size onions
1   red onion
1   small cauliflower
½   pound fresh beets or 1 can cooked beets
1   avocado
1   bunch carrots
1   bunch celery
     Red and green chili peppers
1   bunch parsley
1   bunch radishes
1   bunch watercress
1   small pineapple
1   pound red and green seedless grapes
1   lemon
1   small orange
1   container (16 ounces) dairy sour cream
1   quart orange juice
1   can (1 pound) whole tomatoes
1   bottle red wine vinegar
     Tortilla chips
2   ounces semisweet chocolate
     Almonds
     Walnuts
1   bottle (12 ounces) club soda
1½   quarts red or white wine; or beer or soda
     Rum
     Brandy

To Have on Hand:
- Mustard ● Salt ● Olive oil
- Vegetable oil ● Chili powder
- Garlic ● Ground cinnamon
- Ground coriander ● Anise seeds
- Brown sugar ● Sugar ● Ice cubes

WORK PLAN

1. One or two days beforehand, prepare the Turkey in Chili Mole Sauce through Step 9. Cover and refrigerate.
2. A few hours beforehand, prepare the Mixed Vegetable Salad through Step 2. Cover and refrigerate.
3. A few hours beforehand, prepare the Fruit and Cream Brûlée through Step 3.
4. One or two hours beforehand, prepare the Sangria (Step 1), if using. Refrigerate.
5. An hour beforehand, reheat the turkey (Step 10).
6. Just before serving, complete the salad (Step 3).
7. Complete the sangria (Step 2).
8. Garnish the turkey with red and green chili peppers and parsley, if you wish, and serve.
9. When ready to serve dessert, turn the fruit into a serving bowl. Spoon the sour cream evenly over the top of the fruit. Carefully break the broiled sugar topping into large pieces and place on the sour cream. Garnish with extra grapes, if you wish.

Turkey in Chili Mole Sauce

This variation of the popular Mexican mole sauce is flavored with chili powder, ground nuts and semisweet chocolate. Prepare the dish 1 or 2 days ahead and the flavor will improve.

Bake at 325° for 1 hour and 15 to 30 minutes.
Reheat at 350° for 45 to 60 minutes.
Makes 10 servings.

Nutrient Value Per Serving:
505 calories, 60 g protein, 25 g fat, 10 g carbohydrate, 651 mg sodium, 181 mg cholesterol.

1   fresh or thawed frozen turkey (about 10 pounds), cut up into 8 pieces
4   to 6 tablespoons vegetable oil
½   cup chopped onion (1 medium-size)
½   cup chopped carrot
½   cup chopped celery
2   teaspoons salt
4   cups water
2   to 3 tablespoons chili powder
2   medium-size onions, cut up
2   to 3 cloves garlic, coarsely chopped
1   can (1 pound) whole tomatoes, *un*drained
8   tortilla chips
½   teaspoon ground cinnamon
½   teaspoon ground coriander
¼   teaspoon anise seeds, crushed
½   cup finely ground toasted almonds
½   cup finely ground toasted walnuts
1½   squares (1 ounce each) semisweet chocolate

Garnish *(optional)*:
     Red and green chili peppers
     Parsley

1. Preheat the oven to slow (325°).
2. Brown the turkey pieces, working in batches, on all sides in the oil in a large skillet. Transfer the turkey pieces to a large, deep roasting pan.
3. Sauté the chopped onion, carrot and celery in the same skillet until soft. Stir in the salt and the water. Bring to boiling, scraping up any browned bits from the bottom and side of the skillet with a wooden spoon. Pour the mixture over the turkey. Cover the roasting pan tightly with aluminum foil.
4. Bake the turkey in the preheated slow oven (325°) for 1 hour and 15 to 30 minutes or until tender.
5. Remove the turkey pieces to a platter and keep warm. Strain the broth through a large sieve into a large bowl; there should be at least 4 cups of broth. Discard the vegetables in the sieve.
6. Combine 1 cup of the hot broth with the chili powder in a small bowl. Reserve the other 3 cups of broth.
7. Place the cut up onions, the garlic, tomatoes with their liquid, tortilla chips, cinnamon, coriander and anise seeds in the container of an electric blender or a food processor. Cover the container and whirl until smooth.

(Recipe continues next page.)

Turkey in Chili Mole Sauce —continued

8. To prepare the mole sauce, skim 4 tablespoons of fat from the top of the turkey broth and place in a large saucepan or Dutch oven. Heat the fat and stir in the chili powder mixture. Bring slowly to boiling, stirring constantly, and cook for 2 minutes. Stir in the tomato sauce from the blender and the ground almonds and walnuts. Return the mixture to boiling. Lower the heat and cook, stirring often, for 5 minutes. Stir in the chocolate and cook, stirring, until the chocolate is melted and mixed into the sauce, for about 10 minutes. Add 2 cups of the remaining broth and cook for another 45 minutes, stirring often. Add some additional broth if the sauce becomes too thick. Add salt to taste.

9. Meanwhile, remove and discard the large bones from the turkey. Cut the meat into small pieces. Arrange in a single layer in 1 or 2 shallow baking dishes. Spoon the mole sauce over the turkey. Let cool slightly. Cover and refrigerate for 1 to 2 days.

10. To reheat and serve the turkey, reheat, loosely covered, in a preheated moderate oven (350°) for 45 to 60 minutes or until the mixture is heated through. Garnish with red and green chili peppers and parsley, if you wish.

Mixed Vegetable Salad

Makes 8 servings.

Nutrient Value Per Serving: 230 calories, 2 g protein, 22 g fat, 8 g carbohydrate, 180 mg sodium, 0 mg cholesterol.

¼ cup red wine vinegar
1 teaspoon prepared mustard
½ teaspoon salt
⅔ cup olive or vegetable oil
2 tablespoons chopped parsley
Lettuce leaves
1 red onion, sliced
1 cup sliced radishes
1 bunch watercress
3 cups cauliflower flowerets (1 small head)
1 cup sliced cooked beets, fresh or canned
1 avocado

1. Combine the vinegar, mustard, salt and olive or vegetable oil in a jar with a tight-fitting lid and shake well to blend. Add the parsley. Refrigerate the dressing until ready to use.

2. Line a serving platter or shallow salad bowl with the lettuce leaves. Arrange the onion, radish, watercress, cauliflower and cooked beets over the lettuce in an attractive arrangement. Cover and refrigerate the salad for several hours or until ready to serve.

3. Just before serving, halve, pit, peel and slice the avocado. Add to the salad. Serve the dressing separately.

Fruit and Cream Brûlée

Sangria

A fruity wine punch, made with either red or white wine, is perfect for cooling the spiciness of the Turkey in Chili Mole Sauce.

Makes about 2 quarts.

Nutrient Value Per Cup:
197 calories, 1 g protein, 1 g fat, 17 g carbohydrate, 10 mg sodium, 0 mg cholesterol.

⅓ cup sugar
⅓ cup water
½ cup orange juice
¼ to ⅓ cup brandy
½ lemon, sliced and seeded
1 small orange, sliced and seeded
1½ quarts red or white wine, chilled
1 bottle (12 ounces) club soda, chilled *(optional)*
Ice cubes

1. Combine the sugar and the water in a large, clear glass pitcher. Stir to dissolve the sugar. Add the orange juice, brandy, lemon and orange slices and the wine. Refrigerate for 1 hour.
2. Just before serving the sangria, add the club soda, if you wish, and the ice cubes.

A festive fruit dessert topped with sour cream and caramelized sugar.

Broil the sugar topping for 1 to 2 minutes.
Makes 8 servings.

Nutrient Value Per Serving:
338 calories, 2 g protein, 13 g fat, 54 g carbohydrate, 43 mg sodium, 25 mg cholesterol.

1 small pineapple, peeled, quartered, cored and sliced
1 pound red and green seedless grapes
¼ cup rum
1¼ cups brown sugar
1 container (16 ounces) dairy sour cream
Grapes, for garnish *(optional)*

1. Place the pineapple slices and the grapes in a large bowl. Sprinkle the fruit with the rum and ¼ cup of the brown sugar. Toss the fruit gently to coat. Cover the bowl and chill the mixture for several hours.
2. Butter a cookie sheet. Force the remaining 1 cup of brown sugar through a sieve onto the cookie sheet in a layer ¼ inch thick.
3. Broil the sugar 4 inches from the source of the heat until it is almost melted and forms a lacy pattern, for 1 to 2 minutes. Watch carefully to prevent overbrowning. Cool the cookie sheet on a wire rack.
4. To serve the brûlée, turn the fruit into a serving bowl. Spoon the sour cream evenly over the top of the fruit. Just before serving, carefully break the sugar topping into large pieces and place on the sour cream. Garnish with extra grapes, if you wish.

QUICK TIP

Punch Pizzazz
Give any punch or cold drink pizzazz by adding fruited ice cubes. Fill an ice cube tray about half full of water. In each compartment, place a single piece of fruit. Put the tray in the freezer and allow the water to partially freeze. Fill to the top and allow the cubes to freeze solid. Raspberries, strawberries, maraschino or bing cherries, lemon, lime or orange slices, grapes—try them all!

301

Index